HOLIDAY HOUSE

The First Sixty-Five Years

HOLIDAY HOUSE

The First Sixty-Five Years

RUSSELL FREEDMAN

BARBARA ELLEMAN

HOLIDAY HOUSE · NEW YORK

1935 – 1985 designed by David Rogers
1985 – 2000 designed by Claire Counihan

First Edition

Library of Congress Cataloging-in-Publication Data

Freedman, Russell.
Holiday House, the first sixty-five years /
by Russell Freedman and Barbara Elleman.—1st ed.
p. cm.
Rev. ed. of: Holiday House, the first fifty years. c1985.
Includes bibliographical references and index.
ISBN 0-8234-1559-7 (hardcover)
1. Holiday House (Firm)—History.
2. Children's literature—Publishing—
United States—History—20th century
I. Elleman, Barbara. II. Title.
Z473.H73 F73 2000
070.5'09747—dc21
99-049917

FOREWORD

By 1998, *Holiday House: The First Fifty Years* by Russell Freedman was dated, stock was running low, and another anniversary was coming up. Some familiar questions resurfaced, namely, should there be a history of the succeeding years, and if so, who should write it.

The first part was easy. As before, the book would be a tribute to the authors and illustrators who have defined our lists for the past fifteen years—another opportunity not to be missed. Also, *The First Fifty Years* had proved to be a welcome introduction for those we would be publishing for the first time. The answer to the second question was equally easy: we would ask Russell to continue the story. However, the number of books he had under contract precluded any such undertaking. Our disappointment was mitigated by the knowledge that some of those would be ours.

Now the whole project hinged on whether or not we could find the right person. The qualifications were familiarity with the field of children's books, knowledge of our list, and enthusiasm, not to mention time. It soon became apparent that Barbara Elleman, distinguished scholar of children's literature at Marquette University, former Children's Editor of *Booklist* and Editor in Chief of *Book Links*, and longtime friend of the house was the ideal choice—and she proved us right. Subsequently, we heeded Elizabeth Winthrop's suggestion that the complete history be published in a single volume.

We remain indebted to the representatives who sell our books throughout the country: Krikorian-Miller Associates in New England, Walck-Rikhoff Bookpeddlers in the Middle Atlantic states, George Scheer Associates in the South, Ted Heinecken Associates in the Midwest, and Lee Collins Associates in the West. In Canada we continue to be distributed by Thomas Allen and Son, a fourth-generation family firm that has represented us there since 1935.

And we are also grateful for the job done by those who sell our foreign rights: John Johnson Ltd. in the British Commonwealth, Tuttle-Mori Agency in Japan, International Children's Book Service (ICBS) in the Nordic countries, Silke Weniger Books for Children in Germany, Lora Fountain Literary Agency in France and Italy, Julio F-Yañez Agency in Spain, and Korea Copyright Center (KCC) in South Korea.

Our long relationship with the best warehouse service in the industry continues. Being able to work with Stephen DiStefano, Tony DiStefano, and Charlie Rizzo and their staff at W. A. Book Service has been nothing less than a blessing.

What happens in our office is the result of a lot of talent and effort. Special thanks are due to the following colleagues, not mentioned elsewhere, for their contributions and good company: Dorothy Broschak, Christa Chatrnuch, Michelle Frey, Lisa Morales, and Suzanne Reinoehl. None of us could function properly without our computers, which are maintained by Young Lee, who is always present when needed, is never without a solution to whatever the problem may be, and is forever patient! Karen Estes, who served a ten-year tour of duty here, was recalled to help prepare for publication the manuscript covering the past fifteen years, a task she performed cheerfully and expertly. Also, for the last seven years, it has been a special pleasure and benefit to have our daughter, Ashley Bernhard, working part-time in the production department.

Finally, it has been my good fortune to share thirty-five of these years with Kate. Our jobs by themselves have been enjoyable and satisfying, and we have tried to give our best. The support and friendship authors and illustrators have bestowed on us, however, make it clear we've gotten better than we've given. We have a lot to be thankful for and a lot to look forward to.

John Briggs
February 2000

HOLIDAY HOUSE

The First Fifty Years

1935–1985

RUSSELL FREEDMAN

PREFACE

Sometime in 1980 the idea of publishing a history of Holiday House surfaced during conversations Kate and I had with Glen Rounds on his terrace in Southern Pines, and with Margery Cuyler in New York. The more we talked, the more it appeared that the project, if done properly, would end up being a major undertaking, which magnified some problems that would need to be overcome.

At first, there never seemed to be very convincing answers to why we should make the effort, or for whom. That contributed to the difficulty of rationalizing the expenses that would be incurred. And finally, this was a story close to our hearts, and there didn't seem to be anyone both qualified and willing to write it.

The first concern was overcome by acknowledging that the story itself was worth telling—that to pay tribute to the authors and illustrators was reason enough. That being the case, we agreed on a budget, and a printing in spite of the sales forecast.

The seemingly impossible task of finding a qualified, *i.e.*, perfect, author ended when we realized that in our midst was Russell Freedman, researcher, contributor to the Holiday House list, and friend of the firm for twenty-five years—a person ideally suited for the job. Our confidence was confirmed by the enthusiasm with which he responded to the idea and the result of his considerable efforts.

The fact that Russell became associated with Holiday House has a bearing on this history, since it seems quite certain that no one else would have been asked to write it. He was working for a large advertising agency in 1959, when he came up with the idea for his first book, a collection of biographies about people who earned a place in history before they were twenty years old. He talked about it with his father, a sales representative on the West Coast for a group of publishers, who mentioned it to George Scheer, a Holiday House sales representative, who in turn mentioned it to Vernon Ives. Vernon then called Russell and invited him to his first publisher's lunch at the old "68" restaurant on lower Fifth Avenue, where he asked to see a sample chapter and then surprised the would-be author with the promise of a contract if it was satisfactory. Russell remembers the moment well: "I was terrifically excited. 'That's wonderful,' I told Vernon over dessert. 'Now I can quit my job and become a writer.' Vernon almost spilled his coffee. 'For heaven's sake,' he warned me, 'whatever you do, *don't* quit your job.'

"Well, I ignored Vernon's advice and left my job in order to work on the book, which involved a lot more effort than I expected. Without Vernon's gentle prodding and friendly encouragement, I doubt that I would have finished it.

"I had typed the 250-page manuscript on Eaton's Corrasible Bond, the erasable paper with a waxy coating, and was carrying it in a manila envelope from my apartment in Greenwich Village to the Holiday House office on West 13th Street, when I got caught in the great hurricane of September, 1960. By the time I arrived, all the pages were soaked and stuck together. We had to peel them apart and dry them over a radiator.

"*Teenagers Who Made History* came out in 1961. I've been publishing happily with Holiday House ever since, and I've had the good luck to work with most of the people who have been associated with the firm, from Helen Gentry and Vernon Ives, the founders, up to the present generation. My own feelings about Holiday House were expressed in various ways by the authors and illustrators I interviewed while researching and writing this history; so many of them spoke of their warm personal relationships with members of the staff, of the pleasures and satisfactions of working with a small, independent, quality publisher, and often, of the fun they've had producing books with Holiday House. That's been my experience, too. For me, this project

has been not just the history of a publishing house, but the story of
some of my best friends."

Kate and I share these sentiments and echo them frequently. Nothing at Holiday has been more gratifying than the friendships we have
made. We treasure all of them the way we treasure our relationship
with Russell.

Russell's father, Louis Freedman, started representing our list in the
West in 1965, which marked the beginning of a relationship Kate and I
remember with appreciation and affection. It is easy to underestimate
the importance of representatives, yet difficult to overstate their contribution to this story. Currently we have the good fortune of being represented by Krikorian-Miller Associates in New England, Homer
Roberts and Sandy Rector in the Middle Atlantic States, George
Scheer Associates in the South, Ted Heinecken Associates in the Midwest, and Lee Collins Associates in the West. It follows that we are
equally indebted to the independent bookseller, as well as librarians
and reviewers, and our suppliers.

The formal relationship between Holiday House, William R. Scott,
Inc., and Frederick Warne & Co. is touched on briefly in the pages that
follow, but it was the informal relationship Vernon Ives, Bill Scott,
Dick Billington, and I had that was meaningful. Ideas, business practices, and privileged information were exchanged to the extent that I
doubt there was ever a gathering of two or more of us that would have
met with the approval of the anti-trust people. Regardless, I value those
friendships, and the good counsel I have received from three wise and
astute publishers of children's books.

I would not have had the good fortune of being a part of this story if
it had not been for the generous support of my parents and my Aunt
Jean when it came time to take the plunge in 1965. Walter, Marion, and
Ashley Briggs have all put in time here, their presence and contribution pleasing me no end.

Everyone who has been lucky enough to know Kate is almost as
aware as I am of how much she has meant to Holiday House. My good
luck has been to share the last twenty years, and more, with her, both
in the office and out. Our relationship has been the best—full and full
time.   JOHN BRIGGS
                                                      January 20, 1985

HOLIDAY
HOUSE

cover art for first catalog
by Valenti Angelo (1935)

CHAPTER

1

Fifty years ago, in 1935, a new firm called Holiday House set up three desks in the corner of a printing plant and prepared to publish its first list of books. "The event was unique in at least one respect," *Publishers Weekly* would say. "The new company was the first American publishing house ever founded with the purpose of publishing nothing but children's books."

The first of its kind, then—a specialized publisher with a unique program and a diminutive catalog, small enough to fit in a child's palm. The catalog announced five books, three nursery rhyme broadsides, and the publisher's intentions: "Holiday House is a publishing venture devoted exclusively to the finest books for children [and] is . . . sufficiently small to insure each title the personal attention of the founders, yet large enough to provide adequate and economical distribution. Its editorial policy embraces only such books as are worthy of inclusion in a child's permanent library."

The books had been designed with uncompromising attention to detail by Helen Gentry, an alumna of the Grabhorn Press, the finest printing house on the West Coast. They had been printed by William E. Rudge's Sons, the East Coast counterpart of Grabhorn. Reviewing the first Holiday House list in the New York *Herald Tribune*, May Lamberton Becker wrote: "Books easy to the eye, stoutly made, meant to last. They have the look of rightness a child's book should have. Each is part of a program, part of the fulfillment of a pledge made to itself and the public by a publishing enterprise trying, in its own quiet way, to make its children's books notable examples of typography and thus to train appreciation of a noble art from an early age in the way it should go."

The only original title on the list was *Boomba Lives in Africa* by Caroline Singer and Cyrus LeRoy Baldridge, "a realistic story" of a West African boy and his native village. There was a centennial edition of Hans Christian Andersen's *The Little Mermaid*, with color illustrations by Pamela Bianco, and a twelfth-century Arthurian legend, *Jaufry the Knight and the Fair Brunissende*, translated from the original Provençal by "Vernon Ives, our editor" and illustrated in black and white by John Atherton.

To these were added "two small books for small hands," miniature editions of *Cock Robin* and *Jack and the Beanstalk*, patterned after the English chapbooks popular in the nineteenth century. The two titles inaugurated the Holiday House series of fifty-cent "stocking books," described in the catalog as "tiny volumes in chapbook form to delight small souls, particularly when found in the top of Christmas stockings, where they are meant to be."

Barbara Bader, the author of *American Picturebooks from Noah's Ark to the Beast Within*, has called the Holiday House stocking books "revolutionary little revivals . . . with cut-flush uncovered board sides (or covers) stamped in red; and a red cloth backbone; a petite allover-pattern endpaper—dollhouse wallpaper—with a blank area not, as usual, for the owner's name but for his thumbprint; and inside, instead of the minuscule letters of modern miniature books, good-sized readable type. Type in keeping with the character of the story, set in accordance with its own character, and set around drawings that have the same feel."

Rounding out the list were three nursery rhyme broadsides illustrated in color by Valenti Angelo, "suitable for framing" and designed to be hung on "the walls of any nursery or school room." Barbara

art by Pamela Bianco from
The Little Mermaid (1935)

JACK & THE BEANSTALK

art by Arvilla Parker from
Jack and the Beanstalk (1935)

Boomba
Lives in Africa

by
CAROLINE SINGER and
CYRUS LeROY BALDRIDGE

Holiday House
1935

title page
Boomba Lives in Africa (1935)

art by John Atherton from
*Jaufry the Knight and the
Fair Brunissende* (1935)

art by Anne Heyneman
from *Cock Robin* (1935)

Bader calls the broadsides "a picture of fine design. Selling for fifty cents, they represent a revival of the old English illustrated poem or ballad, printed on a single sheet for posting."

It could not be called a "balanced list," and by choice it never would be. "Each book on that first list appeared to be there for its own sake," said *Publishers Weekly*. "Considerations of an overall publishing program were subservient to concern about each individual book."

The books caused a stir in design circles and among children's book specialists. They were warmly recommended by librarians and teachers. *The New York Times* wrote that the stocking books "in size and content suggest the past, though they differ decidedly from the original chapbooks in the exquisite quality of their design and workmanship." Despite all the praise, some of the titles on that first list—the stocking books and the broadsides, in particular—proved difficult to market. Many bookstores were wary of such unconventional items for children; many libraries did not know what to do with them.

"Our first list was unusual, to say the least," Vernon Ives recalls. "Our publications promptly landed in the A.I.G.A.'s Fifty Books of the Year and the Printing for Commerce exhibitions, but their saleability was something else again. Bookstores did not want to bother with broadsides or miniature books, and the libraries were afraid they would be stolen."

The stocking books were small and easily pocketed, the broadsides big and easily soiled. In an effort to market the broadsides, Holiday House made up a display folder for bookstores and offered all three broadsides as a set; replacements were sent in cardboard mailing tubes. To meet bookstore objections that the stocking books would be buried on busy counters, the publisher came up with another special display, this one for bookstore promotion during the Christmas season of 1935. The little books were tucked into big red Christmas stockings mounted on green display posters—an "ingenious display," reported *Publishers Weekly*.

"We learned the hard way," Ives recalled in 1947. "After such a start, it took us quite a few years to live down the idea that we were a private press, publishing collectors' items."

During its early years, Holiday House expanded its list, gained mar-

Hey! diddle, diddle,
The cat and the fiddle,
The cow jumped over the moon;
The little dog laugh'd
To see the sport,
While the dish ran away with the spoon.

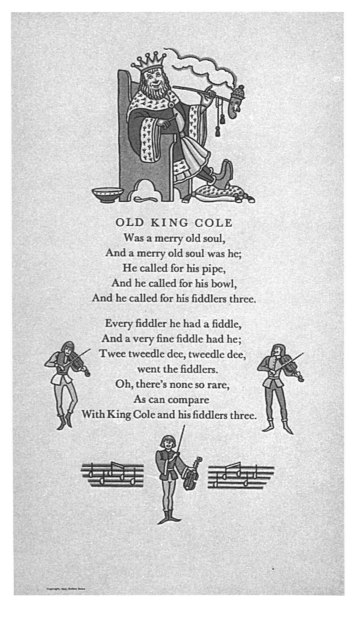

OLD KING COLE

Was a merry old soul,
And a merry old soul was he;
He called for his pipe,
And he called for his bowl,
And he called for his fiddlers three.

Every fiddler he had a fiddle,
And a very fine fiddle had he;
Twee tweedle dee, tweedle dee,
went the fiddlers.
Oh, there's none so rare,
As can compare
With King Cole and his fiddlers three.

art by Valenti Angelo for
Hey! Diddle Diddle and
Old King Cole, broadsides (1935)

keting savvy, and produced books "less exotic in appearance and far more popular in content," as Ives put it. The look of the books changed, but the firm held fast to its original tenets, emphasizing individuality and care in book manufacturing and remaining the small, personal, quality house that its young founders had wanted to create.

Writing in the July, 1935, issue of *The Horn Book*, Helen Gentry said, "Holiday House has been chosen as our name for two reasons. First, because we expect to have fun making the books. Second, because we hope they will have a happy spirit that will make young people fond enough of them to keep them, to lend them only to careful friends, and to hand them down to their children—and, in some cases, to their grandchildren."

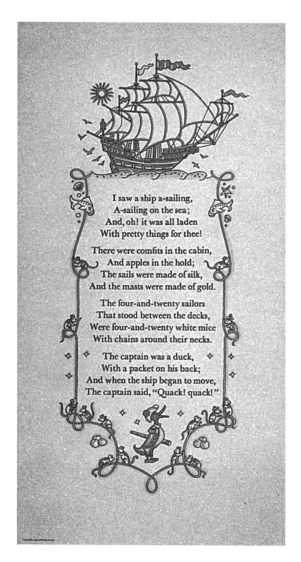

art by Valenti Angelo for
I Saw a Ship A-Sailing,
a broadside (1935)

CHAPTER

2

"The year was 1935," Vernon Ives recalls, "and the Great Depression was at full throttle. Anyone who would start a publishing house then, especially without experience or enough working capital, was stupid or crazy. So we did: Helen Gentry, Ted Johnson, and I. Helen Gentry was a talented book designer with no knowledge of publishing. Ted Johnson was a college acquaintance of mine whose only qualification was his father's money. I had edited publications in high school and college and was a partner in a struggling young printing business. Some team!"

Theodore A. P. Johnson had no publishing experience at all. Ives, however, had worked for five years with a firm that printed and published fine books. Gentry had spent more than a decade at the Grabhorn Press and at her own press in San Francisco. She was well known as a pioneer in the printing trade, an industry that did not encourage women.

Helen Gentry had grown up on a California ranch, graduated from the University of California in 1922, and tried her hand at writing, theater directing, teaching, and advertising before finding her life's work: "I was taken to see an exhibition of books, selected for their beauty

art by Jack Tinker from
The Old Woman and Her Pig (1936)

art by Jack Tinker from
Titty Mouse, Tatty Mouse
(1936)

from the best books since printing began nearly five hundred years ago. Some of them were as magical and unreal to me as the fairy tales I had read long before—they were like the glorious fruit in Aladdin's garden. I went to see them again and again; I could hardly believe they existed. I had not known human hands could make so much beauty. Months later, I began to wonder if mine could. I had been a let-me-do-it child, as well as a bookworm—able to make dresses, to ride horses after cattle, to drive nails—and that gave me confidence. Why not learn printing? So I went to work in San Francisco in a shop where books were made."

Gentry became an apprentice at the celebrated Grabhorn Press, where she did the work connected with the first steps in printing. She was a printer's devil who set type, handfolded and sewed books, and did the bookkeeping. She did not do the presswork, however, because Ed Grabhorn told her it was not a job for a woman. After two years at Grabhorn, she went to work in a private printing plant operated for a big grocery store. It was there that she learned to operate presses, both hand-fed and power-driven, and to design circulars, sale broadsides, and other mailing pieces.

Finally, she borrowed a hundred dollars and opened her own press in one room of a two-room San Francisco studio. She has been called the first contemporary woman printer to do all the presswork and other labor herself. Barely five feet tall, she could not reach the big press she had installed, so she built a special platform to stand on.

At first she did the layouts and printing for advertising and other commercial accounts. Eventually her brother, Bruce Gentry, joined

art by Maxwell Simpson from
Aucassin and Nicolette (1936)

art by Percival Stutters from *How Percival Caught the Tiger* (1936)

her, and together they ran the Helen Gentry Press. They began to print fine editions of adult books and, in 1934, produced three award-winning books for children—*Tom Thumb, Rip Van Winkle,* and *The Nightingale*, which were sold by subscription.

That year her husband, David Greenhood, made a trip to New York. "This was the decisive factor," she says. "I thought I could get a job in New York after all the publicity for my press books. David had found a publisher for his novel, and he liked the literary atmosphere there. So I left the press to Bruce and took a train east, weeping all the way from the knowledge that New York was not the place for a press such as mine. There, while looking for a job, I contacted many of the people who had written me about my books."

One of her correspondents had been Vernon Ives, who was also interested in publishing fine children's books. An upstate New Yorker and 1930 graduate of Hamilton College, Ives had served an apprenticeship in fine printing at The Printing House of William Edwin Rudge. After working in all departments, he had transferred to Rudge's publishing division, known as William Edwin Rudge, Publisher. "I discovered that 1931 was not the year to sell art books and esoteric *belles lettres*," he said later. "But I did learn something about publishing, for as the firm retrenched and the staff was rapidly cut down, I had more and more jobs assigned to me."

In 1932, after the death of Rudge, Ives became one of the founders of a new printing firm, William E. Rudge's Sons, which succeeded the

art by Cyrus LeRoy Baldridge
from *Ali Lives in Iran* (1937)

parent firm. "Our plan was to establish a publishing division later, which I would run. Before this was financially possible, Ted Johnson proposed buying into our young firm. Here was the financial answer to our publishing plans. But since I was the only member of William E. Rudge's Sons interested in publishing, why not start a separate business—children's books?"

By then, Helen Gentry had arrived in New York. Ives had admired her books, had written to her, and was eager to meet her. Johnson had recently returned from Oxford, where he had done graduate work in English literature. He was anxious to settle into a career, and had a father with money to invest. The three of them decided to work together.

"We started, then, with more technical know-how than we needed, and not enough capital; more ideas than we could use, and too little experience," says Ives. "We had no authors, no salesmen, no clerical help.

"At first there were only the three of us, and our 'office' was behind filing cabinets, empty so far, in a corner of the Rudge pressroom, where our first books were printed in 1935. Helen Gentry was, and remained, in charge of design and production, and at first even set much of our display matter by hand from the Rudge cases. Ted Johnson was responsible for accounting and sales, although I often hit the road, too, before we had commission salesmen. My special provinces were administrative and editorial, but here again any of us with a book idea pitched in to build the list. Inexperienced as we were, we knew that a sound backlist was essential to survival.

"Because of our inexperience, we very nearly didn't make it. At the outset, we leaned heavily on reprints, 'fine editions worthy of the child's permanent library,' as our first catalog blithely announced.

art by Stuyvesant Van Veen
from *The Fairy Fleet* (1936)

A was an archer, who shot at a frog;
B was a butcher, he had a great dog;
C was a captain, all covered with lace;
D was a drunkard, and had a red face;
E was an esquire, with pride on his brow;
F was a farmer, and followed the plough;
G was a gamester, who had but ill luck;
H was a hunter and hunted a buck;
I was an innkeeper, who loved to carouse;
J was a joiner, and built up a house;
K was King William, once governed this land;
L was a lady, who had a white hand;
M was a miser, and hoarded up gold;
N was a nobleman, gallant and bold;
O was an oyster girl, and went about town;
P was a parson, and wore a black gown;
Q was a queen, who wore a silk slip;
R was a robber, and wanted a whip;
S was a sailor, and spent all he got;
T was a tinker, and mended a pot;
U was a usurer, a miserable elf;
V was a vinter, who drank all himself;
W was a watchman, and guarded the door;
X was expensive, and so became poor;
Y was a youth, that did not love school;
Z was a zany, a poor harmless fool.

1		2	3		4
One, two, buckle my shoe			Three, four, shut the door		
5		6	7		8
Five, six, pick up sticks			Seven, eight, lay them straight		
9		10	11		12
Nine, ten, a good fat hen			Eleven, twelve, who will delve		
13		14	15		16
Thirteen, fourteen, maids a-courting			Fifteen, sixteen, maids a-kissing		
17		18	19		20
Seventeen, eighteen, maids a-waiting			Nineteen, twenty, my plate's empty		

art by Valenti Angelo for *A Was an Archer*, and
One, Two, Buckle My Shoe, broadsides (1936)

Little Jack Horner
Sat in a corner,
Eating of Christmas pie:
He put in his thumb,
And pulled out a plum,
And said, "What a good
boy am I!"

art by Philip Reed for
Jack Horner, a broadside (1937)

There was an old woman
who lived in a shoe,

She had so many children
she didn't know what to do;

She gave them some broth
without any bread;

She whipped them all soundly

and put them to bed.

art by Anne Heyneman for *Old Woman
Who Lived in a Shoe*, a broadside (1937)

"Our handicap was that, like Caxton, we were more printers than publishers. Helen Gentry and I both had excellent training in the graphic arts, but our combined knowledge of working with authors consisted of my editorship of a college literary magazine. Our standards were higher than our skills."

That first office behind filing cabinets was spartan. Helen Ives, Vernon's wife, made it possible for the new firm to save the expense of a telephone. "I was running the switchboard for William E. Rudge's Sons," she remembers, "and therefore I was entitled to take phone calls for Vernon."

art by Clara Skinner from *Mighty Magic* (1937)

"What saved us," says Ives, "was the arrival of Glen Rounds, trying to peddle some drawings to anyone with a few dollars. How he discovered us I'll never know. He was a young, footloose westerner with a discerning eye, a quick, sketchy style of drawing that had enormous vitality, and a tongue even more facile than his brush. He began spinning Paul Bunyan yarns, and we knew we had a book if he would stop talking and begin writing."

With his Stetson hat, his portfolio of drawings, and his gift of gab, Rounds had walked into the Holiday House office unannounced—a rangy artist from Out West, the genuine article. "We all realized that here was the real thing," said Ives, "not some reprint of the classics." Born in the Badlands of South Dakota, Rounds had grown up on a

Montana ranch and had "prowled the country" as a cowhand, lumberjack, carnival barker, sign painter, and lightning artist. In 1926, he had studied at the Kansas City Art Institute, and in 1930 he had come to New York to attend night classes at the Art Student's League, where he met Thomas Hart Benton and Jackson Pollock. During the summer of 1931, he and Benton had traveled the rodeo circuit in Wyoming and Colorado together, making sketches.

Now, in the summer of 1935, Rounds was back in Manhattan, carrying his portfolio from magazine to magazine, trying to make a living. In April he had sold some drawings to Frank Crowninshield at *Vanity Fair*, illustrating a dude ranch story. Thomas Hart Benton had arranged for an exhibit of Rounds's woodcuts at the Ferargil Galleries. "It wasn't a bad life," he recalls, "but I wasn't really getting ahead much."

Rounds had gone to Holiday House on a tip. A friend had heard about a new publishing firm that was just starting up. "They're working right now on a book about Africa [*Boomba Lives in Africa*]," the friend confided, "and a book about Africa should need a lot of animal drawings."

Rounds went down to the Rudge printing plant on lower Varick Street and found Ives, Gentry, and Johnson sitting at "three old desks behind a barrier of wooden boxes in the corner of the press floor, with old Miehle cylinder presses thumping and wheezing on all sides."

Cyrus LeRoy Baldridge was already doing the illustrations for *Boomba*, so that was out. The talk turned to Paul Bunyan. Rounds had experimented with a Paul Bunyan comic strip that he had hoped to syndicate. "I had finally given it up," he says, "but in my portfolio I had some drawings of the nonexistent animals and folk I'd invented for my project. Ives was entertained by them, and that led to my telling some Bunyan yarns."

As Ives listened, he could see a book in the making. "If you could write some of those stories down, we might publish them," he told Rounds, "and then you could illustrate the book."

Rounds wasn't interested, not at first. He hadn't really thought of writing a book and recalls telling Ives, "I'm an artist. Anybody can write, but being an artist is difficult." Even so, he began to drop in at the Holiday House office—"Ives and Gentry were usually good for a lunch or a drink"—and finally he was persuaded to put a few yarns on paper to see what would happen.

"By then," he says, "I was working more or less regularly for a textile place on Broadway, setting up a silk-screen shop for them. I bought me an old Corona portable, known then as the World War I correspondent's portable, for seven dollars and started writing Paul Bunyan stories at night. Instead of doing research—looking them up—I made them up as I went along. In the spring, Holiday House published the book, and that, my friends, is the true and unexpurgated story of how I got involved in writing and with Holiday House."

Ol' Paul, the Mighty Logger appeared on the second Holiday House list, in the spring of 1936. The firm did not yet have a sales force. Rounds was unknown but undaunted. With his bride, Margaret, a children's librarian who had worked for Anne Carroll Moore in New York, he fixed up a station wagon as a combination sleeping quarters and warehouse, loaded it with copies of his book, and set out on a cross-country barnstorming tour to spread the word about *Ol' Paul.*

ABOVE AND FACING PAGE:
art by Glen Rounds from
Ol' Paul, the Mighty Logger
(1936)

"They drove to the West Coast," recalls Ives, "working with booksellers and librarians on the way. And I mean working. Some of his reports were hilarious but unprintable. The shock waves of that unorthodox trip haven't died down yet.

"Glen was to become a very real part of Holiday House. He not only wrote and illustrated, he made signs, sold books, put on lightning-artist acts, appeared at conventions, did public relations—he can't help it, he *is* public relations—and was generally helpful in raising our spirits. It was Glen's loyalty, honesty, and irreverent attitude toward pretense that helped us through some difficult years and formed a close friendship that still endures."

Glen Rounds was the first Holiday House "discovery." He was soon followed by other writers and artists new to the children's book field who came to the noisy office at 225 Varick Street and left with books to do.

CHAPTER

3

art by Fritz Eichenberg
from *Dick Whittington
and His Cat* (1937)

"Those early years brought our first close working relationships with authors and artists," said the *Holiday House News* in 1960. "To find a new talent, to help it develop into a growing list of fine books, and in the process to enjoy a warm personal friendship—this is, to us, the most rewarding part of publishing."

One new talent was Fritz Eichenberg, who joined the Holiday House list in 1936, the same year as Glen Rounds. Eichenberg had come to the United States in 1933, a refugee from Germany, where he had worked as a newspaper artist and reporter, making quick sketches of people and events, and had taught himself wood engraving to illustrate his first books. In New York, he recalled later, "I made my rounds with my meager portfolio, an unknown young artist with little to show that would be of interest to the American public, who had other things to worry about in November of 1933."

In 1935 he was introduced to Helen Gentry by a mutual friend, the printer Joseph Blumenthal. Gentry commissioned the young refugee to illustrate two new stocking books, *Puss in Boots* and *Dick Whittington and His Cat*. They were Eichenberg's first American children's books.

Puss in Boots was printed from the artist's original woodblocks.

18

art by Fritz Eichenberg
from *Puss in Boots* (1936)

Helen Gentry set the type by hand and made the endpapers herself by combining tiny lead pieces from the print shop into a two-color pattern. "What touched me so much," Eichenberg says, "was the infinite care she applied to every tiny little detail." Gentry also hand set *Dick Whittington*, but she decided that printing from the original woodblocks was too risky, so she had zinc plates made. Both books were selected for the Fifty Books of the Year exhibits sponsored by the American Institute of Graphic Arts. "That was of great consequence to me," said Eichenberg, "as I was trying so hard to break into the American book field."

Irmengarde Eberle's long career as a writer of children's books began with a book of realistic animal stories, *Hop, Skip, and Fly*, published in the spring of 1937 and followed that fall by *Sea-Horse Adventure*. These were the first nature books published by Holiday House, fore-

art by Else Bostelmann from *Hop, Skip, and Fly* (1937)

runners of the firm's Life-Cycle series. Eberle went on to write both fiction and nonfiction on a variety of subjects for Holiday House and other publishers, and she became one of the founders of the Children's Book Committee of the Authors' Guild.

Irma Simonton Black was a nursery school teacher at the Bank Street College of Education when Holiday House published her first book, *Hamlet: A Cocker Spaniel*, with illustrations by Kurt Wiese, in 1938. Black was to contribute titles to the list for more than thirty years. She became a teacher of children's literature at Bank Street and senior editor of *The Bank Street Readers*.

art by Kurt Wiese from *Hamlet* (1938)

art by Fritz Eichenberg
from *Padre Porko* (1939)

Robert Davis, one of Vernon Ives's most prized discoveries, was a foreign correspondent when he published his first book for children at the age of fifty-seven. Davis had gone to Spain in the late 1930s to write a series of articles for the New York *Herald Tribune*. While there he heard the Spanish folktales that he incorporated into *Padre Porko: The Gentlemanly Pig*. He sent the manuscript to an agent in New York, who showed it to Ives. Illustrated by Fritz Eichenberg, the book was published in 1939 and is still in print—"one of the nicest books I ever worked on," the artist says.

In 1940, on assignment in North Africa, Davis took time off to visit some Berber tribesmen in the mountains of Morocco, where he collected the material for his second children's book, *Pepperfoot of Thursday Market*. The handwritten manuscript became an early World War II casualty when the ship carrying it to the U.S. was sunk in the Mediterranean. Davis had to rewrite the book from memory. When it was published in 1941, Helen Gentry copied a Berber rug design for the cloth binding.

art by Cyrus LeRoy Baldridge from
Pepperfoot of Thursday Market (1941)

Davis had been living with his family in southwestern France for about twenty years. With the fall of France, he lost his farm, his 300 dairy cows, and the 30,000-bottle wine cellar that he had been accumulating for his old age. He resettled his family on a Vermont farm, became a history professor at Middlebury College, and continued to write books for Holiday House until his death in 1948.

The war, meanwhile, had given Holiday what Vernon Ives has called "our first real best seller." The book was *Dive Bomber* by Robert Winston, published in the fall of 1939. Winston, a former newspaper reporter, was a naval aviator training recruits at the Pensacola Naval Air Station. *Dive Bomber* presented a dramatic and detailed account of his experiences. "It was a very timely subject," says Ives, "the training of naval aviators, and the book was later used as a text in the Navy's V-12 training program." The first order for *Dive Bomber*, however, dated November 22, 1939, came not from the United States Navy but from the New York Inspector's Office of the Imperial Japanese Navy. "They only ordered one copy," says Ives. "I guess that's all they needed."

art by Walter I. Dothard from *Dive Bomber* (1939)

Gradually, Holiday House was building a roster of talent and a growing list of books. "The reason so many Holiday House authors were discovered by the house in those early days," says Ives, "is that we were hungry for authors of any kind. We would undertake to publish a manuscript that a bigger house wouldn't want to be bothered with, and we would work very hard on it and try to make a producing author of that individual. From a publishing point of view, you want to publish authors and not books, because developing a public interest in an individual is much more productive if you're talking about a body of work by that person, and not just one specific book.

"We never lost an author we wanted to keep. While we were a small operation and couldn't spend as much money promoting the authors as other publishers could, we could spend as much time working with them as anyone could—and we did."

In November, 1939, the American Institute of Graphic Arts sponsored an exhibit of Helen Gentry's work that was eventually shown all over the country. It included samples of Gentry's title pages, jacket and binding designs, and text pages, plus a wide range of the commercial printing she had done at her own press in San Francisco.

Under Gentry's direction, Holiday House had continued to emphasize fine printing and imaginative design. Three of the firm's stocking books had been chosen for the A.I.G.A.'s Fifty Books of the Year exhibits. In 1939, Holiday House issued two other miniature books, *The History of Tom Thumb* and *Thumbelina*, boxed together in a slipcase and sold as a set. The edition was limited to 1200 sets, each with hand-colored illustrations. Watercolors were applied with tiny brushes to Hilda Scott's line drawings by members of the Holiday House staff. (*Tom Thumb* had been published without color illustrations by Helen and Bruce Gentry.) *Library Journal* called the little volumes "miniature masterpieces of good bookmaking."

The Seven Voyages of Sindbad the Sailor, also published in 1939, was another limited edition, a collector's item illustrated with eighteen colored woodcuts by Philip Reed, who set the book by hand and printed it for Holiday House on gray rag-content paper at his Broadside Press in Chicago. Two years later, Reed illustrated and printed a handsome gift edition of *A Christmas Carol* for the firm.

Gentry, however, was not content simply to produce "what printers call fine books." She was an innovator who brought a spark of originality to many of the firm's offerings. All of the stocking books, for example, were bound in printed board, the first time this was used. The first use of Electra Oblique as a text face was in Irmengarde Eberle's *Sea-Horse Adventure*. Holiday House also became the first publisher to use the silk-screen process in book production. And there were other innovations, some rather whimsical. "Don't think we didn't have fun, in spite of our growing pains," said the *Holiday House News* in 1960. "We were small, but we were independent and full of ideas."

art by Hilda Scott from *Thumbelina* (1939)

art by Philip Reed from
A Christmas Carol (1941)

art by Philip Reed from
*The Seven Voyages of Sindbad
the Sailor* (1939)

art by Ilse Bischoff from
The Night Before Christmas (1937)

The Thumb Print of

Owner of This Book

front endpaper design by Hilda Scott
from *The History of Tom Thumb* (1939)

art by Glen Rounds from
Lumbercamp (1937)

One idea was to bind Glen Rounds's second book, *Lumbercamp*, in three-ply firwood. In manufacturing terms, the idea worked out fine. The plywood was durable and the book attracted plenty of attention. However, the edges of the binding were rather treacherous. Librarians began to report that readers were getting splinters in their fingers.

Another idea was to douse the binding of Irmengarde Eberle's *Spice on the Wind* with the oil of cloves. At the time (1940), Holiday House was still doing its own shipping from its office on Varick Street. "Every time we sent out an order," says Ives, "we would open both endpapers of the book, give it a squirt of oil of cloves with an atomizer, then close it fast, so when the book was opened, you would get the scent of cloves. That created a lot of publicity, but the odor of cloves dissipates very quickly, so it was a lost cause. You had to be a first reader to get the full benefit."

That's not the way Helen Gentry remembers it. "What we actually did," she says, "is mix cloves with the binding glue of the book. The scent lasted about fifteen years."

Everyone agrees that the idea to print silk-screened books originated with Glen Rounds, who had worked in silk-screen textile shops. Beginning in 1939, Holiday House issued a series of babies' cloth books without text. While they were not the only cloth books on the market, the version developed by Holiday House was unique among American publications. The books were printed in three bright, nontoxic colors by the silk-screen process on special cloth, not an imitation or a paperbacked hybrid. They were washable, pressable, and "safely chewable." Infants could not tear them, ravel them, cut themselves on stiff edges, or poison themselves by chewing the corners. Three of the cloth books were illustrated with simple but imaginative drawings of familiar objects by Leonard Weisgard, who was just out of art school, two by Glen Rounds, and another by Kurt Wiese.

art by Richard Jones from
Spice on the Wind (1940)

art by Leonard Weisgard from
Cloth Book 1 (1939)

art by Glen Rounds from
Cloth Book 4 (1940)

art by Kurt Wiese from
Cloth Book 6 (1942)

Supplied in cellophane envelopes, the books were a great success until wartime shortages curtailed them. "By 1942," says Ives, "wartime austerity prevented us from getting cloth of the proper quality. That was the end of the cloth books, for when the war ended we were shifting our emphasis from the declining trade market to the expanding library market."

The war also marked the end of such departures from tradition as miniature books and nursery rhyme broadsides, which had never found a solid market. There were nine stocking books in all—"little gems of books," *St. Nicholas* magazine had called them—and seven nursery rhyme broadsides, when both projects were laid to rest in 1939.

Meanwhile, the firm had adopted a small boy sitting on a rock reading a big book. The first Holiday House catalog in 1935 featured a colophon, or device, designed by Valenti Angelo—a boy riding a grasshopper that is jumping over a double *H*. Early catalogs and books carried different versions of this device on their covers and title pages.

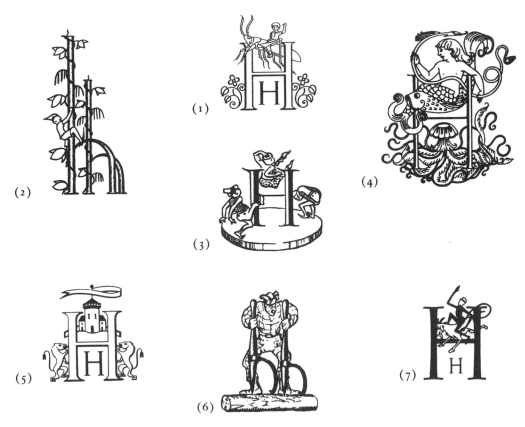

(1) by Valenti Angelo for cover of first catalog (1935), (2) by Arvilla Parker for *Jack and the Beanstalk* (1935), (3) by Stuyvesant Van Veen for *The Fairy Fleet* (1936), (4) by Pamela Bianco for *The Little Mermaid* (1935), (5) by John Atherton for *Jaufry the Knight and the Fair Brunissende* (1935), (6) by Glen Rounds for *Ol' Paul, the Mighty Logger* (1936), (7) by Percival Stutters for *How Percival Caught the Python* (1937)

"Then, in 1938," according to the *Holiday House News*, "we came across Kenneth Grahame's story, 'The Reluctant Dragon,' in *Dream Days*, and asked Ernest Shepard to illustrate it. One of his drawings was of the little boy who read 'natural history and fairy-tales . . . just took them as they came, in a sandwichy sort of way, without making any distinctions; and really his course of reading strikes one as rather sensible.' Both idea and drawing were so fitting that the little boy reading a book inevitably became our permanent device."

The new colophon appeared on the cover of the 1939 Holiday House catalog. Ives told a friend, "The boy has come to stay." He has identified the firm ever since.

art by Ernest H. Shepard from
The Reluctant Dragon (1938)

CHAPTER

4

In May, 1942, Holiday House moved to new offices at 72 Fifth Avenue and marked the event by inaugurating a chatty newsletter that would appear from time to time during the next eighteen years:

"This initial issue of *Holiday House News* is, in a manner of speaking, a celebration of our first moving day. After seven years on Varick Street, we have taken new offices in the genteel neighborhood of lower Fifth Avenue. The proximity of spring, the sidewalk cafes, and Macmillan have proved so invigorating that nothing would do but a newsletter.

"Our only fixed resolve about it is not to be dully commercial. If we mention forthcoming books or backsliding writers, it will be because they're interesting or amusing or important—even if we have to talk about some other publisher's. If we write short biographies of authors or artists (and that is one of our chief purposes), they'll describe people we think you'll really want to know about. If we sometimes toot our own horn, grind an occasional axe, or blow off about our pet peeves, we'll try to be entertaining about it. As for suggestions, if you don't see what you want, ask for it."

The new offices were on the second floor. Directly above, on the

drawing by Glen Rounds from
Holiday House News (1942)

third floor, were the offices of William R. Scott, Inc., which had been founded in 1938 as another small, independent publisher specializing in children's books. Since both firms did their own shipping, they decided to share that task and some others. One of their mutual employees was a young woman named Rose Vallario, who works for Holiday House today. She remembers the Fifth Avenue office:

"We had a shipping spot where we did all the shipping and billing for both Scott and Holiday House. They shared the biller, the receptionist, and the stenographer—all one person, me. I took dictation, typed manuscripts, kept the files, and helped Ted Johnson with the bookkeeping. Two sisters named Janet and Renée did the shipping. They picked; they packed; and they got them out. If there were any orders for over fifty books, then the binder shipped them. Smaller orders were always shipped directly from the office. We were a very friendly office, like a family. After all, there weren't that many people there."

art by Glen Rounds from *The Blind Colt* (1941)

Glen Rounds's classic novel, *The Blind Colt*, inspired by a real blind colt Rounds had known as a boy, had been published in the fall of 1941. After finishing the book, Rounds enlisted in the army. From Fort Bragg, North Carolina, he wrote: "Think of the peace that will settle over the offices of publishers for a while—nothing to upset the cultured quiet. From now on, instead of having to hunt up fellows to fight with, the Gov'ment is going to furnish them to me without cost. Instead of trying to make a Nice Nelly of me they encourage me to be my own nasty self, or even more so. . . . Now is the time to sit back and laugh to beat hell when you think what they have on their hands, trying to handle me and a war too!"

Wartime shortages were to affect Holiday House more severely than

art by Kurt Wiese from
A Puppy for Keeps (1943)

art by Fritz Eichenberg
from *Mischief in Fez*
(1943)

older and larger publishers. Paper rationing was based on a quota system; each firm received a percentage of the paper it had used in the past. With its small lists, miniature books, and brief history, Holiday House hadn't used much paper. "There was nothing we could do under the government regulations," says Ives. "Because of this we had to tighten our belts. Helen Gentry took a leave of absence and went to work for Simon and Schuster. She was gone for most of the war. We struggled along without her as best we could, because she was outstanding as a designer, and up to then, she had been doing all the production.

"The war almost did us in completely. Sales plummeted and debts mounted. Our output of new books dropped to virtually nothing. Almost half our backlist, small as it was, went out of print for lack of paper and working capital. We barely survived."

During the war, the firm introduced its Lands and Peoples series, which came to occupy an increasingly important place on the shrinking list of new books. The series had originated in England with four titles written and illustrated by Rafaello Busoni. "He showed them to Holiday House in hopes that we would import and sell the British edition," says Ives. "We liked the books, but the texts were so Commonwealth-oriented that we bought only the rights to the illustrations of *Australia* and *Mexico and the Inca Lands*, and I completely rewrote both texts, although Busoni was still credited as author. These were published in 1942, during the first full year the United States was in the war. All further titles in the series, eventually over twenty, originated from Holiday House, with Busoni doing the illustrations.

art by Rafaello Busoni from
Mexico and the Inca Lands
(1942)

"When we first started the series and were considering what countries to include, we discovered that, unbelievably, there were no books for young people on the history of Russia since the 1917 revolution. With Russia our wartime ally, there certainly should have been such a book, even though the subject was highly controversial. I decided to write it myself; not because I was an expert (it was entirely a research job), but because we wanted a viewpoint we could be sure was as objective and unbiased as possible. *Russia* was published in 1943 and immediately welcomed, particularly by librarians, as something long needed."

The firm's major discovery during the war years was Jim Kjelgaard, an avid outdoorsman and writer, whose agent was Lurton Blassingame. After reading some of Kjelgaard's stories in outdoor magazines, Ives got in touch with the young writer and asked if he'd be interested in doing a boys' adventure book. Yes, Kjelgaard replied, he'd like to try a book about forest rangers. He had once lived with his brother, a ranger in Pennsylvania, and he had worked part-time as a ranger himself.

Forest Patrol, Kjelgaard's first book, was published in 1941. His second book was *Rebel Siege*, a historical novel about rebel frontiersmen during the Revolutionary War. His third book, *Big Red*, was the one that made him famous as an enormously popular writer of animal and outdoor adventure stories.

Kjelgaard was working in a Wisconsin defense plant when he wrote *Big Red*. "The book was his way of ecaping from the daily routine of the factory, work he disliked intensely," says Ives. "He solaced himself by writing the book at night. He just poured his heart into it, and that's why it's such a wonderfully moving story of a boy and a dog."

Big Red became the most successful book that Holiday House had ever published, appearing in translation throughout the world and enjoying a wide distribution at home. It was also the first Holiday House book to be made into a movie. Forty years after the book appeared—and twenty-six years after the author's death—fan letters are still coming in from youngsters who have just discovered *Big Red*.

"He was a natural storyteller," says Ives. "He wrote simply and unaffectedly. His wild animals were completely believable. You had the feeling that Jim just knew the motivations of animals and why they be-

art by Charles Banks Wilson
from *Rebel Siege* (1953)

haved as they did and how they reacted and fought. It was a gift.

"I remember visiting him in Wisconsin years ago. There was a dog, a German shepherd, which had turned vicious and was locked up in a room. Jim wanted to see the dog, and he took me along. When we opened the door, the dog began snarling and barking. Obviously he wanted to take a piece out of one or both of us. Jim was completely unruffled. He just talked to that dog slowly and calmly, and gradually the dog stopped snarling and quieted down enough so that Jim was able to walk into the room. He showed his fearlessness and understanding of animals in that one episode, and I've never forgotten it."

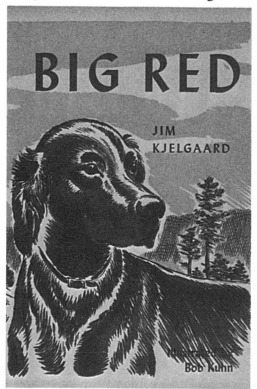

jacket art by Bob Kuhn for *Big Red* (1945)

Published in 1945, *Big Red* couldn't have come at a better time. The book's immediate success helped pull Holiday House through a financial crisis. During the war, the firm's output had dropped steadily— from twelve new titles in 1939 to a low of five new titles in 1944 and in

1945. By then, a substantial part of the backlist was out of print. For the spring 1947 season, only one book was in production. "Holiday House was barely breathing," Ives recalls. "Paper rationing had meant that we couldn't grow. We were virtually bankrupt; our largest creditor refused to print any more books until bills were paid. We had ground to a halt."

That year, Holiday House underwent an extensive reorganization. Ives bought out Ted Johnson and borrowed enough money to keep the firm going. Helen Gentry, who had worked at Simon and Schuster throughout the war, agreed to return on a part-time basis, and her husband, David Greenhood, joined the staff as an editor. Greenhood had done some free-lance editing for the firm in the past; he was the author of *Down to Earth*, a book on mapping published by Holiday in 1944.

During this period, Holiday House and William R. Scott decided to move their offices. "We both rented space in a tiny building at 513 Sixth Avenue," says Ives. "We shared a bookkeeper, Sophie Schwartz, in the larger Scott office; in ours were four people, for we now had a production assistant. The view was a brick wall ten feet away. In this office I spent two or three nights a week, sleeping on a folding canvas cot. Other nights I was in Warwick, for I began doing editorial work at home, including an extra job of editing a series for Pocket Books. This working-at-home arrangement lasted from then on."

Helen Ives, also working at home in Warwick, New York, undertook the job of building up a joint mailing list for both Holiday House and Scott. Before long, Frederick Warne & Co. was invited to come in with them and share the expense. The three firms began to exhibit together at library and other conventions, taking turns staffing the exhibits. Each publisher's books were displayed separately but in one booth. "Vernon and I many times discussed the pros and cons of merging our two little firms," Bill Scott recalls, "but we could never see that there was anything to be gained over our informal partnership."

As Holiday House began to rebuild, Vernon Ives, Helen Gentry,

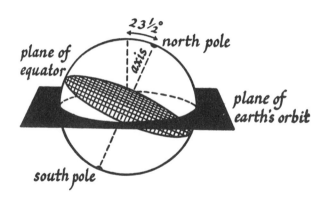

diagram by Ralph Graeter
from *Down to Earth* (1944)

art by Charles Banks Wilson
from *Henry's Lincoln* (1945)

and David Greenhood all worked as active editors. Ives handled most of the fiction, Greenhood the nonfiction, and Gentry the Life-Cycle and other nature books, and later, the few picture books the firm did. The Greenhoods had arranged to work on half-year schedules, so they could spend time at their new home in Santa Fe, New Mexico.

"There were no rigid separations," says Ives. "David read most of the manuscripts that came in 'over the transom.' He had good judgment, but he would spend almost as long writing a sympathetic and helpful letter of rejection as he would editing a publishable book. Our editorial duties just evolved. We wisely made no attempt to have a balanced list with something for all ages."

In 1948, Glen Rounds, back from the army, returned to the Holiday House list with *Stolen Pony*. Jim Kjelgaard became a prolific contributor, writing exclusively for Holiday House and publishing one or two new books a year. New titles were being added to the popular Lands and Peoples series; new authors were joining the list, and out-of-print titles from the backlist were being reissued in new editions.

art by Glen Rounds from
Stolen Pony (1948)

While the stocking books were never revived, Holiday House used one of the titles to start a vogue for sending miniature books as Christmas cards. *The Night Before Christmas*, originally published in 1937, was reissued as a twenty-five-cent booklet, sold with its own mailing envelope and "designed to be mailed to your friends as Christmas remembrances." It was so successful that the firm issued a second Christmas booklet, *Holiday Cheer*, a miscellany of Christmas recipes, customs, sayings, and songs from around the world, with color illustrations by Philip Reed.

By 1950, there was an active backlist of some sixty titles and a new mood of optimism. On the firm's fifteenth anniversary, Vernon Ives was able to tell *Publishers Weekly:*

"Today, after fifteen years of changing conditions that have radically affected many older and larger publishers, we are still doing business at the old stand. Our books are now less exotic in appearance and far more popular in subject matter than they were at first. But we still hold fast to our original tenets: high quality of content and format, and a small, personalized list. We're still 'choosey' about what books we accept, and still try to give each one a little something extra in idea or design to keep it from being just another book."

art by Philip Reed from
Holiday Cheer (1946)

CHAPTER

5

During the 1950s, the primary market for children's books was shifting rapidly from bookstores to schools and public libraries. "Bookstore sales had virtually stopped—at least for the kinds of books we were doing," says Vernon Ives. "We were now publishing mainly for the school and library market."

The Life-Cycle books, introduced in 1951 with *Garden Spider* by Mary Adrian, were aimed specifically at that market. Each volume presented the life cycle of a familiar creature in story form, using simple language, large type, and lots of detailed, three-color illustrations. The books were checked for scientific accuracy by authorities. "Every one [is] distinguished for its interesting text and excellent illustrations and bookmaking," reported *The Horn Book*.

To meet the demand for sturdily bound books that would stand up under heavy library use, Holiday started to issue many of its titles in side-sewn editions. When the firm decided that all the Life-Cycle books should be side-sewn, a number of the titles had already been published in regular bindings.

"Helen Gentry was a perfectionist," Ives recalls. "She had designed the books very well indeed, and she didn't like the idea of side-sewing

art by Ralph Ray from
Garden Spider (1951)

because you couldn't open a book as fully if it were Smyth-sewn. She agreed to have the books side-sewn if she could remake all the plates of the existing books, so there would be more room in the center margins. That would satisfy her aesthetic and perfectionist sense. We did it at considerable expense, which we could not very well afford at that time. But we did it."

The Lands and Peoples series, started during the war, had also found wide acceptance in schools and libraries. In 1947, *Publishers Weekly* called the series "outstanding in presenting young people's books about world trouble spots—India, Turkey, Palestine, etc. The various volumes present concise, unbiased surveys of the history, geography, economy, and sociology of different countries, their present position in the world, and their probable future."

One of these titles became the storm center of a censorship controversy in 1954. The disputed book was Vernon Ives's thirty-two-page volume, *Russia*, published in 1943. "*Russia* had made all the recommended lists," says Ives, "and had sold the best of any of our Lands and Peoples series—until the McCarthy era of the early 1950s." The book had been revised slightly in 1951, when a paragraph was added noting the deterioration of U.S.-Soviet relations and commenting that "a way of life not our own is not necessarily the wrong way."

The controversy erupted when Mrs. Maude Willdig of New Hyde Park, Long Island, signed a copy of the book out of a school library and refused to return it, charging that the book was "pro-Russian propaganda," "anti-American," and "lies from beginning to end." Mrs. Willdig demanded that the eight copies of the book remaining in the community's public schools be destroyed and that the librarian responsible for purchasing the books be fired.

"All hell broke loose," Ives recalls. "Involved were the librarian, the school board, the people who made up the recommended lists, the National Association of Book Publishers, the American Legion, and every newspaper and television station in the New York area."

One newspaper carried a photograph of the library shelf from which *Russia* had been removed. "In the space that my book had taken up, which was about a quarter of an inch, they had a space at least two inches wide," says Ives. "You'd think it had been an encyclopedia."

After twice voting to retain the book in its schools, the New Hyde Park School Board finally agreed to remove *Russia* from all library shelves, pending a decision by the New York State Textbook Commission. In its first ruling since its establishment in 1952, the three-member commission dismissed the complaint that the book was "subversive." However, it recommended that local school boards "would be well-advised to exclude the book from their school libraries" because it had become an "object of controversy" and because, in the light of current events, it contained "half-truths" and "inaccuracies," which were never specified.

The temper of the times was expressed by a Long Island high school principal who commented, "This opinion expresses my own about most any book. I can't see keeping any book if it involves any kind of controversial issue like communism or religion. There are so many hundreds of books on any topic, every school board should be able to have books that no particular group is opposed to."

Other educators refused to ban the book, and the Commission's decision was widely protested by the press and by professional organizations. "Book banning by the individual is presumptuous and can tear a community apart," said *Publishers Weekly*. "That the banning found the support of a state agency is disheartening." The Long Island newspaper *Newsday* ran a series of articles condemning censorship and said in an editorial: "It is shocking that an education official would throw out a book because it stimulates argument, discussion and thought. . . . If controversy is stifled in the schools, the future is destined to see a generation of boneheads, bringing with them the collapse of civilization as we know it."

As a result of the controversy, the American Association of School

Lenin and Stalin

art by Rafaello Busoni
from *Russia* (1943)

Librarians issued a statement reaffirming The Library Bill of Rights of the American Library Association. Another statement came from C. F. Shepherd, Jr., chairman of the Committee on Intellectual Freedom of the New York Library Association: "This would seem to be a very questionable policy, for how many books are absolutely free from such possible criticism? If such action jells to make a precedent, tremendous numbers of books could be removed from school or public library shelves. A closer look at 'half-truths' or 'inaccuracies' in any book may readily reveal that it is simply a matter of opinion."

The controversy gradually faded away, and the book that had caused it was allowed to go out of print. Looking back at these events many years later, Ives tried to put it all into perspective: "The attendant publicity was typical of the hysteria of the McCarthy era, but the little book did help resolve the question of who was to be responsible for book selection in the schools, professionally trained librarians or self-appointed critics."

art by Paul Galdone from *Night Cat* (1957)

The Holiday House list had long reflected Vernon Ives's enthusiasm for boys' adventure stories. One of his prized discoveries during the 1950s was an ex-actor and magazine writer who called himself Zachary Ball. Born Kelly R. Masters, he had spent thirty years traveling with small-town stock companies as an actor, director, and musician before selling his first story to *True Detective* for sixty dollars. He picked his pen name, "one they'd remember," by compounding Zachary Ball from the names of two show people, and at the age of forty-five started a new career as a writer. He was the author of two adult novels, and of stories for *Collier's, Esquire,* and *The Saturday Evening Post,* when his agent warned him that television was going to put an end to the magazine short-story field and suggested that he try writing adventure novels for boys, or what Ball liked to call "youth novels."

While living in Miami, Florida, Ball had become interested in the Seminole Indians and had visited a number of Seminole villages. His first youth novel was *Joe Panther,* the story of a Seminole boy of the Everglades, published in 1950. It was followed by eleven other popular titles during the 1950s and 60s.

Ball's best-known novel was *Bristle Face,* a classic boy-dog story published in 1962. It was an American Library Association Notable Book, a winner of the Dorothy Canfield Fisher and William Allen White awards, and was eventually filmed by Walt Disney. "I got the idea while writing the book that I wanted it to be an adult novel about a boy, rather than a juvenile story," Ball recalls. "So when the book was finished, I sent it to my agent, who at that time was Maurice Crane, and I told him what I had in mind, that I wanted it to be published as an adult novel and that I'd like him to send it to Random House.

"Well, I heard from Maurice a few weeks afterward, and he said in his letter, he said, 'Zach, I think you have painted yourself into a corner. This is a juvenile story. It is by no stretch of the imagination an adult book. I showed it to Random House, as you suggested, and the editor immediately sent it to the juvenile department. The juvenile editor at Random House wants it, and the Junior Literary Guild wants it, too.' "

At that point, Ball demurred. "I wrote him back and said, 'If that's the case, then I don't want it to go anywhere except to Vernon Ives at Holiday House. Vernon has done so well by me that if it's going to be a

jacket art by Elliott Means
for *Joe Panther* (1950)

jacket art by Charles Banks Wilson
for *North to Abilene* (1960)

jacket art by Louis Darling
for *Bristle Face* (1962)

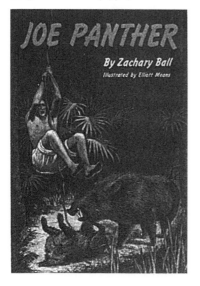

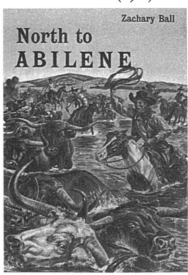

juvenile book, then that's where I want it to go. You call Vernon and explain the whole thing to him, and tell him that I want him to have the first chance at it.' "

As Ives remembers the story, Louise Bonino, the juvenile editor at Random House, phoned him and said, "Look, this is your author, and we don't have any intention of trying to take him away. And you might be interested to know that the book has already been chosen by the Junior Literary Guild."

And so the manuscript found its way to Ives's desk. "Vernon later told me," said Ball, "that it was the only time in all his publishing experience that he had ever bought a story without reading it."

With the success of authors like Zachary Ball and Jim Kjelgaard, Holiday House was turning its attention more and more to the young adult market. In 1960, Ives told *Publishers Weekly*, "The young adult reader is the one too frequently lost between 'juvenile' and 'adult' publishing departments. I think more books should be aimed specifically at this group." Holiday House was doing exactly that. Jane and Paul Annixter had joined the list with a series of historical novels such as *Buffalo Chief* (1958) and *Wagon Scout* (1965), and wildlife adventures such as *The Great White* (1966) and *Vikan the Mighty* (1969). Another husband-and-wife team, Pauline Arnold and Percival White, wrote solid informational books for young adults, including *Homes: America's Building Business* (1960), *The Automation Age* (1963), and *Food Facts for Young People* (1968).

For beginning readers, the Holiday House list emphasized science, nature, and animal stories. All of these elements were combined in the work of Gladys Conklin, who became the firm's most popular and prolific nature writer for younger readers. Before publishing her first book,

jacket art by Charles Geer
for *Wagon Scout* (1965)

jacket art by Robert J. Lee
for *Vikan the Mighty* (1969)

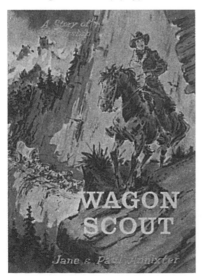

Conklin had spent thirty years as a children's librarian, working with Anne Carroll Moore at the New York Public Library, and at libraries in California. In 1950, she became head of the children's department of the Hayward [California] Public Library. Some of the children asked her to start a science club: "After giving it some thought, I said, 'We can study insects and call our club the Bug Club.' The children agreed, and the following Friday, forty boys and girls filled the clubroom at four o'clock. I didn't know a thing about insects, but I found out rapidly by raising them along with the youngsters. Hayward was a small country town at that time, and insects were plentiful."

It was the Bug Club that suggested the topic for Conklin's first book, and a Holiday House book by Dorothy Koch that inspired her to write it. "All my life I had wanted to write," she recalled. "I had recently finished a course in writing, and the teacher, Howard Pease, had said, 'When you find the type of book you would like to see your name on, use that book as your pattern.'

"In 1955, Holiday House published a perfect pattern for me. It was *I Play at the Beach* by Dorothy Koch, with illustrations by Feodor Rojankovsky. It was for the youngest readers and lookers, illustrated in beautiful color—what more could I wish for? I read the book over and over, trying to capture the rhythm of the words. I decided to do a simple book on caterpillars. I had been reading and buying children's books for thirty years and had never seen a book on caterpillars. The children, even the seventh- and eighth-graders, loved them.

"I sent the typed manuscript to Holiday House. They accepted it. I was on cloud nine for weeks. That enthusiasm stayed with me through my twenty-fifth book. None of my books was ever disappointing. The editors chose the illustrators with great care, and I have liked every one of them." Among her illustrators were Barbara Latham, Artur Marokvia, Joseph Cellini, Matthew Kalmenoff, Charles Robinson, Leslie Morrill, Leonard Everett Fisher, and Glen Rounds.

art by Feodor Rojankovsky from *I Play at the Beach* (1955)

art by Artur Marokvia
from *We Like Bugs* (1962)

art by Matthew Kalmenoff
from *Chimpanzee* (1970)

art by Charles Robinson from
Cheetahs, the Swift Hunters (1976)

art by Leonard Everett Fisher from
Journey of the Gray Whales (1974)

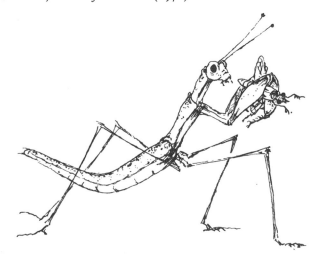

art by Glen Rounds from
Praying Mantis (1978)

art by Leslie Morrill from
Black Widow Spider—Danger! (1979)

art by Barbara Latham from
I Like Caterpillars (1958)

I Like Caterpillars, her first book, was published in 1958. From then on, Conklin wrote at least one nature book a year for the firm. One of her titles, *Elephants of Africa*, was the first Holiday House book ever sold to the Book-of-the-Month Club. After retiring as a librarian, Conklin spent much of her time traveling and speaking at schools and libraries: "One school down South made me a quilt. This was from the third- and fourth-graders. The children read the books, then made drawings from them. They used crayons on white paper, and then the P.T.A. used a warm iron and pressed the pictures onto the quilt squares. The squares were soft colors of green, yellow, and blue. I was dumbfounded. It would take hours to tell all the nice things that happened to me. I guess that's why I always liked my work so much."

art by Joseph Cellini from *Elephants of Africa* (1972)

Another popular addition to the list during the 1950s was Glen Rounds's pint-sized cowboy, Whitey. Rounds had created the character back in 1937 for *Story Parade* magazine. Whitey turned up at Holiday in 1938 in *Pay Dirt*, and again in 1941 as the boy who adopts and trains the horse in *The Blind Colt*. In 1951, beginning with *Whitey and the Rustlers*, he became the hero of a series of easy-reading "westerns" animated by Rounds's wry humor and waggish illustrations.

Jim Kjelgaard had been producing one or two novels a year for Holiday House and had become a close friend of Vernon Ives. Their relationship epitomized the advantages that a small firm can offer to an author. Ives wrote in the twenty-fifth anniversary issue of the *Holiday House News*, "Whether we were exchanging ideas and manuscript drafts with Jim by mail, watching his dogs run in Wisconsin, or fishing with him in Arizona, we never ceased to wonder at his understanding of nature, his love of dogs and boys, his modesty as a writer and, in later years, his magnificent courage in the face of increasing pain and discouragement. We are proud to have had a part in shaping the legacy that he has left to young readers."

Kjelgaard had died in 1959 at the age of forty-nine. All nineteen of his books were still in print, and every one a success. Two additional novels were published after his death. "I edited over twenty of his books," said Ives, "and became able to think as he did, with the result that in his last book, *Boomerang Hunter*, which I finished, his widow couldn't tell Jim's writing from mine."

Edna Kjelgaard told Ives in a letter: "I'm very grateful to you for all the work you've done on the book. I know Jim is, too. I believe I said before—but it's gospel—Jim has told me many times that you and you alone are the one person he could work amicably with. He said you were the most capable editor he knew. And so I am truly certain that the final version is one he will be proud to have his name on. . . . Sentimental or no, this I think is poetic justice—that you finished the book he couldn't."

art by Brinton Turkle from
Camp-in-the-Yard (1961)

In 1960, Holiday House was twenty-five years old. Its volume of business had increased every year since World War II, and about 90 percent of that business was now with schools and libraries. The 1960 catalog announced ten new books, included an active backlist of some 135 titles, and restated the Holiday House philosophy:

"In the quarter-century that Holiday House has been in existence, the world of children's books has come of age. To have been a part of this development has been an exhilarating experience.

"When our first catalog was issued, in 1935, it said that Holiday House would be 'a publishing venture devoted exclusively to the finest books for children' and that it would be 'sufficiently small to insure each title the personal attention of its founders, yet large enough to provide adequate and economical distribution.' We still mean it. To survive in a highly competitive field and to become a modest success as a small, independent, highly personalized specialist in publishing has not been easy. At first we were inexperienced, unknown, and financially insecure. Later, there were temptations to be resisted—a bigger list at the expense of editorial standards, books written to formula or for quick success, and economies of design and manufacture, regardless of good bookmaking practices.

"Through the years of growth, certain convictions emerged.

"We have never attempted to have a 'balanced' list. It has always seemed to us that a small publishing house should concentrate in areas where its interest, knowledge and enthusiasm are strongest. Consequently our backlist—two-thirds of which is still in print—is heavy in fiction for older boys, in books for beginning readers, in nature and geography and history and one-worldliness.

"We believe that not only illustrations but the type page and all other visual aspects of a book should make a unified, appealing presentation to the reader. This appeal should be aesthetic, but also practical in its contribution to ease of reading.

"We have, over the years, become more and more concerned with books that inform as well as entertain, until today our primary editorial consideration is the needs of schools and libraries. This is evidenced not only in the very high percentage of our books that appear on standard lists, but even in our bookmaking. All our books are bound in cloth, those for younger readers are nearly all side-sewn and reinforced, and as a service to librarians we double-jacket the first printing of new books.

"Finally, we have always been content to be small and specialized, so long as we felt that what we were doing we were doing well."

art by Jane Castle from *Watch the Tides* (1961)

CHAPTER

6

art by Lilian Obligado
from *Sad Day, Glad
Day* (1962)

After World War II, Helen Gentry and David Greenhood spent half the year in New York and the rest at their home in Santa Fe, New Mexico. When Holiday House celebrated its twenty-fifth anniversary, the Greenhoods decided to move to Santa Fe for good. Gentry arranged to sell her shares in the business to Vernon Ives. She and her husband phased themselves out gradually, completing their projects at hand and helping Ives through the transition period. "This was not retirement to us but a desire to pursue other interests and leave New York," says Gentry. "We had already bought a house in Santa Fe. David wanted to spend all his time writing, and I was the designer for the University of New Mexico Press."

In 1962, Gentry hired Leslie Pap, who had once run his own small press in Budapest, to replace her as the Holiday House designer and production manager. Later that year, Ives advertised in *Publishers Weekly* for a new editor.

art by Tom Funk from
I Read Signs (1962)

"When I made the arrangement to buy Helen out," he says, "I was aware that I desperately needed a good editor, someone who could be an executive in the business. I interviewed quite a few people and I finally chose Marjorie Jones, because I realized that she was not only a good editor, but had considerable executive ability as well. She did turn out to be a fine editor—and an executive."

Marjorie Jones had arrived in New York from Hebron, Ohio, a decade before, seeking a career in journalism. Her first job was as a reporter on a weekly newspaper in Westchester County. "I had never thought of book publishing," she recalls, "but a year on a weekly newspaper proved to me that I was not a foot-in-the-door reporter type. I knew that I wanted to do something that involved the printed word. Book publishing seemed like a nice idea, though I knew very little about the field."

She found a job at Prentice-Hall, then located on lower Fifth Avenue. (Around the corner, at 8 West 13th Street, were the offices that Holiday House had occupied since 1950.) Jones worked at first in advertising and promotion, and later as an assistant to Marjorie Thayer, who had come from Knopf to start the children's department at Prentice-Hall. Jones wrote catalog and jacket copy, and under Thayer's tutelage began to edit some books. "Marjorie Thayer was very generous with her time," Jones says. "She gave me my first chance to learn something about editing children's books. I've always been extremely grateful to her."

When Thayer went to California on a business trip in 1958 and sent a telegram back announcing her resignation, Jones was appointed the juvenile editor at Prentice-Hall. "I got the job because I was there," she says. "I was the only one who knew where the manuscripts were, I guess. It was a lucky accident for me to have been in the right place at the right time." One of the authors she worked with during this period was Glen Rounds, who wrote and illustrated three nature books for Prentice-Hall. (One title, *Wildlife at Your Doorstep*, was later reissued by Holiday House with new illustrations.)

Early in 1962, Jones moved on to Putnam, and later that year she was hired by Vernon Ives: "I remember very well the day I started. It was the week of Thanksgiving, a short work week. I walked in and

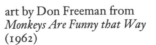

art by Don Freeman from
Monkeys Are Funny that Way
(1962)

found Vernon stretched out on that couch in the reception area. He was having one of his attacks. As I found out later, he had a chronic back problem.

"Helen Gentry had already left for the winter in Santa Fe. Vernon was planning to go to Bermuda [where he had a vacation home called Holiday Hill]. So I sat down and he told me very clearly and concisely what I was to do to carry on my editorial duties while the two of them were gone. I had been there one day. I was taking frantic notes about authors I had never heard of and books I knew nothing about.

"On Wednesday, having made it through the first two days, I came in after lunch and found a pile of money on my desk. 'What's this?' I asked. Sophie Schwartz, the bookkeeper, was sitting at her old-fashioned roll-top desk with all the cubbyholes; it was certainly a collector's item. She looked at me and said, 'What's that? It's payday.' And I said, 'This is it? What about deductions?'

" 'Oh, you want to know about deductions,' Sophie said. So she took a pencil and a little slip of paper, wrote some figures, handed it to me and said, 'There you are.' We were always paid in cash; it wasn't even in an envelope. It was all very casual."

For someone who had come up through the ranks at Prentice-Hall, the casual setup at Holiday House was "quite different, to say the least." There were no formal departments at Holiday, no time clocks, no memos. "If you had an idea," says Jones, "you simply turned your chair around and said, 'What do you think of this?' "

The Holiday House offices on West 13th Street were in an apartment building: "It was a very pleasant and convenient apartment. We had a regular bathroom with a shower and a tub, and we had our own kitchen, with kitchen duty—buying coffee and cookies when it was your turn. And cleaning up, too. You hoped you didn't get kitchen duty when it was time to defrost the refrigerator. It certainly was not what you would think of as an official, impersonal office in any sense."

At the time, Holiday was publishing five or six books a season. "It sounds like a small amount," says Jones, "but we all did everything. We didn't have the support of secretaries and copy editors. The Annixters, Ball, Rounds, and White and Arnold were producing regularly

art by W. T. Mars from *Castle, Abbey, and Town* (1963)

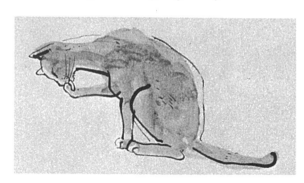

art by Brinton Turkle from *Mr. Blue* (1963)

for us. We did indeed need some new talent, but at that point we had talent and we were continuing to work with the same people who were well established.

"One of the first things Vernon told me was that it wasn't important to have a balanced list. We should do the books we were interested in and enthusiastic about, and that we could do well. That was the philosophy.

"My job was to fit in and maintain the reputation of the house. I was proud of the things they were doing. It was an excellent list. These were quality books. They were well designed; they were well received. Every detail in them was important. Everybody cared very much about what we were doing. If something wasn't right, the book was postponed. It was important to publish books we could all be proud of.

"It was a team effort. We all read everything that was being done. If someone had edited a book, probably someone else read the galleys. There was never that much emphasis on 'I am responsible for this.' We all felt that they were our books."

art by Charles Schwartz from *When Animals Are Babies* (1964)

One project that involved the entire office—it had been in the works for some time before Jones arrived—was *Rain Makes Applesauce*, a picture book with nonsense verse by Julian Scheer and complex, double-page, full-color illustrations by Marvin Bileck. This was to be Helen Gentry's last major effort for Holiday House. "It was Helen's pride and joy," says Vernon Ives. "She was the one who thought the unusual quality of the text could best be done by an artist she knew, Marvin Bileck. I think he spent three years making the illustrations. They were incredibly detailed and beautifully executed."

"I picked Marvin Bileck because I had informed myself about his work," says Gentry. "He seemed the ideal artist for the text and the kind of book I wished to make. That statement covers my selection of all illustrators. I spent much time and effort searching for the right artist for each book."

Gentry decided to have the book printed in Belgium and the sheets shipped back to the United States for binding. "At that time there was no printer in this country who could handle the complex color-reproduction problems," she says. "Other European countries had comparable printers, but Belgium was being favored by many of the American production people I knew as dependable, inexpensive, and excellent."

As things developed, the book took an inordinate proportion of the firm's time, effort, and money in relation to other books. "The artwork was redone completely at least two times," Marjorie Jones recalls. "It was practically a life's work that Bileck put into it. He was a perfectionist. And Helen Gentry approached every project I can recall in exactly the same way, in terms of perfection. And this was certainly very special art and a very special book. The technique was such that it was going to be very difficult to reproduce.

"It was in the works so long that the project became extremely expensive. We would send an urgent cable asking, 'When are the sheets due?' Two weeks later we would get a polite note in reply. Vernon said at one point that he hadn't thought that one book could put us out of business, but he was beginning to wonder. When everything was finally ready, and we were simply waiting for notice of shipment, we were informed that the sheets were being sent on a ship called the *Black Heron*. That seemed ominous. We were sure it would sink.

"As soon as we got the first sheets in, we rushed them out to reviewers and award-committee members. There was no time or money left to spend promoting the book. It was simply a matter of sending out unbound sheets. It certainly must have been very late being received by the reviewers. It's a perfect example of a book that was recognized on its own. It took off from the beginning."

Helen Gentry had wanted to make *Rain Makes Applesauce* a testament. Published at last in the fall of 1964, it became the firm's first Caldecott Honor Book and a perennial favorite on the Holiday House backlist.

art by Marvin Bileck from *Rain Makes Applesauce* (1964)

Helen Gentry and David Greenhood had left for Santa Fe in 1963. With their departure, Vernon Ives decided to hire a science editor to work with Marjorie Jones. The job went to Ed Lindemann, a soft-spoken naturalist, photographer, and science enthusiast who had been working as a free-lance copy editor. Lindemann took over the science desk in April, 1964, and set three long-term objectives for himself:

"I wanted to bring the science list more up to date, so it would reflect current advances. I also wanted to produce the kind of science books that would stimulate the thinking process in both teenagers and children. And finally, I was hoping to do books on subjects that had been neglected by other publishers, in science areas that had had very little attention paid to them."

Vernon Ives, meanwhile, was also planning ahead. He was beginning to think of retirement: "Holiday House was prospering modestly to the point where larger firms were beginning to make offers to buy. The value of a publishing house is its backlist, and ours was of top quality, though small. What made me think seriously of a sale was an ashtray.

"Helen [Ives] and I had driven to Lancaster, Pennsylvania, the Amish country, where I was to make a speech. In the hotel gift shop were the usual gimcracks, but a pottery ashtray caught my eye—or, rather, the inscription on it: 'We grow too soon oldt and too late schmart.' I bought the ashtray and still have it on my desk, a reminder of a 'schmart' decision.

"It seems to me that to change one's work and/or abode once or twice in a lifetime is salutary, but not one's spouse if you're as lucky as I have been. Otherwise, there is the danger of feeling in a rut. One day, at my desk in Warwick, looking at my ashtray, I began figuring and realized that I had edited over fifty books for teenage boys, plus many books in other categories. I was growing stale editorially and bored with administration, which I had never liked, really. I didn't want all the money in the world, just enough to live on comfortably while I developed new interests. Our girls were through college. That expense was over. The time had come when Helen and I should see whether we could afford to retire.

"I had offers from some of the larger publishing houses because of the strength of our backlist and the appearance of the books, but I knew that if the business was sold to a large publishing house, the list would be absorbed, the name would be forgotten, and that would be the end of it. I didn't want that to happen, because I had put thirty years of hard work into it. So I waited until John Briggs came along."

art by Ernest H. Shepard from
The Reluctant Dragon (1938)

CHAPTER

7

John H. Briggs, Jr., was born in Cleveland, Ohio, the same year that Holiday House was founded in New York. He was twenty-nine years old when he met Bill Scott and learned that Holiday House was for sale.

"I was looking for a new job when I met Bill Scott," Briggs recalls. "I can't say I was searching for a publishing house, but it looked like an opportunity. I was excited by the idea. I had been in the book business since leaving college, and I wanted to stay in it."

At Yale, Briggs had majored in English and served as chairman of the *Yale Literary Magazine.* He graduated in 1957, married Kate Halle, his childhood sweetheart, and applied for a job at The World Publishing Company in Cleveland, where he started out checking invoices and worked his way up to the special sales department. Nights and weekends he moonlighted as a salesclerk in the book department at Halle Brothers, the Cleveland department store that had been founded by Kate's grandfather.

After two years in Cleveland, Briggs went on the road as a trade salesman for World, calling on bookstores and wholesalers in New England and New York State, selling Bibles, dictionaries, adult trade

books, Skira art books, Meridian paperbacks, and children's books. In
1962 he transferred to World's editorial offices in New York City and
began to sell subsidiary rights. He then did brief stints at Horizon
Press and at Farrar, Straus and Giroux; he was working in Farrar's
New York sales department when he met Bill Scott late in 1964.

"I was young and foolish and wanted to be on my own," he says, "so
I went over and saw Vernon. Then I became intrigued."

"I remember John saying, 'Oh, I met somebody who knows somebody who's selling a publishing house,' " says Kate Briggs. "After John
and Vernon had met, off we went in a horrendous blizzard to Warwick.
I thought, 'What are we doing? We'll never get there.' We finally arrived, and I liked both Vernon and Helen from the start. It was a get-
acquainted meeting, a chance for them to get to know us and for John
to talk some business. We had lunch in their wonderful house, and it
was just very comfortable. It seemed that everything was right."

"There was interest on both sides," John Briggs recalls. "Vernon
said he was burned out. It wasn't fun anymore. It was an effort. He had
knocked himself out for thirty years and wanted to pursue other interests. I was attracted by the adventure of setting out and doing something on my own. I wanted to be independent."

The negotiations went quickly. Less than three months elapsed between the first meeting and the closing. "There were no hitches," says
Briggs, "no problems with copyrights or anything else. I remember
one of the lawyers saying that the sale was a standard textbook case. It
just went straight through."

The final papers were signed in March, 1965. Ives was to act as a
paid consultant for three years, but first he wanted to get away. The
day John Briggs took over, Vernon and Helen Ives flew to Bermuda.
"He said he was doing that as a favor to me," says Briggs, "and he was
absolutely right. Vernon had been there for thirty years, and even with
him out of the picture, there was always the thought, 'What would
Vernon say? What would Vernon do?' He foresaw that. If he had hung
around the office, I'd have just been in his shadow."

The sale came as a surprise to the Holiday House staff. "My first reaction was shock," says Marjorie Jones. "Vernon was not really at retirement age [he was fifty-seven]. I had had no indication that he was
planning to do this.

"We were assured by Vernon, and later by John when he did take over, that Holiday House was to continue on very much the same basis and there were to be no staff changes. Certainly there have been situations since then with publishers where that had been announced and not followed—but that's exactly what happened. Things did continue as before.

"We all had respect for Vernon. If he was willing to sell the business that he had established and obviously cared very much about, whatever his reasons for doing so, then I would trust his judgment. In retrospect, I would say that Vernon and John are actually somewhat alike. They are both totally honest, straightforward, self-contained people. There's not a lot of talking around—if you have something to say, you say it. I don't recall ever hearing either of them raise his voice.

"It couldn't have been easy for John, either. He came into a group of people who knew more about Holiday House than he did. But it was very clear very quickly that he was serious about this and wanted to learn. He was not going to make any changes without careful thought.

"The changeover was accomplished quickly. They signed the contracts over lunch, Vernon came back and said goodbye, got on a plane for Bermuda, and that was it."

In a letter dated March 10, 1965, Ives wrote Gladys Conklin: "Holiday House is being sold, and the details have been extremely time-consuming. The buyer is a young man named John Briggs, who wants to continue the firm as it has been built up over the years: a small, independent, quality publisher of children's books. I am very happy over this aspect, for it will mean the continuation of the pleasant, intimate relations between authors and staff that we have always enjoyed. As for myself, I'll be staying on as a consultant and editor, with free time in the future to do some writing myself and develop editorial projects that I've had little time for.

"So this will be the last contract I'll be signing with you, but not the last one between you and the house, I can assure you."

Briggs eased cautiously into the day-to-day operations of Holiday House: "My advocate and loyal adviser at World, Roy Chennells, told me, 'Don't do anything for six months.' That was good advice. Holiday House had a very fine reputation as a quality children's house. As far as any vision of what the house would become, that evolved over a period of time. Starting out, the idea was just to keep it as it was."

As Briggs studied the list, he began to formulate some long-range plans. The firm had been averaging five or six new titles a season, with an emphasis on older fiction and natural science books. "The list was static," he says. "It needed new authors and new illustrators, as well as new kinds of books. As fine as the list was, something had to be done, or down the road it was going to dry up. I spoke with Marjorie Jones about what I felt was needed. We wanted to do more books and get some new talent."

"We agreed that Holiday House needed some new blood," says Jones. "We had perhaps been relying too much on the people who were well established and continuing to produce books regularly. That was one of John's first concerns. He was interested in expanding, in the sense of bringing in new authors."

Another objective was to expand the firm's promotional efforts. In September, 1965—exactly six months after taking over—Briggs hired Dagmar Greve as the firm's first full-time, professional publicity director. Greve had worked in publicity at Henry Z. Walck, a children's house, and at Random House. "She was bright, young, and enthusiastic," says Briggs, "and she knew something about promoting books. We wanted to become more aggressive and more active in our promotional activities. That meant changing the sample list and attending more meetings and conventions."

To start with, Greve took care of a mundane but necessary task. "When I arrived," she says, "the review-copy list was not on stencils. So that was the first thing I did. I had it stenciled to avoid the horrendous job of typing all those labels." With that taken care of, Greve turned her attention to school and library conventions and exhibits. She began to branch out to other areas, too, displaying the Holiday House list at meetings of the International Reading Association, at audio-visual conventions, and at other educational get-togethers that

photograph of Jules Verne
from *Jules Verne* (1965)

relatively few trade publishers attended at the time. "Dagmar went out and showed the flag," says Briggs. "She also developed a new sample list for us, the importance of which can't be exaggerated. I think more sales were generated from those sample books than from anything else."

"It was a wonderful place to work," Greve remembers. "Because it was a small company, all of us were directly involved in every aspect of the operation. When art came in, Marjorie immediately showed it to me—her office was just five feet away. If John wanted to discuss something, he just stepped out of his office. There were no formalities. John let me do exactly what I thought was right. I didn't have to write long memos explaining what I wanted to do. He trusted me."

art by Lorence F. Bjorklund from *Horses: How They Came to Be* (1968)

In 1966, Holiday House left its Greenwich Village apartment and moved to midtown offices at 18 East 56th Street. It was the best of times for children's book publishers. The federal government's Elementary and Secondary Education Act had allocated huge sums of money for school libraries, and the Holiday House list was slanted toward that market. The firm's sales for 1966 were nearly double those of 1964. "I was lucky to have started out when business was on the upswing," says Briggs. "It made settling in easier and helped prepare me for the less prosperous times that lay ahead."

As Briggs had planned, the list was beginning to expand. Ed Lindemann recruited several new authors and signed up books that reflected current scientific advances. His books for older readers included Daniel S. Halacy's *Bionics*, Herbert Kondo's *Adventures in Space and Time*, Vladimir and Nada Kovalik's *The Ocean World*, and Paul W.

art by Jean Zallinger from
They Turned to Stone (1965)

Hodge's *The Revolution in Astronomy*. Julian May, an established science writer for younger readers, joined the list in 1965 with *They Turned to Stone* and eventually wrote fifteen books for the firm, illustrated by artists including Lorence F. Bjorklund, Leonard Everett Fisher, Symeon Shimin, and Jean Zallinger.

art by Symeon Shimin
from *Before the
Indians* (1969)

Gladys Conklin, meanwhile, began to work with Ed Lindemann, producing one or two books every year. Conklin and Lindemann often conferred on the telephone. They once had a lengthy discussion about some rare banana slugs that the author had discovered in her California garden. Lindemann asked if she could please send him a specimen. She did, and the slug arrived alive and well in an airmail package. Lindemann examined it with great interest, then went through the office showing it off to the staff. Some of them were not amused. "It was whitish and yellowish, yucky and icky," says Dagmar Greve. When Lindemann sent Conklin a thank-you note, he wrote: "I showed it around the office, and everyone admired it to the best of their ability."

art by Leonard Everett Fisher
from *To Unknown Lands*
(1956)

Marjorie Jones was also signing up new talent. At Putnam she had edited two books written by Anico Surany and illustrated by Leonard Everett Fisher. Fisher had illustrated the second children's book of his career, *To Unknown Lands* by Manly Wade Wellman, for Holiday House in 1956. Jones brought him back to the list. Beginning with *The Burning Mountain* in 1965, Fisher illustrated four of Surany's picture books.

Vivian L. Thompson's collections of Hawaiian myths and legends were noteworthy additions to the list. A long-time resident of Hawaii, Thompson had become a scholar of Hawaiian culture. She had done a great deal of original research, tracking down old legends and folktales

art by Leonard Everett Fisher
from *The Burning Mountain* (1965)

that were part of an oral tradition; many of them had never before appeared in print. Her first collection, *Hawaiian Myths of Earth, Sea, and Sky*, published in 1966 and dedicated to Helen Gentry, was illustrated by Leonard Weisgard, who had illustrated three of the Holiday House cloth books.

Marjorie Jones edited two novels during this period that represented a departure for Holiday House. "Problem novels now seem to be the rule rather than the exception," she says, "but fiction in the mid- and late sixties was still centered more on happy families and happy endings. We did two books in those years that I was very proud of, and still am. They weren't the first in the field, perhaps, but they were among the early books in what is now a common category."

One was Lois Baker Muehl's *The Hidden Year of Devlin Bates*, about "one of fiction's early ten-year-old rebels," says Jones. The other was Margaret Embry's *My Name Is Lion*, the story of a Navajo boy who resists "adjustment" to a Bureau of Indian Affairs boarding school. Embry wrote the book while teaching at a Navajo reservation school in New Mexico. "She had done some earlier books for Holiday, including *The Blue-Nosed Witch*," says Jones, "but *My Name Is Lion* was definitely a departure for her and for the house."

Jones was also the editor of Florence Parry Heide's *The Shrinking of Treehorn*. "One hardly thinks of *Treehorn* as a problem book," she says, "but we had some letters of complaint from people who didn't believe it was proper in a younger-age book to depict a child with such insensitive parents."

Heide was new to the Holiday House list. Although she had written a dozen children's books for other publishers, no one seemed to want *The Shrinking of Treehorn*. Her agent, Marilyn Marlow, sent the manuscript to Holiday, and Marjorie Jones grabbed it. "This was also a different kind of book for the house—and a different kind of book, period," she says. "The manuscript certainly needed no creative editing. I remember my first meeting with Florence. We discussed the manuscript. I think we agreed we would change maybe two words, one sen-

art by Edward Gorey from
The Shrinking of Treehorn (1971)

tence, and a couple of commas. She was absolutely delighted when she heard that Edward Gorey was going to illustrate the book."

Treehorn gained immediate critical acclaim; it was an A.L.A. Notable Book; it appeared on *The New York Times* list of the year's ten best-illustrated books; and it was published in several foreign editions. "It's a key book in our history," says Briggs, "one of the books that helped change our image and bring a new luster to the list. I remember Gorey saying that it was the only book he had illustrated, other than those he had written, that he really liked."

By the time *Treehorn* was published in 1971, Marjorie Jones had left to become the editor-in-chief of the Junior Literary Guild. "Marjorie was very talented, very likable," says Briggs. "She contributed stability to the list during a period of transition, and she helped move the house in new directions. She was able to provide the continuity that we needed during the changeover, because she was an expert editor and had excellent relations with the authors and illustrators. I relied on her a lot. I'm very thankful she was here.

"Before Marjorie went to the Guild, we talked about who her successor might be, and she brought up Eunice Holsaert's name."

art by Glen Rounds from
Wild Horses of the Red Desert (1969)

CHAPTER

8

Eunice Holsaert had entered children's publishing as an author of nonfiction books (*Life in the Arctic, Outer Space, Ocean Wonders,* and others). She became an editor at Knopf, went to Prentice-Hall in 1962 to replace Marjorie Jones, and then moved on to Hawthorn Books. John Briggs hired her in 1971. "She impressed me as having the ability to bring in new authors and illustrators," he says, "and that was an important consideration. She had done some very distinguished books for both Hawthorn and Prentice-Hall."

Holsaert brought a number of names to Holiday House. She signed up picture books by Mehlli Gobhai, Dahlov Ipcar, and Edna Miller; fiction by Mary Francis Shura and Ruth Chew; a series of science books by Seymour Simon; and three imaginative concept books by

art by Mehlli Gobhai from *The Legend of the Orange Princess* (1971)

art by Dahlov Ipcar from *A Flood of Creatures* (1973)

art by Edna Miller from *Duck Duck* (1971)

Sam and Beryl Epstein. She also introduced Marilyn Hirsh and Tomie dePaola to the list. She initiated the firm's list of Judaica books and was the editor of some of the earliest children's stories by Native American authors and illustrators.

"If there had been any children's fiction published by American Indians, it was extremely limited," says Briggs. "There may have been some books at the time put out by small specialty presses, and others may have come and gone, but there wasn't much around. *Jimmy Yellow Hawk* was certainly among the first."

In 1971, Virginia Driving Hawk Sneve had received an award from the Council on Interracial Books for Children for her unpublished manuscript, *Jimmy Yellow Hawk*, the story of a Sioux boy. Sneve had spent her childhood on the Rosebud Sioux reservation in South Dakota. Briggs met her at the awards ceremony in New York and suggested that she send the manuscript to Eunice Holsaert, who had expressed a long-standing interest in American Indian culture and concerns. The book, Sneve's first, was published in 1972 with illustrations by Oren Lyons, and was followed by four other Sneve novels on American Indian themes.

Three of Sneve's books were illustrated by Lyons, a chief of the Turtle Clan of the Onondaga Nation and an associate professor of American Studies at the State University of New York at Buffalo. One evening while visiting Holsaert at her New York apartment, Lyons told a story about a childhood experience with a dog he had owned. The story was so moving, and so well told that Holsaert burst into tears. The next day at the office she repeated the story to John Briggs. "She broke into tears again, and I did too," says Briggs. "It was a magnifcent story. We asked him to write it out, and we published it as *Dog Story* in 1973."

art by Oren Lyons from
Jimmy Yellow Hawk (1972)

art by Marilyn Hirsh from
Ben Goes into Business (1973)

The Holiday House Judaica books originated with Marilyn Hirsh, who had worked with Holsaert at Hawthorn. When they first met, Hirsh had just returned from India, where she had been a Peace Corps volunteer and had written and illustrated her first four picture books, published in New Delhi by the Children's Book Trust. ("For me, India was the land of opportunity," she later said.) Back in New York, mutual friends introduced Hirsh to the Indian author and artist Mehlli Gobhai, who at the time was working on a Hawthorn book for Holsaert. "You should meet my editor," he said. "Her daughter is living in India, and she'd love to hear about your experiences there." Hirsh and Holsaert became good friends, and Hirsh designed a couple of book jackets for her.

Hirsh's first book for Holiday was inspired by a story that Holsaert had told her. "Eunice had always wanted to write a story about her father's childhood," says Hirsh. "She didn't want to do it as a biography, yet she felt that it was too personal for her to fictionalize. Her family had come to this country as immigrants at the turn of the century and settled on the Lower East Side. When her father was a boy, he earned money by selling lollipops at Coney Island. Eunice told me about some of his adventures and suggested that I might write the story for her." The result was *Ben Goes into Business*, published in 1973 and dedicated to "Ben's Daughter."

Hirsh's second picture book for Holiday House was suggested by her friend Mehlli Gobhai. "He phoned me one night and said, 'I've just read this wonderful Yiddish folktale in a collection by Leo Rosten. It's a classic. You've got to read it right away.'" Hirsh's own retelling of that old tale, *Could Anything Be Worse?*, was followed by other picture books based on Yiddish folktales, Talmudic legends, and Old Testament stories.

art by Marilyn Hirsh from
Could Anything Be Worse? (1974)

"At the time," she says, "Jewish folklore was not being covered in children's books, at least not by general publishers. There were plenty of ethnic folktales around, but not Jewish ones. I wanted to do a Jewish folktale for its humor and its humanity, like any ethnic folktale, not for any religious message. And so *Could Anything Be Worse?* led to other books. They seemed to fulfill a need in the market, and they fulfilled a need in myself to explore my own background."

Could Anything Be Worse? was published in 1974. Holsaert had also edited Irving Howe and Eliezer Greenberg's *Yiddish Stories Old and New,* published the same year. These were the first Holiday House books on Jewish themes, the beginning of a growing list of Judaica books. "Marilyn Hirsh's early books, along with *Yiddish Stories,* made us aware that there was a market out there for Judaica," says Briggs.

Tomie dePaola had also worked with Holsaert at Hawthorn. He had illustrated science books by other authors and was just beginning to write and illustrate some books of his own. "Eunice held my hand at a crucial point in my career," he says. "I was living in San Francisco at the time, teaching at Lone Mountain College. Eunice came out and spent four days with me, just the two of us in my apartment, talking about ideas. She let me know that she liked my work very much, and she encouraged me to do more books of my own—original science books and stories based on my childhood. She had a master plan for me to do my own material."

When Holsaert moved to Holiday House, she asked dePaola to illustrate Sam and Beryl Epstein's concept books, *Pick It Up, Hold Everything,* and *Look in the Mirror.* They also discussed projects for

art by Tomie dePaola
from *Pick It Up* (1971)

original books by dePaola and came up with the idea for *The Cloud Book*. "I had done science books for other people," he says, "so I thought, 'I can do this myself.' I felt that the science books I had illustrated weren't as funny or as entertaining as they might be. *Sesame Street* was at its peak, and I was impressed by how very difficult concepts could be made simple and entertaining. I wanted to do something like that. I wanted to do my own concept books with as much humor as possible." He started working on *The Cloud Book*.

Marjorie Weinman Sharmat, meanwhile, had turned up in the Holiday House slush pile. "The first Sharmat manuscript came in without an accompanying letter," John Briggs recalls. "Eunice picked it out of the slush pile, read it, and gave it to me, recommending it. I gave it back to her and said I didn't like it. The next day she returned it to me and said, 'Would you mind reading this again?' I did, and realized I had made an awful mistake. Thank goodness Eunice persevered. She was dead right." The book *Morris Brookside, a Dog*, was published in 1973 with illustrations by Ronald Himler.

Sharmat had written several children's books for other publishers. When Holsaert asked her why she had sent *Morris Brookside* to Holiday House, Sharmat explained it this way: "My son came home from school one afternoon holding a book and said it was the best book he had ever read. 'Let me see that,' I said. It was *The Shrinking of Treehorn*. So I thought, 'Well, I have this manuscript here; maybe I should send it to that publisher.' I did, and I've felt like part of the family ever since."

During those years, Ed Lindemann was expanding his roster of science writers. "When I first went to Holiday House," he says, "I sat down and picked out a list of names from science magazines. I wrote to them and asked if they'd like to do books. Some of them accepted, and gradually the list began to grow."

Several of Lindemann's authors were professional scientists who had never written for children before. Marie Jenkins, a professor of biology at Madison College in Virginia, did a number of books, including *Animals Without Parents, Embryos and How They Develop*, and *Goats,*

art by Ronald Himler from
Morris Brookside, a Dog (1973)

art by Matthew Kalmenoff from
Goats, Sheep, and How They Live (1978)

Sheep, and How They Live. Philip S. Callahan, an entomologist at the University of Florida, wrote *Insects and How They Function, The Magnificent Birds of Prey,* and *Birds and How They Function.* William Stephens was a marine biologist in Florida. His first book was *Southern Seashores,* and he co-authored several Life-Cycle books with his wife, Peggy Stephens. Lindemann's most prolific author turned out to be Dorothy Patent, a zoology instructor at the University of Montana. Her first book, *Weasels, Otters, Skunks, and Their Family,* with illustrations by Matthew Kalmenoff, was published in 1973. By the spring of 1985, Patent had written twenty-eight Holiday House science books for all age groups.

"Ed was an excellent editor," says John Briggs, "and his books added prestige to the list."

art by Matthew Kalmenoff from *Weasels, Otters, Skunks, and Their Family* (1973)

Kate Briggs was responsible for bringing the novels of Helen Griffiths to the firm. She had discovered Griffiths's work in 1968 while she and John were in London looking for new authors. At the time, Griffiths had published ten books in England (her first was published when she was sixteen). Kate was visiting the offices of Hutchinson, Griffiths's English publisher, when Paul Langridge showed her a copy of the author's most recent book. "I read it and showed it to John, and we both fell in love with it," she says. "But it was on option with another publisher, who took it. So John went to Rosemary Macomber,

art by Shirley Hughes
from *Moshie Cat* (1970)

the agent for Hutchinson's children's list in the U.S., and asked her to please keep us in mind if Griffiths ever became available. When Helen's American publisher decided not to exercise its option on a subsequent book, *Moshie Cat*, we signed it up. The book was published in London by Hutchinson in 1969 and by Holiday House in 1970. Since then, Helen's novels have appeared regularly on the list and we've also had the privilege of publishing two other English novelists, Gillian Cross and Robert Swindells."

Kate Briggs had been working at Holiday House all along. "I had been brought up in a family business," she says, "and I felt terribly divorced from John's professional life when we were first married. It was distressing, because I wasn't used to that. His business world was his own, and it was hard for me to be separated from it. So when he took over Holiday House, I began to think, 'Ah, maybe there will be an opportunity for me here.'

"I came in doing just odds and ends. I did whatever was necessary. For a while I helped Rose with the inventory. My first real job was billing.

"In 1966, I went directly from the office on West 13th Street to have Ashley [the youngest of three Briggs children]. I billed from six-thirty to nine that morning, and then I went over to St. Vincent's. I had to

jacket art by Victor Ambrus for
Blackface Stallion (1980)

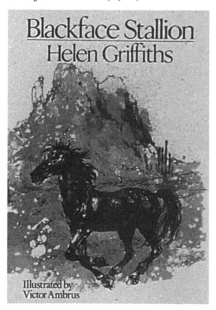

jacket art by Mark Edwards for
Born of the Sun (1984)

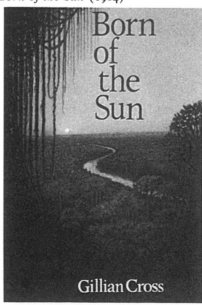

jacket art by Allan Manham for
Brother in the Land (1985)

take a few months off, so at that point John had to hire a replacement. That took my job away, which concerned me, because I'd gotten a taste of working and I liked it. So I asked John if there wasn't somewhere else where I could fit in."

Kate returned to full-time work in 1967 and became Dagmar Greve's publicity assistant. "I started out very gradually," she says. "My first real project was doing a bookmark. I mean, that was the most exciting thing I could ever remember doing. A bookmark!" Greve moved to John Day in 1969, and soon afterward Kate Briggs stepped in as the Holiday House publicity director.

"I learned by asking a lot of questions," she says. "Dagmar was my mentor, and also Mimi Kayden at Dutton. Those two were just wonderful. The other person who was enormously helpful was Eunice. She had a real flair for promotion. She'd say, 'Now this is somebody you should get to know.' She got me thinking about the differences between public libraries and school libraries, about so many things. Lots of people were helpful, but those three—Dagmar, Mimi, and Eunice—really got me started. Then Margery Cuyler arrived with her energy and ideas. She has been totally supportive and encouraging of all my efforts, and a joy to work with."

Eunice Holsaert had been with Holiday House just over three years when she fell critically ill. She set up an office in her hospital room and for a time worked on manuscripts and held bedside conferences with her authors. She died in the spring of 1974. "The books Eunice did were different," says John Briggs. "She brought new talent to the list, and she added some snap—a word she liked to use—and vigor to our image. She was a pivotal figure. With Eunice, we started on a new road."

decoration by Oren Lyons
from *Betrayed* (1974)

CHAPTER
9

Margery Cuyler was the juvenile editor at Walker and Company when she heard that Holiday House was looking for a new editor. "I kept sending people over who I thought would be interested in the job," she says. "They kept coming back and saying, 'This is an incredible job, Margery. Thanks so much for telling me about it.'

"About five people reported this. I hadn't been planning to leave Walker, but suddenly I thought, 'Gosh, that job really does sound terrific. I'm kind of interested in it myself.' When I realized that I might have the opportunity to work for a company that publishes only children's books, I phoned John Briggs and asked if I could have an interview. And he said, 'Sure, how about today?' "

They met for lunch at the Autopub in the General Motors Building, Cuyler's choice. "I found out later that John didn't like the place," she says, "but he was too gentlemanly to tell me that. We sat in a cramped antique car in the dark. There was just a dim little lamp, so we could hardly see each other. We had all these elbows and knees all over the place, because John is as bony as I am. Every time I moved, my knees banged against his or my elbow went scrunching into his ribs. We were terribly uncomfortable.

art by Barbara Cooney from
Burton and Dudley (1975)

"Within ten minutes of meeting John, I knew I wanted to work for him. I was going to land the job no matter what. So I sold myself. I pulled out all the stops. And I told him he'd be crazy not to hire me."

Briggs had already interviewed several candidates for the job. He had more interviews scheduled, and he would talk to Cuyler again before making up his mind. Looking back, however, he concedes that his decision had jelled during that lunch at the Autopub: "I was very impressed by her energy, her enthusiasm for the field, and her vision—what she wanted to do, what she felt she could do. Margery loves children's books. She really had few laurels to rest on; everything was in front of her and very little behind her. She had worked in publishing for only about three years, but she was knowledgeable and had this great sense of commitment. She wanted to be the absolute tops in her field—bring superior books to the list and publish them well—and that's exactly what she's done."

Cuyler started working at Holiday House in June, 1974. "It was the beginning of a long and happy relationship," she says. "John Briggs hired me to be an editor when I was twenty-five years old—a full editor in a very responsible job. Now that says something about him, doesn't it?"

To hear Margery Cuyler tell it, she had a calling and she knew it: "I decided when I was sixteen that I wanted to be a children's book editor. I had no ambivalence about it at all. The educational path I chose was geared to fulfilling my goal."

Growing up in Princeton, New Jersey, she was "one of those very lucky children who was read to by both parents daily, at lunch and after dinner. My father was a commuter. He would come home from his job exhausted, and he'd escape with me into these books. It was a special time I had alone with him, away from my noisy siblings. He would really sit down for an hour every night and read me stories that he adored as much as I did. He instilled in me a marvelous feeling for books. And my mother did the same thing. I'd come home from school on my bicycle for my lunch break, and she'd sit down and read me *David Copperfield* and *The Scarlet Letter* and other great books. My brothers and sisters, who were much older than I, also read to me, so my childhood was filled with books."

art by Matthew Kalmenoff from
Animal Architects (1971)

The educational path she chose led to Sarah Lawrence. The college had an excellent early-education center, but its chief attraction for Cuyler was Remy Charlip, who was teaching courses in children's literature and theater. "I was determined to go to Sarah Lawrence," she says, "because it was one of the only colleges that had a flexible enough curriculum to accommodate my interest in children's books."

After graduating in 1970, Cuyler became the assistant to Emilie McLeod at the Atlantic Monthly Press in Boston. "Emilie was my mentor," she says. "She was a great woman, and she taught me a lot. I learned from her that as you develop books with authors, you also develop friendships, and that the personal angle is critical to the editorial process."

In 1972, Cuyler moved to New York to become an associate children's book editor at Walker. She was twenty-three. It was an opportunity to create a list, and the books she acquired sold well. "I learned there that I had good commercial instincts," she says. At Walker she became friends with Millicent Selsam, who had been hired to develop a science list for the firm. From Selsam she learned how to help authors present scientific concepts simply and clearly, and how to convey the excitement of scientific discovery. "Millicent made me realize the importance of publishing science books in the children's field," Cuyler says.

Shortly after starting at Holiday House, Margery Cuyler was introduced to one of the firm's authors [Russell Freedman] at an American Library Association convention in New York. "I'm so happy to meet you," she said. "I've read all your books."

"It's nice of you to say so," the author replied, "but you haven't really read *all* of them, have you?"

"Oh, but I have," said Cuyler. And in truth, she had. During the

drawing of Samuel Colt by Arthur Shilstone from *Teenagers Who Made History* (1961)

art by Leslie Morrill
from *Growing Up Wild*
(1975)

previous weeks she had read practically every Holiday House title by the authors and illustrators she would be working with. She had studied the backlist diligently, from *Animal Architects* to *Yiddish Stories Old and New*. And she had plenty of ideas.

"There were some very fine books on the list and some wonderful talent," she says, "but in my view, the list was too conservative. Many of the books looked dated. They lacked exciting formats. They didn't seem to be exploring new territory. There was no pizzazz. I felt that Holiday House needed to head in a new direction. It should be nudged toward capturing more of the trade market, which was emerging as a vital force in the field.

"I thought, 'Holiday House is a terrific publisher. It has a really exciting promotion person—Kate; she's got a lot of style. It has a new art director, Kay Jerman, who started two months before I got here, and it has a president who is committed to children's books. Everybody is a top-notch person, and with a staff like this, we can really go places.' "

She had entered children's publishing at a time when paperback reprints were becoming more and more important. "I felt that the backlist could be partly rejuvenated by selling paperback rights. I didn't feel that the house had taken enough initiative in pushing subsidiary rights sales to a developing, softcover reprint market."

She picked through the backlist and began plucking out slumbering titles by old-timers such as Jim Kjelgaard and Glen Rounds, and more recent titles by authors such as Florence Parry Heide, Helen Griffiths, and Marjorie Weinman Sharmat. "I just went through the backlist and had a field day. I had a wonderful time. I sold lots of rights. It was so much fun! The excitement was that these books were going to have a new life. It was one of the things I accomplished in my first few months at the firm."

Another priority was to keep the list growing, a goal that Cuyler and Briggs had discussed at their first meeting. Holiday House was pub-

art by Matthew Kalmenoff
from *Frogs, Toads,
Salamanders, and How
They Reproduce* (1975)

lishing eight or nine books a season. "In my first year," says Cuyler, "there were eight books on the spring list, and they were shared between two editors. I felt that I could handle a lot more titles, and that that would contribute to the profitability of the company. To be a good editor, you have to have a good head for business."

One way of expanding the list was to produce more picture books, "exciting picture books" that would sell well in both the institutional and bookstore markets. "I love picture books," says Cuyler. "That's my first passion as an editor. I wanted to go out and acquire the best picture-book list I could, with some really well-known illustrators. There were so many things I hoped I could do. For instance, the name Holiday House. I thought, why not do a lot of books with holiday themes?"

art by Kelly Oechsli from
Walter the Wolf (1975)

art by Lisl Weil from
The Candy Egg Bunny (1975)

art by Tomie dePaola from
The Tyrannosaurus Game (1976)

Holidays were one of Cuyler's special interests (she has written three books on holiday themes for other publishers: *Jewish Holidays, The All-Around Pumpkin Book,* and *The All-Around Christmas Book*). "Holidays are important because they offer children a chance to experience their traditions," she says. "Most children today are isolated from those traditions, since we live in a very 'now' society. Halloween, Christmas, Passover—they all have ancient roots, and holiday books can put children in touch with those roots."

There was another item on Cuyler's agenda that would eventually change the Holiday House image: "I wanted to take the talent that was already on the list and try to focus it differently. I was very impressed by what many of these people had done, but I felt that they needed another sort of challenge. So that was an objective—to take what was already there and try to lead it to its full potential."

art by Glen Rounds from
*Mr. Yowder and the Lion
Roar Capsules* (1976)

CHAPTER

10

Tomie dePaola had illustrated three books for Holiday House when Margery Cuyler arrived on the scene in 1974. "He had fallen into my lap," she says, "so I thought, why not go after him to do some really interesting books of his own? He was at a critical point in his career where he was shifting gears from illustrating nonfiction books to using his imagination to come up with a whole different kind of picture book, the kind where his storytelling skills, both visually and verbally, were beginning to shine.

"*Strega Nona* [Prentice-Hall] hadn't been published yet. There were certain books he had done up to that time, like *Nana Upstairs, Nana Downstairs* [Putnam], that showed he was 'an original.' But I didn't feel that his genius quality had been fully developed. Where I really saw a potential to encourage him to go in a new direction was when he published *Charlie Needs a Cloak* [Prentice-Hall]. In a sense, it is a nonfiction book, but it's a very imaginative nonfiction book."

DePaola was now living in New Hampshire, and Cuyler paid him a visit. He was working on *The Cloud Book*, his first original text for

art by Tomie dePaola from *The Cloud Book* (1975)

Holiday House, a project he had planned with Eunice Holsaert (the book is dedicated to her). He and Cuyler discussed future projects. "The idea was for him to do several concept books—*The Cloud Book, The Quicksand Book, The Popcorn Book,*" says Cuyler. "They were all innovative books because, like *Charlie Needs a Cloak,* they presented information in a humorous way, within the context of a storyline.

"It's extremely hard to write a nonfiction book using a fictional technique. In the early '70s, the market wouldn't accept such a project, because buyers wanted a clear demarcation between fiction and nonfiction. But if you were an artist like Tomie, knew the material cold, and knew how you could present it by using a clear but humorous and charming storyline, you could bridge the gap between fiction and nonfiction.

"He did it first with *The Cloud Book* and more successfully later with *The Quicksand Book,* a 1978 A.L.A. Notable Book. Quicksand was the perfect subject for this kind of experimental format. The book is a marvelous blend of information, storyline, and humor.

"I felt he should continue with this type of book, but in addition to that, he should branch out. He should have the opportunity to try some ideas that he wanted to do very much that didn't fit into a particular category, ideas that could be considered experimental. Also, I knew that he was deeply religious, and that that was an area where he could express himself. I think he was beginning to think of these things too, so the timing was perfect."

DePaola agrees that the timing was right. "Margery and I hit it off very well personally," he says. "For one thing, we share the same sense of humor. She urged me to be as humorous as possible in my books. With *Quicksand* she encouraged me to just take it and run. We also

art by Tomie dePaola from *When Everyone Was Fast Asleep* (1976)

art by Tomie dePaola from *Nuestra Señora de Guadalupe* (1980)

art by Tomie dePaola from *The Night Before Christmas* (1980)

share a strong interest in religious themes. I can't imagine any of my other publishers allowing me to do *Francis: The Poor Man of Assisi* or *The Lady of Guadalupe* the way they were done. Holiday House allowed me to do them just because I was interested. And they let me do them the way I wanted to without having to force them into a commercial mold."

Francis: The Poor Man of Assisi was a 1983 A.L.A. Notable Book. *The Lady of Guadalupe*, published in 1980, was perhaps the first children's book ever issued in four editions simultaneously: an English-language edition in both hardcover and paperback, and a Spanish-language edition, translated by Pura Belpré, in hardcover and paperback. These were also the first paperbacks to carry the Holiday House imprint. DePaola's other unusual books for Holiday House— "projects that other publishers wouldn't touch," he says—have included *When Everyone Was Fast Asleep, Songs of the Fog Maiden,* and *The Hunter and the Animals,* a wordless full-color picture book. "The only classics we've asked him to do," says Cuyler, "are *The Night Before Christmas* and *Mary Had a Little Lamb,* which is an A.L.A. Notable Book."

"I've always thought that Holiday House gave me a chance to grow as a visual artist—not just as a book person. They gave me a chance to develop my art," dePaola says. "Everyone there has helped in some way. Margery pulled it out of me. John Briggs backed me because he was willing to take risks. Kate Briggs has influenced me, too, through her taste, her whole approach; she has a very keen artistic sense. With Kay Jerman, I could always count on my books being beautifully produced. I could show them to other publishers as examples of what could be done in a production sense. Holiday House has allowed me to do the books that interested me, and to do them the way I wanted to."

art by Tomie dePaola from
The Hunter and the Animals (1981)

art by Tomie dePaola from *Francis:
The Poor Man of Assisi* (1982)

art by Tomie dePaola from
Mary Had a Little Lamb (1984)

art by Leonard Everett Fisher
from *The Railroads* (1979)

In 1978, John and Kate Briggs were attending a conference at Old Sturbridge Village in Massachusetts, when they ran into Leonard Everett Fisher. Fisher had illustrated a number of Holiday House picture books and science books during the 1960s and early 1970s, but had done nothing for the firm since then. A conversation in an aisle with John and Kate that afternoon resulted in his highly praised Nineteenth Century America series, which John edited.

Fisher had already illustrated more than 200 children's books written by himself and others. He had been producing distinguished books on American history for more than two decades (including the Colonial Americans series published by Franklin Watts), using his well-known scratchboard technique for the illustrations. But he was also an award-winning painter, and it was that side of his talent that caught Margery Cuyler's eye.

"I felt that he should be doing some full-color picture books," she says. "When I visited his house in Connecticut, I looked at his walls and realized why he had won a 1950 Pulitzer award for painting. His house was filled with his own paintings. I wondered, why wasn't more of this in his recent books?"

Fisher was eager to do some full-color books. He discussed several ideas with Cuyler, including one for a picture book about the creation of the world. "But what would I use as a text?" asked Fisher. "The Bible?"

"No, that would be too difficult for the picture-book level," Cuyler

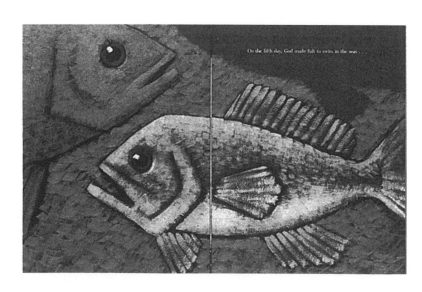

art by Leonard Everett Fisher from
The Seven Days of Creation (1981)

art by Leonard Everett Fisher
from *The Olympians* (1984)

replied. "I think you should adapt the biblical text. You should rewrite it very simply, so it's accessible to a young child."

"Rewrite it? But I can't rewrite the Bible."

"You're going to recreate the world, aren't you? Then you may as well go all the way and rewrite the Bible."

Fisher adapted Genesis 1:1–31 and 2:1–2 and used acrylic paints for his illustrations. The result was *The Seven Days of Creation,* a 1982 A.L.A. Notable Book. Fisher went on to write and illustrate in full color *Star Signs* and *The Olympians,* and he did the full-color illustrations for Myra Cohn Livingston's *A Circle of Seasons* (a 1983 A.L.A. Notable Book) and *Sky Songs.*

"Fisher needs challenging subjects," says Cuyler. "He's no good at illustrating a book about Sally Rabbit who goes out and hunts for Easter eggs. He needs to illustrate the creation, the seasons, the universe. He's got to have huge ideas."

Florence Parry Heide had not appeared on a Holiday House list since the 1971 publication of *The Shrinking of Treehorn.* She had written many books for other publishers, including picture books, novels, and a series of juvenile mysteries co-authored with her daughter, Roxanne. Cuyler was anxious to meet the author of *Treehorn* and bring her back to the Holiday House list, and when Heide visited New York, they got together for lunch.

"When I first met her, I realized that she was one of the wittiest people I'd ever met," says Cuyler, "and I felt she should write a funny book. *Treehorn* is funny, of course, but I wanted her to write a funny novel. She had done so many serious novels for other publishers, and they were sensitive and well written. I wanted to take her and throw her into a whole new genre. So I begged her to write a humorous novel."

jacket art by
Marylin Hafner for
Banana Twist (1978)

art by
Marylin Hafner from
Time Flies! (1984)

"We did have a marvelous time," Heide recalls, "and we've grown to be very good friends. I think we were friends from the beginning." Heide had never attempted a humorous novel, but she liked the idea. She responded to Cuyler's urging with *Banana Twist*, *Time's Up!* (both A.L.A. Notable Books), *Banana Blitz*, and *Time Flies!* "She's one of the few writers who can handle the genre successfuly," says Cuyler. "Humor is extremely hard to write, especially the type she writes, which is witty and satirical." Along with her humorous novels, Heide has written two *Treehorn* sequels edited by John Briggs, *Treehorn's Treasure* (an A.L.A. Notable Book) and *Treehorn's Wish*, both illustrated by Edward Gorey.

Cuyler says that Heide has the "thickest, heaviest, most unwieldy correspondence file of any author we have ever published. She writes almost every day, wonderfully enthusiastic letters about her thoughts, her ideas, what she's been doing, her children, her grandchildren. I love getting her letters, and I love writing her back. She's a real pen pal. But I think she's pen pals with something like four hundred people in America. She becomes pen pals with all the kids who write her fan letters, with authors, and with her other editors. That's how she reaches out beyond the boundaries of Kenosha, Wisconsin."

"When I first started writing books," says Heide, "I felt very isolated out here in Kenosha. Writing is so solitary, and the letters were a bridge for me. Letter writing has helped me stay in touch with others in the children's book field and with my readers. I'll begin a correspondence with youngsters who have read my books, and then the first thing you know, they're in college or married and we're still writing. I love to write letters. It warms me up to write a book."

art by Edward Gorey from
Treehorn's Wish (1984)

Marjorie Weinman Sharmat had published two books with Holiday House during Eunice Holsaert's tenure. "I was lucky that she was already represented on the list," Cuyler says. "She had a wonderful talent for writing picture-book stories with a moral that she could relay with tremendous humor and subtlety. You came away from her books feeling that you had learned something, or maybe that you had been changed in some small way, though you weren't necessarily aware of it consciously. Besides, she's terribly funny. She's got a terrific sense of humor and a keen ear for dialogue. You could see that in the books she had already done for Holiday House, *Morris Brookside, a Dog* and *Morris Brookside Is Missing*."

Cuyler wanted Sharmat to keep it up, to do more of the same. "I also wanted to crank Marjorie up to do a lot more books, because she's so talented. I thought we should have at least one book a season from her, which we pretty much have had."

art by Kay Chorao from
I'm Terrific (1977)

art by Lilian Obligado from
The Best Valentine in the World (1982)

Dorothy Patent had joined Holiday House in 1973 as one of Ed Lindemann's science writers. When Lindemann left the firm in 1979 to work as a free-lance editor, Patent already had fourteen active titles on the list, all substantial natural history books for older readers. Patent's books required a great deal of research. Cuyler felt that the same research could be recycled and presented in a different format for younger readers. She discussed this idea with John Briggs and they agreed

The Lives of Spiders
(1980)

Spider Magic
(1982)

to divide Dorothy Patent between them. "John would do all the editing of the older-level books," says Cuyler, "while I would try to help her use the same material for the younger level." Thus, *The Lives of Spiders* (ages ten and up), a Golden Kite Award winner, became the A.L.A. Notable Book *Spider Magic* (ages six to nine), while the information gathered for *Horses and Their Wild Relatives* (ages ten and up) was used in *A Picture Book of Ponies* (ages five to eight), and *Bacteria* (ages twelve and up) provided the idea for *Germs!* (ages eight to eleven).

Glen Rounds had been publishing with Holiday for nearly forty years when Cuyler flew down to Southern Pines, North Carolina, to get acquainted. "I felt he should get back to writing some novels," she says. "He had written two classics, *The Blind Colt* and *Stolen Pony*, and I knew he had at least one more novel in him. Of all the books we've worked on together, the one that was most satisfying to me, because it was the hardest one to pull out of him, was *Blind Outlaw*. It took a lot of work to get him to do it. It had been sitting inside him for thirty-five or forty years, waiting to come out. But I knew it was there. Every now and then he'd talk about it.

"And also, he's just terrific as a tall-tale storyteller. He hasn't really been given the homage he's due as an original American humorist. I think history will judge him as one of the best. He's made an extraordinary contribution.

"Glen is also one of the most professional writers I've ever worked with. He is so hard on himself that by the time I have a draft, I don't have to edit it. He's done my work for me. It's the same with his artwork. It's perfect when it reaches the office."

art by Glen Rounds from
Blind Outlaw (1980)

CHAPTER

11

John Briggs and Margery Cuyler had agreed that the list should be expanded. It grew from seventeen new titles in 1974, the year Cuyler joined the firm, to thirty-eight in 1985.

During that decade, Holiday House signed up more than thirty new authors and illustrators. Some were people with established reputations; others were newcomers who had never been published before. They came to the house through agents and through friends of friends, through chance meetings and fortuitous circumstance. A couple of gifted illustrators simply walked into the office with their portfolios. And some talented authors were discovered unexpectedly in the mail.

Steven Kroll was one of Cuyler's earliest discoveries. They met in 1973, while she was still at Walker. Kroll had worked as an adult fiction editor at Holt and in England. He had published a number of short stories and book reviews. He had also written some unpublished children's stories, and Cuyler asked to see them.

"They all showed that he had this uncanny ability to think visually," she says, "which is the key talent when you're writing a picture book, if you can't illustrate your own work. You certainly have to write in a way that illustrators can appreciate. You have to be able to think in images.

art by Dick Gackenbach from
Is Milton Missing? (1975)

art by Tomie dePaola from
Santa's Crash-Bang Christmas (1977)

"A lot of picture-book authors who don't illustrate their own work have problems with that, because they're not visually oriented. They're word-oriented. Steven is both word-oriented and visually oriented. This was clear from the first draft I read of the book that Holiday House finally published, *Is Milton Missing?*"

That was Kroll's first published book. "I rewrote it completely," he says, "using Margery's advice as my guide." Kroll was soon writing a picture book a season for the firm, giving Cuyler a chance to recruit some new illustrators and to practice her intensely personal style of editing: "We worked best when we were alone, so we might spend eight or nine hours closeted in a room. I'd edit and Steven would rewrite; I'd edit and he'd rewrite—we'd just spend as many hours as necessary until it worked. Steven would rewrite on the spot and test it out on me. He likes to work that way. He doesn't want to lose his thoughts."

One of Kroll's early books, *Santa's Crash-Bang Christmas*, went through something like eight or nine drafts. Santa wasn't even in the first draft, which was about a little girl who lives in a house that begins to collapse. Santa didn't appear in this collapsing house until the fifth draft. "That was a book that went through lots of stages," says Cuyler. "But it was worth it, because it has been through several printings and

art by John Wallner from
One Tough Turkey (1982)

art by Jeni Bassett from
The Biggest Pumpkin Ever (1984)

has become a perennial holiday favorite. Also, it was one of Steven's early books, and he was still learning the craft of writing a picture book. Now he writes a draft, and it usually needs just one or two revisions."

"We work so well together after all these years," says Kroll, "that the amount of work has decreased. In the early days we'd often work right through dinner and sometimes up to midnight. We don't need to do that anymore; things come right much more quickly. Even so, I look back with longing at those midnight editing sessions with Margery, because they were so special.

"Nowadays we'll talk about a story idea before I've written a word. When we first sit down to talk, we might not have much to go on, but when we finish we'll have a full-blown idea that I can start working on. I'll do a couple of drafts on my own. After Margery has read it, it will go through another full draft, and after that, it just needs polishing. We have plenty of disagreements, of course, but we always wind up compromising. I'll often disagree when she first makes a suggestion, but later, on reflection, I'll acknowledge that she's right. It's a marvelous experience to work with Margery. It's as close as I can get to working inside someone else's head besides my own. She's not just my editor, she's my collaborator."

Whenever possible, Cuyler likes to work face-to-face with her authors, revising on the spot. Many authors have spoken of their marathon editing sessions with her. "It's all very personal," says Tomie dePaola. "I always work with Margery in person. She comes up to visit, stays two or three days, and we hash out what projects we're going to do. When I'm working on a manuscript, she comes up again and we work revising. Often she stays a few days, and when she leaves, the manuscript is finished. It's very exciting to work with her, very intense."

Another of Cuyler's early discoveries was T. Ernesto Bethancourt, a singer-guitarist who performs professionally as Tom Paisley. They met through a mutual friend, who arranged a lunch to introduce them. It was obvious to Cuyler that Bethancourt was extremely bright and imaginative. "He began to talk about his childhood—he had grown up as a poor kid in Brooklyn. It was just fascinating," Cuyler recalled later. "I asked him if he had ever tried writing about it and he said, 'As a matter of fact, I have four chapters of a novel sitting in my bureau drawer at home.' "

Cuyler asked Bethancourt to send her the chapters. "I read them, took them in to John Briggs, and he agreed that we should give Bethancourt a contract immediately. He had never published anything before that."

Bethancourt's first book, *New York City Too Far from Tampa Blues*, was published in 1975 and was made into an NBC Afternoon Special. By 1985, Bethancourt had published seventeen novels on the Holiday House list, including *The Dog Days of Arthur Cane* and eight popular *Doris Fein* mystery books.

jacket art by Bernard Colonna for *The Dog Days of Arthur Cane* (1976)

jacket art by Brad Hamann for *Doris Fein: Murder Is No Joke* (1982)

jacket art by Emily McCully for *That's Mine* (1977)

jacket art by Emily McCully for *Marathon Miranda* (1979)

Three of the authors that Cuyler signed up during these years were children's book editors. Elizabeth Winthrop had been a classmate of Cuyler's at Sarah Lawrence. She had worked as an editor in the children's book department at Harper & Row, which published her first children's books. Her first title for Holiday House was *Potbellied Possums*, a picture book; it was followed by *Knock, Knock, Who's There?*, a young adult novel. She became the only author on the Holiday

House list other than Glen Rounds to write both picture books and novels.

Betty Ren Wright had been an editor at Western Publishing in Racine, Wisconsin, for many years (when she became managing editor in 1968, she supervised twenty-two different lines of children's books). During that time she wrote magazine fiction for adults and some thirty-five picture books for children, many of them Golden Books. When she retired from Western, she wrote her first novel, *Getting Rid of Marjorie*, published by Holiday House in 1981. ("The title tugged at my heart," says Cuyler.) Wright has since written both problem novels and mysteries. *The Dollhouse Murders* was an Edgar Award nominee.

Ann M. Martin was the young editor of Scholastic's Teenage Book

jacket art by
Pat Sustendal for
Getting Rid of Marjorie
(1981)

jacket art by
Stephen Mancusi for
The Dollhouse Murders
(1983)

jacket art by
Eileen McKeating for
Bummer Summer
(1983)

jacket art by
Blanche Sims for
Stage Fright (1984)

Club when Holiday House published her first novel, *Bummer Summer*, in 1983. It was followed by *Inside Out*, based on Martin's experiences working with autistic children, and by a humorous novel, *Stage Fright*. "She's an expert at taking a problem and exploring it with humor," says Cuyler.

Other new authors were found among the unsolicited manuscripts brought in by the mail. Betty Bates, an Evanston, Illinois, housewife and mother of four grown children, sent in a manuscript addressed simply to "Holiday House." She had picked the firm's name from a list of publishers supplied by The Children's Book Council. "The manuscript wasn't acceptable," says Cuyler, "but it showed that she understood how twelve-year-olds think. It also showed that she had a fresh, humorous, easygoing style. Style is very important as far as slush-pile reading goes. That's one of the first things I look for—a style that kids will really like."

Cuyler wrote an encouraging letter to Betty Bates, turning down her first submission but asking to see something else. Bates quickly sent in three chapters and a synopsis for *Bugs in Your Ears*, which became her first published book in 1977. It was later filmed as an ABC Afternoon Special, which was nominated for an Emmy Award. By 1985,

jacket art by
Harold James for
Bugs in Your Ears
(1977)

jacket art by
Linda Strauss Edwards
for *Call Me Friday the
Thirteenth* (1983)

jacket art by
Leslie Morrill for
*Judge Benjamin:
Superdog* (1982)

Bates had written nine successful novels for Holiday.

"Out of all those books, I've had just one go through without major changes," she says. "When I was working on my first book, I almost got mad at Margery because she asked for so many changes. Really, my temperature was rising! I was writing and rewriting for a year before she accepted it. But look what happened. It was worth it."

Judith Whitelock McInerney was a Decatur, Illinois, housewife and mother of four when she sent in an unsolicited manuscript about their family pet, a 200-pound Saint Bernard. It was too short, only twelve pages, but it looked promising. Cuyler wrote to McInerney and asked her to turn those twelve pages into a 150-page novel, which she did. It was published in 1982 as *Judge Benjamin: Superdog*, the first of McInerney's popular *Judge Benjamin* titles, all illustrated by Leslie Morrill.

Bill Wallace, another slush-pile discovery, was the principal and physical education instructor at the same school he had attended as a child in Chickasha, Oklahoma. Wallace had published short stories in periodicals such as *Western Horseman, Hunting Dog Magazine*, and *Horse Lover's Magazine;* he also had collected several rejection slips from book publishers before sending a manuscript to Holiday. Cuyler

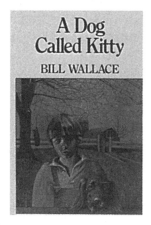

jacket art by
Judy Clifford for
A Dog Called Kitty
(1980)

jacket art by
Ken Mitchell for
Shadow on the Snow
(1985)

turned down that manuscript, but she wrote a long, encouraging letter to Wallace, saying that he had a gift for telling boys' adventure stories and urging him to send in more of his work. His first published book, *A Dog Called Kitty*, received the 1983 Texas Bluebonnet Award and the 1983 Oklahoma Sequoyah Award. This was followed by *Trapped in Death Cave* and *Shadow on the Snow*.

Holiday House receives between 3,000 and 4,000 unsolicited manuscripts a year, and everything that comes in gets a reading. About one fourth of the submissions receive a personal letter and an individual critique in reply; the others get a form letter. Kate Briggs is in charge of these submissions and does most of the initial screening, helped out by practically everyone on the staff. "After so many years of reading these manuscripts," says Kate, "the concern over missing a good script and the thrill of finding one remain."

"Some publishers have stopped reading their slush piles because of the overhead," says Cuyler, "and I am against that. I think it's absolutely the worst thing a children's book department can do. This is one of the few ways an editor can read books by unpublished writers. Even the best agents in New York, who are very good about sending in manuscripts, often don't represent the housewife who lives in the northern stretches of Idaho and has written a great novel. One reason we have a Bill Wallace or a Judy McInerney or a Betty Bates is that we feel that discovering writers is exciting. Often what we get is very raw. It needs of lot of work, but we're willing to do that. The slush pile is a great way of finding new talent."

One of Cuyler's prime objectives was to develop "a really top-notch picture-book line." Some of the artists she signed up were Dick Gackenbach, Victoria Chess, Marylin Hafner, Lillian Hoban, John Wallner, Lisl Weil, and Stephen Gammell. To recruit more artistic talent, she invented Daisy Wallace.

"The whole Daisy Wallace series was designed in part as a way of bringing important artists to the list," she says. "Also, I felt there were not nearly enough poetry anthologies aimed toward the five-, six-, and seven-year-old. Poetry opens a lot of doors for children. So I decided to bring five books onto the list that were visually stimulating—so we could sign up some strong artists—and that also would introduce chil-

art by Victoria Chess
from *Poor Esmé* (1982)

art by Stephen Gammell from
The Best Way to Ripton (1982)

art by Trina Schart Hyman
from *Witch Poems* (1976)

art by Kay Chorao
from *Monster Poems* (1976)

art by Margot Tomes
from *Giant Poems* (1978)

art by Tomie dePaola
from *Ghost Poems* (1979)

art by Trina Schart Hyman
from *Fairy Poems* (1980)

dren to first-rate poetry. That's why the subjects of the anthologies are both visual and popular—fairies, ghosts, giants, monsters, and witches. But the poetry that's represented in them is of high quality, and much of it was commissioned by us. Since I had such a specific vision of what these books should be, I decided to do the anthologies myself and use the name Daisy Wallace."

Cuyler signed up artists for the Daisy Wallace books (and for future projects): Kay Chorao for *Monster Poems*, Trina Schart Hyman for *Witch Poems* and *Fairy Poems*, and Margot Tomes for *Giant Poems*. *Ghost Poems* was illustrated by Tomie dePaola.

One of the poets represented in the Daisy Wallace series was Myra Cohn Livingston. Cuyler had admired her work ever since attending Sarah Lawrence College, also Livingston's alma mater. When Cuyler was doing research for the Daisy Wallace books, she realized the extent of Livingston's contribution to the field. Says Cuyler, "I can't think of anyone who has done more for poetry and children." So she asked Livingston to collaborate with Leonard Everett Fisher. Fisher wanted to do a full-color picture book on the changing of the seasons, and Cuyler suggested that the text be done by a poet. "I thought Myra Cohn Livingston would fit the bill beautifully," she says, "so I approached her and her agent, Dorothy Markinko. Myra's such a giant in the field, it really took me a while to work up my confidence. I was thrilled when she agreed."

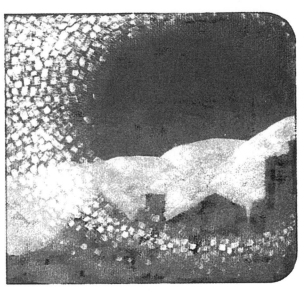

art by Leonard Everett Fisher
from *Sky Songs* (1984)

art by Leonard Everett Fisher
from *A Circle of Seasons* (1982)

Livingston wrote a single long poem that accompanied Fisher's acrylic paintings for *A Circle of Seasons*. They also collaborated on a companion volume, *Sky Songs*, and on *Celebrations*. Livingston, meanwhile, began to edit a series of poetry anthologies with holiday themes, beginning with the 1984 publication of *Christmas Poems*, a 1985 A.L.A. Notable Book with illustrations by Trina Schart Hyman.

Hyman, the illustrator of more than a hundred children's books, had first worked with Cuyler at Walker. "She's an artist's artist," says Cuyler. "I don't know an artist in the field who doesn't admire her work. And children . . . well, it must mean something that her books

art by Trina Schart Hyman
from *Christmas Poems* (1984)

show up sooner or later in every child's private library."

Hyman's Holiday House books have included full-color editions of three classics: *Rapunzel,* a 1983 A.L.A. Notable Book retold by Barbara Rogasky; *Little Red Riding Hood,* a 1984 Caldecott Honor Book; and a landmark edition of *A Christmas Carol,* published in 1983. "I can honestly say that Holiday House kept me from leaving this business," says Hyman. "I've known John and Kate Briggs for many years. John suggested that I illustrate *Rapunzel.* At the time, I was dissatisfied with my work and with publishing; I was going through one of those personal crises. But working with Holiday House on *Rapunzel* was so much fun and so satisfying, I decided it's not so bad after all to be a children's book illustrator. They take a personal interest in you at Holiday House. You feel as though you're working with people who appreciate what you're doing. They've given me a free hand on all my projects; if I could, I'd work for them exclusively. They're one of the last remaining publishers in the old tradition—small, independent, personally owned, and caring."

art by Trina Schart Hyman
from *Rapunzel* (1982)

art by Trina Schart Hyman
from *Little Red Riding Hood* (1983)

art by Charles Mikolaycak
from *A Child Is Born* (1983)

art by Charles Mikolaycak
from *He Is Risen* (1985)

Charles Mikolaycak joined the list in 1979 as the illustrator of Elizabeth Winthrop's *Journey to the Bright Kingdom*. He also did the full-color illustrations for Winthrop's *A Child Is Born: The Christmas Story* and *He Is Risen: The Easter Story*, and for his own retelling of *Babushka: An Old Russian Folktale* which was selected by *The New York Times* as one of the year's ten best-illustrated books. "His work is classy with a capital *C*," says Cuyler, "and it's also deep. He goes right to the core of the unconscious."

"If she means that I believe in mythological or primordial beginnings of things, she's probably right," says Mikolaycak. "That's the kind of story I'm always looking for."

Mikolaycak's retelling of *Babushka* was inspired by a boyhood memory. "I've known the story since I was a kid," he says. "My parents gave me a book called *Merry Christmas*, published by Knopf during the 1940s, an anthology of Christmas carols, poems, and stories, with "Babushka" among them. I loved that book. I used to lie on the floor and pore over it. A couple of years ago, while driving through the Finger Lakes region, I walked into a small-town bookshop, and there

art by Charles Mikolaycak
from *Babushka* (1984)

was the book sitting on a shelf. It was in pristine condition, the old wartime edition. When I looked through it, I was seven years old again. Back in New York I told Margery Cuyler, 'I've got to tell that story in my own way,' and she said, 'Go ahead.' I felt on top of the world. For the next twenty months she held my hand while the book went through something like eighteen drafts."

art by Janet Stevens from *The Tortoise and the Hare* (1984)

In addition to working with these well-known illustrators, Cuyler was looking for new talent. One of the newcomers she found was Janet Stevens, an artist who had attended a workshop given by Tomie de-Paola in Colorado. DePaola had praised her work and asked her to get in touch with Cuyler: "He called me and told me to watch out for her, but nothing came in the mail. Finally, when I was visiting Tomie in New Hampshire, I called her to confirm our interest and offer encouragement. She sent in a dummy of *Animal Fair*, and we bought it immediately." From then on, Stevens appeared on virtually every Holiday House list, illustrating picture books by Steven Kroll and Marjorie Sharmat, and adapting Hans Christian Andersen's *The Princess and the Pea* and Aesop's *The Tortoise and the Hare*.

art by Janet Stevens from
The Princess and the Pea
(1982)

art by Janet Stevens from
Lucretia the Unbearable
(1981)

art by
Tricia Tusa from
Libby's New Glasses
(1984)

Tricia Tusa, another Holiday House discovery, came into the office one day to show her portfolio to the art director, David Rogers. Her timing was perfect. She ended up getting her first illustrating job, which was *Loose Tooth* by Steven Kroll. Also, Rogers got Cuyler to encourage her to work on a dummy she'd brought about a girl who hated her new glasses. The result was *Libby's New Glasses*, the first book written and illustrated by Tusa, which was published in the fall of 1984.

Olivier Dunrea was another discovery. He was unpublished when he came to the office to show his portfolio to David Rogers. "He was a real find," says Rogers, "very impressive. Margery was out of the office that day, but when she returned, I urged her to get in touch with Dunrea and see for herself."

Cuyler contacted the artist at his home in Philadelphia while she was there for an A.L.A. convention. They met for breakfast, and she looked at his work. "I loved it," she says. "I had been thinking of asking him to illustrate a picture book by someone else, but when I saw his work I realized he was an original talent and that he should do his own book. A character named Ravena—a wild-haired banshee—kept turning up in his drawings; he had done a partial dummy with a tentative storyline about Ravena's adventures. I showed his work to John and Kate, who were also in Philadelphia for the convention, and they reacted the same way I had. We offered him a contract on the spot." Dunrea's *Ravena*, published in the fall of 1984, was followed by *Fergus and Bridey* in the spring of 1985.

art by Olivier Dunrea from *Ravena* (1984)

art by Olivier Dunrea from
Fergus and Bridey (1985)

art by Donna Diamond
from *Rumpelstiltskin*
(1983)

Donna Diamond came to Holiday House through a lucky coincidence. She was just starting out as a children's book illustrator and was moonlighting as a babysitter. Elizabeth Winthrop hired her to do some babysitting and steered her in Cuyler's direction after seeing her portfolio. She had already illustrated *The Bridge to Terabithia* by Katherine Paterson, a Newbery winner published by T. Y. Crowell, and was eager to illustrate picture books.

"Her work was very original," says Cuyler, "very sophisticated, the kind of work you can't really pin down to children's books." Cuyler happened to have a manuscript on her desk, *The Dark Princess* by Richard Kennedy, "which needed unusual art—the kind of pictures to which you can't assign an age level." And so Diamond was signed up to illustrate *The Dark Princess*, a 1979 A.L.A. Notable Book. Since then she has adapted and illustrated *Swan Lake, The Pied Piper of Hamelin*, and *Rumpelstiltskin* for the firm.

Gail Gibbons brought a new look to the Holiday House list of nonfiction picture books. A television graphics designer, she had worked on a children's show and was sent to Holiday by Florence Alexander, who was also the agent for Tomie dePaola and Marilyn Hirsh. She saw John Briggs, and out of their conversation came the idea for *Tool Book*. Gibbons lives in Corinth, Vermont, in a passive solar house that she and her husband built themselves. All of the tools pictured in *Tool Book* had been used in the construction of the house. "I just went down into the basement and did my research," she says.

Tool Book, published in 1982, was followed by *Boat Book* and *Tunnels*, a selection of the Book-of-the-Month Club, and by a series of nonfiction books on holidays, beginning in 1982 with *Christmas Time.*

art by Gail Gibbons from *Tool Book* (1982)

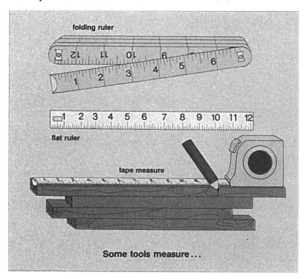

art by Gail Gibbons from *Thanksgiving Day* (1983)

"Gail's books are outstanding for their design," says John Briggs, who has been her editor. "She also has a special knack for writing nonfiction that's accessible to five-, six-, and seven-year-olds—and she's a delight to work with."

Gibbons's approach as an artist stems directly from her background in TV graphics. "The graphics have to be very simple and clear, and in a colorful style, because they're only on for ten seconds," she says. "They have to let you know what the announcer is talking about in a very short time. It's a style that works very well for young children."

Throughout this period, Holiday House had been publishing a growing list of books that celebrate holiday themes. By 1985, the list included more than twenty-five books for holiday reading, produced by some of the firm's most popular authors and illustrators. Among these books were noteworthy new editions of two classics: *A Christmas Carol*, with illustrations by Trina Schart Hyman, and *The Night Before Christmas*, illustrated by Tomie dePaola. The first Holiday House edition of *A Christmas Carol*, illustrated by Philip Reed, had been published in 1941. And the first Holiday House edition of *The Night Before Christmas*, illustrated by Ilse Bischoff, had been published as a stocking book back in 1937.

Several books on Jewish holidays had been written by Malka Drucker, David A. Adler, and Marilyn Hirsh. Drucker, who was sent to the firm by a college classmate of Briggs, joined the list in 1978 as the author of Holiday's first sports biographies, *Tom Seaver* and *The George Foster Story*. The five titles in her Jewish Holidays series have all been praised as distinguished contributions to the field. Adler, an editor at the Jewish Publication Society, has written *A Picture Book of Jewish Holidays*, *A Picture Book of Hanukkah*, and *A Picture Book of Passover*, all illustrated by Linda Heller. His other titles include *A Picture Book of Israel*, a riddle book, and a mystery for very young readers.

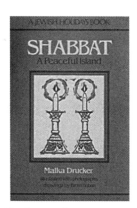

jacket art by
Ed Sibbett, Jr. for
*Shabbat: a Peaceful
Island* (1983)

Celebrating Life
(1984)

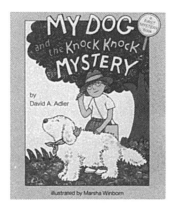

jacket art by Marsha Winborn for
My Dog and the Knock Knock Mystery
(1985)

Over the years, John Briggs had been editing books by a number of Holiday House authors. He had worked at one time or another with Glen Rounds, Gladys Conklin, Florence Heide and Marjorie Sharmat. When Ed Lindemann left the firm, Briggs became the editor of Dorothy Patent's older-level books. As the list grew, he edited Leonard Everett Fisher's Nineteenth Century America series, a number of Malka Drucker's books, and all of Gail Gibbons's picture books. By 1984, he was editing several titles a year, trying to heed Vernon Ives's advice that a wise publisher is always an active editor.

art by Linda Heller from
A Picture Book of Passover (1982)

CHAPTER

12

The first Holiday House edition of *A Christmas Carol*, illustrated with colored woodcuts by Philip Reed and published in 1940, stayed in print about twenty years. In 1966 the Reed edition was reissued by Atheneum under the supervision of David Rogers, director of design and production for Atheneum's children's department. Rogers became director of design and production at Holiday House in 1981, following Kay Jerman's retirement. Within a year he had the chance to work on a brand-new edition of *A Christmas Carol*.

The idea for the book originated with Margery Cuyler. Then she, John Briggs, and David Rogers decided they wanted to produce the finest edition of the work ever published. Rogers saw the project as "an opportunity for me to go back thirty years and do the kind of book I started out doing at Knopf—a solid, old-fashioned book-book." The

jacket art and (facing page) decorated initial and tailpiece by Trina Schart Hyman from *A Christmas Carol* (1983)

new edition was designed and produced with the same uncompromising attention to detail that had distinguished Helen Gentry's work for the firm nearly a half-century earlier.

Trina Schart Hyman illustrated the book in classic Dickensian style with a series of six full-color plates, four black-and-white tailpieces, and decorated initials opening each chapter. The tipped-in plates were printed on ivory-toned sheets to match the color of the text paper. The page edges at the side and foot of the book were rough cut, contributing to the volume's old-fashioned look.

The Holiday House version of Charles Dickens's text was edited by John Briggs, who wanted this edition to follow Dickens's original intentions as closely as possible. Many changes had crept into the text since the book's first publication in London in 1843. Briggs worked from a facsimile of the original edition, and he wrote a historical note on the text that was included in the Holiday House edition, published in the fall of 1983, 140 years after the book was first published in London.

"The latest version of *A Christmas Carol* shows bookmaking skill and a keen sense of literary history," said *Publishers Weekly*. The Book-of-the-Month Club offered the work in its holiday prospectus, and both the Metropolitan Museum of Art and the Boston Museum of Fine Arts included the book in their Christmas catalogs.

Quality bookmaking had been a founding principle at Holiday House in 1935, and the firm's deluxe edition of Dickens's masterpiece expressed a continuing commitment to that tradition.

Both Margery Cuyler and David Rogers seek out illustrators and work closely together. "He is tops in the field," says Cuyler. "In the short time he's been here, he's already brought a new look to the list. And he has a keen eye for new talent."

"Margery and I work together very comfortably," says Rogers. "We've both wanted to make the books a little more imaginative, more lively and appealing. I prefer a very plain, simple design. My basic attitude has always been that the best design is when you don't even realize that the book has been designed. The whole point of design is that people read the text and see the pictures and don't stub their toe over some cutesy little design element. Occasionally a book is written with

art by Lillian Hoban
from *Attila the Angry*
(1985)

the idea in mind that design will be a paramount factor, but basically—and this is true of picture books as well as anything else—if you're aware of the design, then it's bad design."

Besides designing all the books on the list, Rogers handles every stage of production himself, including the mechanicals. "I still work in the mold that prevailed at Atheneum and at Knopf, where I started, where the design-production department is one, and where it has as strong a voice as the editor's."

John Briggs agrees that both voices are important. "You can't consistently publish quality books without a quality editor," he says. "It's the better editors who attract and establish successful relationships with the better authors and illustrators. But there are other elements involved in establishing a good list of children's books, and one of them is design. A quality book should have quality design. If a publisher is indifferent to this, it will show. It's not something that can be taken for granted, and there's no one in the business who makes that more apparent than David."

Changing times have taught Briggs that nothing in children's book publishing can be taken for granted. In 1960, when Holiday House was publishing primarily for schools and libraries, Vernon Ives predicted that "the education 'boom' and an increasing school population [will provide] a continuing, stable market for children's and young people's books." Two decades later, the institutional market had proven neither as predictable nor reliable as Ives had foreseen, and Briggs had to make his own more sober assessment: "Today, rising costs have limited the number of books that schools and libraries can purchase with budgets that are more austere than they used to be."

One effect of a less generous library market has been that books no longer stay in print as long as they once did. "Because of restricted budgets, inflation, and more emphasis on the purchase of new titles," says Briggs, "the security of a solid backlist isn't as comforting as it used to be. Backlist sales have fallen off sharply, and the sale of new

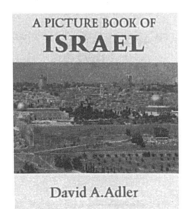

A Picture Book of Israel
(1984)

five paperback reprints by Tomie dePaola (1984)

books, as a percentage of total sales, has increased. Reduced backlist sales have made it more difficult to keep books in print, and since one way to make up for the lost sales is new books, more are being published. Publishing more books that have shorter lives and that are chasing fewer constant dollars means that we are in a considerably less conservative business than we used to be in."

Another effect of the changing library market has been a greater emphasis on bookstore sales and on the sale of subsidiary rights. "When it comes to selling stores," says Briggs, "for us it's been a matter of getting commission representatives who are interested in children's books and who will give them equal treatment when they present their lines to buyers. Experience has taught us—and keeps reminding us—that hardcover titles that are popular with libraries are not necessarily popular in stores. Although we are selling more books in more retail accounts than ever before, I think all of us feel that there is a lot more potential in this area."

Changing market conditions have also resulted in new promotional strategies. "I think we're much more flexible, much more daring," says Kate Briggs. "We've turned out some exciting promotional materials, and we've become more professional in presenting authors and illustrators. Appearances are important because they get the personalities of the authors and illustrators across to the public. Don't you remember as a child wondering about the person whose picture appeared on

photograph from *Rattlesnakes* (1984)

the dust jacket? I met Marguerite Henry as a child, and I was thrilled to discover that there was a living person who really did write all those books. So that's been an interesting trend in the last twenty years—how much more emphasis has gone into promoting authors and illustrators."

From the beginning, virtually everyone who has been associated with Holiday has testified to the benefits and pleasures of working with a small, independent publishing house. "I don't have a plush office, but there are plenty of compensations," says Bob Spencer, who has been the controller since 1970. "I like working for a small company like this—it's fun and it's comfortable. There's not a lot of politics. We all get along very well." Spencer, of course, performs the most important task in the entire firm—he turns out the royalty statements. "We have basically the same equipment as when I started," he says, "an adding machine and a typewriter. We do have a new typewriter and a new adding machine, but nothing has been automated. I still type out all of the royalty statements, every one of them."

"And they're accurate," adds Briggs. "Bob's work has always been first rate."

"There are enormous advantages to working for a small firm like Holiday House," says David Rogers. "You don't waste half your life going to conferences and meetings. Here the people are very comfortable with each other and really able to work together. You can accomplish so much with a minimum of time and discussion."

"Do you know why I can edit so many books?" asks Margery Cuyler. "It's because Holiday House is small and we don't have meet-

art by Gail Gibbons
from *Halloween* (1984)

ings. We don't have paperwork. We just sit down and do our work, and we get books out fast. That's what's nice about a small house—the list reflects the vision of a couple of people instead of a committee. I don't believe in publishing by committee."

"It's very satisfying being a small publisher," says John Briggs. "You hear people in large houses frequently complaining about bureaucracy and meetings, and the stultifying atmosphere they have to work in. Small has different connotations; it can mean weak. But we're not second to anyone, I don't think, as publishers of the kind of children's books we do. I'm not saying that you can't be big and good. I'm just saying that you can be small and be very good. The idea is to try to do everything, including every little thing, at least as well if not better than everybody else."

art by Marilyn Hirsh
from *I Love Hanukkah* (1984)

art by Gail Gibbons
from *Playgrounds* (1985)

At Holiday, being small has always meant a sense of involvement and community for the entire staff. "We're all part of everything that's done in the house," says Kate Briggs, "and that's exciting."

Barbara Walsh, the managing editor, arrived in 1974, not planning to stay. "I came in as a temp for two weeks and just stayed on," she says. "I started doing everything. The more responsibility I took on, the more I was given. Because the house is small, if you're doing the right thing—or the wrong thing—it's noticed right away." Walsh was soon engaged in proofreading, copy editing, and photo research. She began to correspond with authors, keep track of production schedules, handle

photograph from *Whales*
(1984)

copyright applications, and perform a multitude of other chores. "I couldn't have found a better place to work," she says. "There's a very nice family-kind of feeling here. That's an old-fashioned expression, I know, but it's true."

"Barbara has her own responsibilities, but she also assists me in every area of my work," says John Briggs. "I depend on her a lot."

"This has always been a very friendly, family-type office," says Rose Vallario, the senior member of the staff. "A couple of years ago Glen Rounds came by for a visit. He came over to my desk and said, 'Rose!' and gave me a big kiss. 'How come you didn't do that thirty years ago?' I asked him. And he said, 'Because I was stupid.' " Vallario joined the firm in 1942, left after World War II to raise her family, and then was persuaded by Vernon Ives to return. Eventually, she would oversee the billing department, keep track of all inventory and sales records, handle customer relations, and perform many other duties essential to the operation of the firm. "Working here is the greatest thing that ever happened to me," she says. "I told John Briggs that I want to die with my boots under the desk, and he said, 'Rose, please don't do that!' "

"Rose is a dream," says Briggs. "I can't imagine working here without her."

Rose's desk is a keepsake from the old Holiday House office on West 13th Street. A couple of items in the current office (Holiday House moved to 18 East 53rd Street in 1975) go all the way back to the firm's beginnings on lower Varick Street. John Briggs enjoys showing visitors the oak filing cabinets that once separated Vernon Ives, Helen Gentry, and Ted Johnson from the thumping and wheezing presses of the William E. Rudge pressroom.

Briggs speaks with unabashed pride about the firm's many long-term relationships. Until 1951, Holiday House shipped books from its offices and binderies. When this became impractical, it retained the services of W. A. Book Service, which had been founded the year before. W. A. was named after its president, William Aiello, who had started the company with his brother-in-law, Joe Motise, and nephew, Stephen DiStefano, who took over in 1970. Another member of the family, Edward LaCorte, joined the operation in 1968. "As obvious as the importance of order fulfillment is," says Briggs, "warehouse operations usually don't get the recognition they deserve. The importance of Stephen and W. A. to the Holiday House story, and the pleasure of working with them over the years, cannot be overstated. They are the best.

"Feffer and Simons has done a fine job of representing us overseas for over twenty years, but our longest relationship in the export market has been with Saunders of Toronto, formerly J. Reginald Saunders, who have been distributing our books in Canada since the first list was published in 1935."

Holiday House has always used commission salesmen to sell its books to the trade. George Scheer, the dean of the commission men, took on the firm's line in 1949 and has represented it in the South ever since. Scheer was the editor of *Cherokee Animal Tales*, published by Holiday in 1968. His brother, Julian Scheer, wrote *Rain Makes Applesauce* and *Upside Down Day*.

One of the greatest advantages a small publisher has is the opportunity to give personal attention to its authors and illustrators. "Our biggest asset is represented by the authors and illustrators on our list," says John Briggs. "Our future is dependent on them; they, along with the reader, are our reasons for being. From a financial as well as a personal point of view, the most desirable and satisfying publishing involves continuity—establishing long-lasting relationships—publishing authors, not just a number of one-shot titles. Holiday House is fortunate to have had a number of those relationships."

"What's exciting about Holiday House," says Kate Briggs, "and about John's and my involvement, is that we've made so many very good friends. Authors and illustrators have become personal friends and a part of our lives. I really treasure that aspect of my job, as well as

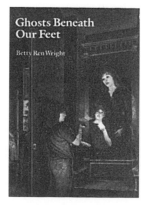

jacket art by
Stephen Mancusi for
Ghosts Beneath Our Feet
(1984)

jacket art by
Peter Catalanotto for
Child of War (1984)

art by Janet Stevens from
The House that Jack Built (1985)

working side by side with my husband. There's a warmth at Holiday House you can't help but notice.

"The thing that's fascinating is that some authors like Glen Rounds and Fritz Eichenberg are still around to be friends with. Even after all these years, here's Glen with a new book on our fiftieth anniversary list. We go down to Southern Pines regularly, and he comes up here to visit us."

Margery Cuyler had learned from her mentor, Emilie McLeod, "that as you develop books with authors, you also develop friendships." It is hard to imagine Cuyler working in any other way. "My relationships with authors and illustrators," she says, "are different from my other, nonprofessional friendships. They are based on sharing imaginations, and that is a very intimate, invigorating, and delicate kind of relationship. You don't have that kind of bond with most people."

In 1935, when Holiday House announced its first list to the trade, it was a small, independent, specialized publisher—the first firm in America to publish children's books exclusively. In 1985, still small, independent, and specialized, the house is flourishing as never before.

"As they say, we live in a changing world," says John Briggs, "and the role of the small independent publisher of children's books is no exception. One unavoidable result of change has been that there aren't as many of us around as there used to be. Although the fortunes of publishing children's books have fluctuated for better as well as for worse over the years, there has been an inexorable decline in the number of small houses. Among the reasons have been financial difficulties on the one hand, handsome offers on the other, and the retirement of one or more of the principals. Since we're about the only house of our kind left, I'm hopeful the decline has ended."

art by John Wallner
from *Easter Poems* (1985)

Briggs intends for the firm to remain small and independent. While the list has doubled in size during the last decade, he believes that further growth would require a fundamental change in the nature of the house. "We think we're going to continue doing thirty to forty titles a year," he says. "We can't do more without expanding the staff significantly, and that would mean changing the character of the place. I'm happy here, and the authors and illustrators seem to like what we have to offer. If we start getting assistants in the different departments, then there's going to be a little more distance between the authors and illustrators and us. We don't want to let that happen."

Looking to the future, Margery Cuyler says: "I want to build up a larger and stronger fiction list. I'm reading more of the slush pile than I've ever read before. Just in the past month we acquired three new novels from the slush pile by new writers. There are also plenty of nonfiction possibilities that haven't been explored. A lot has to do with format, not just subject. I'd like to do more nonfiction books where there's an artistic idea behind the concept."

Is there any kind of book that she doesn't want to do? "Certainly," says Cuyler. "I don't want to do boring books."

The list will change in the years to come, but the character of the house will stay the same. "Holiday House is like an old-fashioned family business," says Tomie dePaola, "yet it is innovative and experimental. They're right up there with the biggest and the best, but they've never lost their personal approach. That's very refreshing these days."

art by Marylin Hafner from
Happy Mother's Day (1985)

John Briggs intends to keep it that way: "Common corporate wisdom, in this country anyway, has been to diversify—the thinking being that it is dangerous to have all your eggs in one basket. As far as books are concerned, the theory is that if one publishes different kinds—children's, school texts, college texts, general adult fiction and nonfiction, and so forth—the risk is spread, and it is less likely that all departments will suffer, if not collapse, at once.

"So what can we do? Small independents tend to have more clearly defined financial limitations than the large companies and thus do not have as much choice when it comes to diversification. For most of us, reality seems to offer two options—we can either stay the way we are or sell out. As for Holiday House, we plan to go on in our independent way and continue to publish for our favorite audience and, we hope, a better world."

art by Leonard Everett Fisher from *Celebrations* (1985)

HOLIDAY HOUSE

Books for Young People

Spring 1985

Our 50th Anniversary
1935-1985

HOLIDAY HOUSE

1985–2000

BARBARA ELLEMAN

HOLIDAY HOUSE
Books for Young People
1985

catalog cover art by Trina Schart Hyman from
A Child's Christmas in Wales (1985)

CHAPTER

13

Holiday House's fiftieth-anniversary year, 1985, was an exciting and energizing time for the independent company. While determined to adhere to its mission of "publishing books that children want to read," the firm was poised to meet the expanding market in children's trade books. Literature-based curriculum had a firm hold in schools in the mid-1980s. Teachers were looking for books that fit the curriculum and had high child appeal, and librarians were tying into those needs. And parents, eager to advance their children academically, were visiting bookstores at an increasing rate. Holiday House was ready to serve all these audiences.

While reminiscing about the year, John Briggs commented, "We could look back and see that the heart and soul of the company hadn't changed. To honor and say thank you to the authors and artists, we gave a fiftieth-anniversary party, which coincided with the publication of Russell Freedman's masterful history of our first fifty years. So many people from Holiday House's early days were able to be there: Vernon Ives, Helen Gentry, Rose Vallario, Fritz Eichenberg, Glen Rounds, and more

jacket design by David Rogers for
Holiday House: The First Fifty Years (1985)

than one hundred others, including authors and illustrators we no longer published and staff who were no longer working here. I must say it was one of the best parties I've ever been to. It was like a love-in."

In fact, it was a love-in, if one subscribes to the view of Briggs's dinner partner, Lisl Weil, who wrote,

> Dear Kate, Dear John, Dear Margery: I am just coming from your wonderful party—wonderful for all that *love* I felt coming from everyone to you all! It was and is so rare—so very special, and it is exactly what I too feel for you all! Bless you and Happy Birthday and many, many more!!! Thank you for letting me be part of Holiday House. Love, Lisl

Commented John, "You can see why I loved the party—and still love Lisl!"

The fall 1985 season included Trina Schart Hyman's newly illustrated edition of Dylan Thomas's *A Child's Christmas in Wales*, a classic originally published in 1954. In approaching this tale based on a special day in the Welsh author's childhood, Hyman, accompanied by her sister, traveled to Wales to find his birthplace. There in Cardiff she saw a town much changed from Thomas's time. Its industrial landscape didn't have the ambience she wanted to portray. At the suggestion of someone they met, the two traveled on to Laugharne, where Thomas actually wrote the story.

"It was a glorious place," Hyman remembers. "We spent two weeks there. I sketched and my sister took photographs. The only problem was that we went in November, when it was still balmy. The roses and holly trees were in bloom, and I had to think how the village would look under snow. We met a man who was a strong Welsh nationalist. He told me in no uncertain terms that I shouldn't be illustrating this story because 'I wasn't Welsh.' When the book was published, I sent him a copy anyway, and he wrote back saying, 'You have captured the feeling

art by Trina Schart Hyman from
A Child's Christmas in Wales (1985)

art by Lilian Obligado from
One Terrific Thanksgiving
(1985)

art by Victoria Chess from
*The Twisted Witch and
Other Spooky Riddles* (1985)

of Wales; I am making you an honorary Welsh woman.' I was touched and still have his letter."

Two best-selling works of fiction were released that fall. One was *The Castle in the Attic* by Elizabeth Winthrop, which won the Dorothy Canfield Fisher Award in Vermont, the California Young Reader Medal, and was a selection of the Book-of-the-Month Club. *Castle* began as a picture book about a young boy's unhappiness at losing his nanny.

"As a picture book," Margery Cuyler said, "the plot didn't really go anywhere, and I urged Elizabeth to turn it into a novel. I dragged her to a series of lectures that Joseph Campbell was giving on courtly love in the Middle Ages, to get her creative juices going."

And while this did get her thinking about quests and knights, Winthrop remembers, it wasn't until she took her son Andrew to a museum and they perused the Knights and Armor section that, she said, "my thoughts really became charged. Then, shortly after that, Andrew [Mahony] and I bought some tiny, one-inch knights. One had a broken sword, and on it I found in tiny letters the name Sir Percivale carved at the bottom. That got me reading the Arthur stories and researching the Arthurian cycle, and eventually *The Castle in the Attic* came about."

It was (and remains) enormously popular, and, in 1993, in response to its popularity and hundreds of children's requests, Winthrop continued the story in *The Battle for the Castle*. "It took that long," Winthrop

jacket art by Trina Schart Hyman
for *The Castle in the Attic* (1985)

jacket art by Robert Sauber for
The Battle for the Castle (1993)

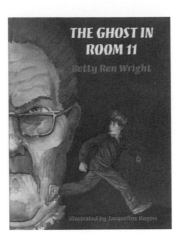

jacket art by Jacqueline Rogers for *The Ghost in Room 11* (1998)

jacket art by Stephen Mancusi for *Christina's Ghost* (1985)

relates, "because I didn't want it to be just a sequel, but, instead, a good story on its own."

Also published that fall was *Christina's Ghost* by Betty Ren Wright, which garnered a lot of attention and won Wright her second (after *The Dollhouse Murders*, 1983) Texas Bluebonnet Award. Wright, who has published seventeen books with Holiday House over the years, says, "I treasure my relationship with Holiday House. They have been a wonderful presence in my life ever since I first met John and Kate and started working with Margery. And when Regina came, she wrote a warm letter introducing herself, making me feel comfortable about the transition. Everyone is caring—and gentle! As an editor, Margery was understanding of the fragility of an author's feelings, yet her comments were to the point. For example, when I sent in the manuscript for *The Scariest Night*, she said, 'We can publish this as is, but I think readers will quickly lose sympathy with the protagonist—she is too defeated and doesn't take an active enough part in solving her own problems.' When I re-read the story, I could see Margery's point immediately, and I changed the character to reflect this. It made a much better book."

jacket art by Stephen Johnson for *The Scariest Night* (1991)

jacket art by Karen Ritz for *The Ghost of Popcorn Hill* (1993)

jacket art by Ronald Himler
for *Beauty* (1988)

jacket art by Jean Jenkins
Loewer for *Ferret in the
Bedroom, Lizards in the
Fridge* (1986)

Bill Wallace, who has eighteen state awards to his credit, began his career with *A Dog Called Kitty* (1980), a poignant tale about the love that grows between a boy and a stray pup, which won the Texas Bluebonnet Award. When asked which book Wallace considers his best work, he said, "I have no idea. It seems like everyone has a different book they think of as my best." As for his favorite, Wallace names *Beauty*. "Since I really had Beauty [a horse], it was the most difficult story ever for me to write. She was a friend, and I wanted her story to be just right."

As for the easiest? "Without a doubt," Wallace says, "*Snot Stew*. I wrote it in about two days. Not long before the book was to be published, Margery Cuyler called and said, 'We have to change the title.' I replied, 'But you can't. There's nothing else we can call that book.' And she said, 'Well, we simply can't publish it with that title. It will cut sales.'" At that point, Wallace told her not to send the second half of the advance, because he would not change the title. "Margery told me that John was the publisher, and the final decision would be his.

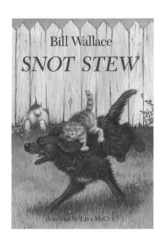

jacket art by Lisa
McCue for *Snot Stew*
(1989)

jacket art by Paul Tatore
for *Red Dog* (1987)

jacket art by Deborah
L. Chabrian for *Aloha
Summer* (1997)

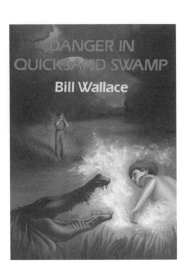

jacket art by Chris Cocozza
for *Danger in Quicksand
Swamp* (1989)

"About forty-five minutes later, she called back with the news that John had said that he got into this business to publish books *for children.* He said that if he couldn't keep doing that, he might as well get out. I imagine a number of publishers would have loved the title," Bill said, "but none with the quality reputation of Holiday House. John's reasoning—his putting kids first—well, not many publishers would do that. It brought Holiday House to a totally new level of respect, as far as I was concerned."

And did it cut sales? "Yes, initially," Wallace admitted. "But eventually it sold well and won the Texas Bluebonnet Award. Kate mentioned to me, 'Maybe the title wasn't so bad after all!' As my friend and fellow author Mary Francis Shura told me, 'There's not a kid in the country that won't want to get his or her hands on this book and not a grandmother in the country who will buy it.'" In 2000, Wallace won a Lifetime Achievement Award from the Oklahoma Center for the Book.

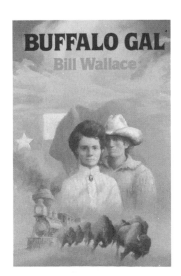

jacket art by Ronald Himler
for *Buffalo Gal* (1992)

jacket art by Leslie Morrill
from *Totally Disgusting!*
(1991)

art by Glen Rounds from
Cowboys (1991)

art by Glen Rounds from *Old MacDonald
Had a Farm* (1989)

art by Glen Rounds from
*I Know an Old Lady Who
Swallowed a Fly* (1990)

In 1984, Glen Rounds, a steady contributor to Holiday House since its second list, found himself put out of business by arthritis in his right hand. Not wanting to go back to making his living at horseshoeing or some other dull trade, he spent most of the summer on the beach, learning to draw with his left hand. By the following spring, he was back in business again, publishing *Washday on Noah's Ark*, and has been drawing with his left hand ever since.

Loreen Leedy's long association with the firm began in the fall of 1985 with *A Number of Dragons*, a counting book that *Publishers Weekly* called "a knockout attraction." The following season brought a companion book, *The Dragon ABC Hunt*, in which the dragons go on a scavenger hunt. This concept book for very young readers was also well received, motivating Leedy and Cuyler to think about other titles of this nature.

Leedy retraces her introduction to Holiday House: "After college, I started a crafts business, making jewelry and chess sets. Creating children's books was only a distant dream when I met children's author-illustrator Olivier Dunrea through a mutual friend. He gave me a tour of his studio, and for the first time I saw the steps in the bookmaking process—a book plan, character sketches, manuscripts in revision, a dummy, final artwork—and was completely fascinated. I decided to try

art by Loreen Leedy
from *A Number of
Dragons* (1985)

art by Loreen Leedy
from *The Dragon
ABC Hunt* (1986)

art by Loreen Leedy from *Blast Off to Earth!* (1992)

my hand at it and dropped my other projects to concentrate on drawing whimsical animal characters based on my jewelry and chess pieces. I took a pile of sketches to show Olivier, who was very encouraging."

Shortly thereafter, Dunrea showed Leedy's drawings to Cuyler, who "called me and said she liked my wacky sense of humor, and then asked, 'Can you write?' I had been a frustrated writer in school because we were rarely assigned creative writing, usually only reports and the like. But I told Margery, 'I'll give it a try.' I worked for several months to come up with three reasonably decent manuscripts that hopefully wouldn't be too horrible. Then I made an appointment with her and took the train to New York. When I got to Holiday House, Margery was running around with bare feet and I thought, hey, this is my kind of place."

art by Loreen Leedy from
The Great Trash Bash
(1991)

art by Loreen Leedy
from *The Furry News*
(1990)

Cuyler chose the counting story because it was the closest to being publishable. "I went home and incorporated her suggested revisions into a dummy. I finished it within a week—I didn't want her to forget about me—and sent it to her. She called back in a few days and said, 'We want to publish it.' I would never have entered the children's book publishing field if it hadn't been for that serendipitous sequence of events."

After her dragon books, Loreen Leedy started using different animals and even alien robots in books such as *The Furry News: How to Make a Newspaper*; *The Great Trash Bash*; and *Blast Off to Earth!: A Look at Geography*.

The year 1986 saw the publication of *Time Enough for Drums* by Ann Rinaldi, her first historical novel and the second of four young adult novels she wrote for the firm. This title, along with *The Last Silk Dress*, launched her career as a popular author of historical fiction.

A new name to come on the list that year was Brooklyn freelance journalist Brett Harvey, who used her grandmother's diaries to shape a story about prairie life at the end of the nineteenth century. Titled *My*

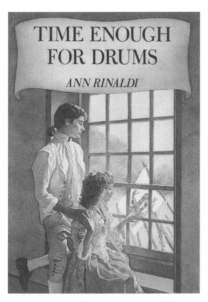

jacket art by Ellen Thompson for
Time Enough for Drums (1986)

jacket art by Ronald Himler for
The Last Silk Dress (1988)

Prairie Year, the book had an unusual inception. Cuyler had read and been intrigued by a magazine article Harvey had written about her grandmother's journals. In a remarkable coincidence, illustrator Deborah Kogan Ray, who had also read the article, came to Cuyler with the idea of turning Harvey's text into a children's book that she (Ray) would illustrate. "I didn't have such a developed idea," Cuyler remembers, "so I contacted Brett, and the three of us worked together. It is a wonderful example of synergy that sometimes happens in publishing."

art by Deborah Kogan Ray
from *My Prairie Year* (1986)

art by Deborah Kogan Ray from
Cassie's Journey (1988)

CHAPTER

14

art by Robert Casilla from *Martin Luther King, Jr.* (1986)

Over several years, David A. Adler had delivered riddle books, books about holidays, and mysteries to Holiday House. He then switched to biographies at the suggestion of Cuyler. "Margery called," Adler says, "and suggested I write a picture book biography. In response, I wrote *Martin Luther King, Jr.: Free at Last*. I told her I knew it was too long for a picture book biography, but I wasn't sure what to cut. Instead of suggesting cuts, Margery asked me to add material, and the resulting book was an older-level biography. Then I began working in earnest on the *Picture Book Biography* series, which now includes almost thirty titles."

The first two, *A Picture Book of George Washington* and *A Picture Book of Abraham Lincoln*, both with illustrations by John and Alexandra Wallner,

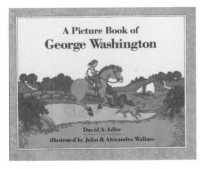

jacket art by John and Alexandra Wallner for *A Picture Book of George Washington* (1989)

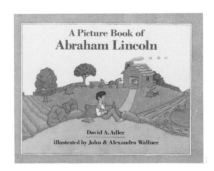

jacket art by John and Alexandra Wallner for *A Picture Book of Abraham Lincoln* (1989)

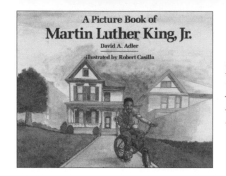

jacket art by Robert Casilla for *A Picture Book of Martin Luther King, Jr.* (1989)

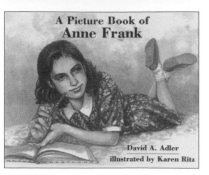

jacket art by Karen Ritz for *A Picture Book of Anne Frank* (1993)

were launched in the spring of 1989 to excellent reviews and a welcoming audience of young readers. In the fall, *A Picture Book of Martin Luther King, Jr.* with illustrations by Robert Casilla was published. "Writing picture book biographies," says Adler, "is challenging. The books must be accurate, interesting, and concise. What I truly hope to do is give a child a picture of the sort of person my subject was and how she or he is important historically while still presenting the person as a human being. I always try to quote my subject, which, I think, makes him or her come alive for the reader."

Another area Adler has delved into is the Holocaust. His first foray was *A Picture Book of Anne Frank.* He was motivated to research and write it, the author says, "because Anne's life paralleled my mother's. They were both born in Frankfurt, Germany, and traced their families back in that city for many generations. They both went to Amsterdam to escape Nazi persecution, but when the Nazis came to Holland, my mother left and Anne Frank went into hiding. I felt it was important to teach children about the Holocaust and the Civil Rights movement. With adults, when we teach them the horrifying effects of prejudice, all we can hope to do is affect their actions. With children, we can affect the way they think *and* act."

Adler followed the Anne Frank book with *Hilde and Eli: Children of the Holocaust; Child of the Warsaw Ghetto;* and *Hiding from the Nazis.* Although the titles tell different stories, their common bond, the Holo-

jacket art by Karen Ritz for *Hilde and Eli* (1994)

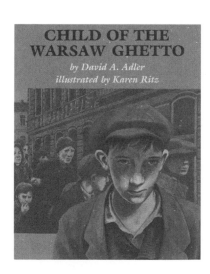

jacket art by Karen Ritz for *Child of the Warsaw Ghetto* (1995)

jacket art by Karen Ritz for *Hiding from the Nazis* (1997)

jacket art by Nancy Tobin for *Shape Up!* (1998)

art by Nancy Tobin from *Fraction Fun* (1996)

jacket art by Nancy Tobin for *How Tall, How Short, How Faraway* (1999)

caust, is linked through Karen Ritz's poignant illustrations. Adler now works with Cuyler's successor, editor-in-chief Regina Griffin. He says, "Margery and Regina are strong editors and very bright women. I have enjoyed working with them both. With Regina, I also learn a great deal from her experiences with other publishing houses."

"David is representative of the long-term relationships—not to mention friendships—we value so highly," says John Briggs.

The Holocaust, which continues to evoke interest and, in some states, is mandated as part of the curriculum, brought another noteworthy contribution, *Smoke and Ashes: The Story of the Holocaust* by Barbara Rogasky, an ALA Notable Book, a Best Book for Young Adults, and a landmark book on the subject. *The Bulletin of the Center for Children's Books* called it "a wrenching and thoroughly documented picture of the Holocaust, with historical photographs that document the horror more graphically than words," and *Booklist* said it was "to be recommended with classics such as *The Diary of Anne Frank.*" A revised edition of *Smoke and Ashes* is in the works.

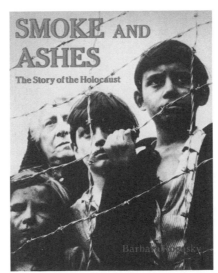

Smoke and Ashes (1988)

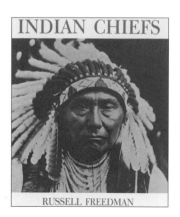

Indian Chiefs (1987)

Buffalo Hunt (1988)

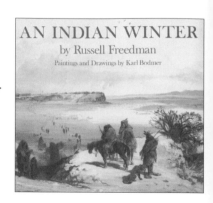

An Indian Winter
(1992) jacket art
by Karl Bodmer

Spring 1987 heralded *Indian Chiefs*, a new book by Russell Freedman, who was drawn back to biography after several years of researching and writing about natural history and animal behavior. In 1961, Holiday House had published his first book, *Teenagers Who Made History*, which included profiles of eight young people who had earned a place in history before they were twenty years old.

Indian Chiefs was followed by *Buffalo Hunt* in 1988 and *An Indian Winter* in 1992. Among them, they earned fourteen starred reviews. These books were inspired by the research Freedman had done for *Children of the Wild West* (Clarion). "I included a chapter on Indian children, and that opened up a vast new area of interest for me in Native Americans," says Freedman. "*Indian Chiefs* was a natural follow-up. I had immersed myself in the period, and the more I learned about Indian culture and lifestyles, the more ideas I had for books on the subject."

Meanwhile, *The Wright Brothers: How They Invented the Airplane* came out and was a Newbery Honor Book. More honors settled on Freedman with the awarding of *The Washington Post*/Children's Book Guild Nonfiction Award in 1992, the Regina Medal in 1996, the Laura Ingalls Wilder Medal in 1998, the DeGrummond Medallion in 1999, and his fourth Golden Kite Award, also in 1999.

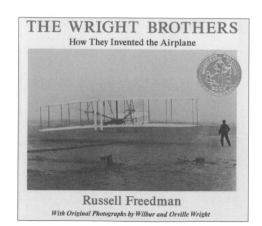

The Wright Brothers
(1991)

According to Margery Cuyler, Freedman is "an easy edit. He writes practically perfect manuscripts, is an expert craftsman, grammarian, and wordsmith, and has three sources for every fact. His writing is always well polished and highly readable. Only with *The Wright Brothers* do I remember asking him to revise a bit, and then just to make the story as dramatic as possible. He's terrific."

With the publication of *Dinosaurs*, *Trains*, *Easter*, and *Monarch Butterfly*, Gail Gibbons's reputation as one of the preeminent author-illustrators of nonfiction for the very young continued to grow. In 1987, she won *The Washington Post*/Children's Book Guild Nonfiction Award.

For several years Gibbons had been promoting the idea of a book on monarch butterflies, but Briggs wasn't enthusiastic and kept trying to put the project off. Fortunately, his reluctance was overcome by Gibbons's irresistible enthusiasm, and *Monarch Butterfly* became one of her best-selling titles. "Dear Gail forgave me," recalls Briggs.

By taking the risk of publishing a 469-page fantasy, the company demonstrated its commitment to older readers as well. *The Hounds of the Morrigan* by Pat O'Shea came out in the spring of 1986 and is still revered by many. The author, who was born in Galway, noted in the book's flap copy that she grew up "close to the sea and surrounded by unspoiled countryside where old people had a lot of time for children and told us many stories of long ago." *The Horn Book* called the novel "a remarkable book, rich and satisfying," and *Booklist* stated, "The brilliant tapestry that this first-time author has woven will delight and enrich those who pursue its multilayered threads."

jacket art by Stephen Lavis for *The Hounds of the Morrigan* (1986)

art by Gail Gibbons from *Dinosaurs* (1987)

art by Gail Gibbons from *Easter* (1989)

art by Gail Gibbons from *Trains* (1987)

art by Gail Gibbons from *Monarch Butterfly* (1989)

art by Leonard Everett Fisher
from *Space Songs* (1988)

art by Leonard Everett Fisher
from *Earth Songs* (1986)

art by Leonard Everett Fisher
from *Sky Songs* (1984)

Another title on that spring list was *Sea Songs*, one of four "song" poems written by Myra Cohn Livingston and illustrated by Leonard Everett Fisher. Fisher tells of an amusing incident following its publication. "My wife and I were in California, and we invited Myra and her husband, Dick, to join us for dinner to celebrate the book's recent publication. The restaurant was right on the water, and it was a very stormy evening. Dick was facing the ocean. Pretty soon we noticed that he was becoming green-faced, and soon he excused himself—he was seasick! After a bit, he returned and was fine. We all had a great laugh, but it was quite ironic for the launching of a book with that title."

Thanksgiving Poems, selected by Myra Cohn Livingston and illustrated by Stephen Gammell, was "a feast for all the seasons," according to *School Library Journal* in a starred review.

"Poetry was a genre Margery had been expanding," commented Briggs, "and she continued to do so with great success."

Eileen Dunlop's first book for Holiday House was *Clementina*, a chilling mystery placed in her Scottish homeland, which has "well-

art by Leonard
Everett Fisher from
Sea Songs (1986)

art by Stephen
Gammell from
Thanksgiving Poems
(1985)

jacket art by Mark O'Neill for
Clementina (1987)

jacket art by Mike Heslop for
The House on the Hill (1987)

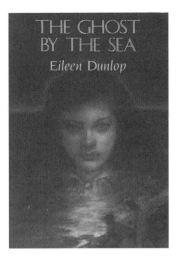

jacket art by Stephen T. Johnson
for *The Ghost by the Sea* (1996)

delineated characterizations and a fascinating plot," according to *Booklist*. Dunlop followed with another novel, *The House on the Hill*, an ALA Notable Book. The firm has published eight of her novels, the most recent being *The Ghost by the Sea*.

"No one writes about Scotland the way Eileen does," says Briggs. "She has a sure sense of drama and impeccable timing."

Tom Birdseye's first novel, *I'm Going to Be Famous*, relates a boy's attempt to break the banana-eating record for *The Guinness Book of World Records* and heralded the author's arrival on the Holiday House scene. The idea for the story, Birdseye says, came from watching his fifth-grade class in Oregon, where he was teaching at the time, constantly pore over *The Guinness Book of World Records*.

"One day," Birdseye remembers, "when the class was supposed to be doing math, one boy was devouring *The Guinness Book*, and I asked him what he was doing. He said he was trying to find a record he could break. That intrigued me. I took *The Guinness Book* home that evening and just happened on the banana-eating bit. Later, I asked my class

jacket art by Irene Trivas
for *I'm Going to Be Famous*
(1986)

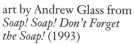

what they thought of a story about someone trying to break the banana-eating record, and they agreed it would be a great theme for a book, so I started writing." He says, "My books tend to come out of my work with the kids, who are a great inspiration for me and often take me back to incidents in my own childhood."

While Birdseye continued to write novels, he decided to challenge his writing skills with a picture-book story. His first, *Airmail to the Moon*, is about a young girl whose tooth, which she is saving to give to the tooth fairy, disappears. In the course of the book, she tells what she threatens to do with the thief—as revealed in the title. Stephen Gammell's home-spun illustrations echo the story's great spirit and fun.

"At that time," the author says, "I had begun teaching kindergarten and was reading lots of picture books to my class and found out how much fun they were—the stories and the kids. The idea for the tooth-fairy book came about because kindergarten is the grade when many children lose their teeth, and they are so passionate about the process and also very funny."

Children also took to their hearts *Soap! Soap! Don't Forget the Soap!*, illustrated by Andrew Glass, which was nominated for four state awards. "I grew up with that story," Birdseye tells. "My father used to tell a similar tale he called 'The Forgetful Boy.' I had forgotten it, however, until one day when I was teaching fifth grade and didn't have a book to share at read-aloud time. So I started telling it, and the kids loved it. The story came out of the oral tradition but then grew into my own personal version." This was followed by *She'll Be Comin' Round the Mountain* by Tom and his wife, Debbie Holsclaw Birdseye.

Cry Uncle! was Mary Jane Auch's first published book. An amusing comedy about a family coping with an elderly uncle's memory loss, it

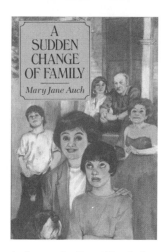

jacket art by Richard Williams for *Cry Uncle!* (1987)

jacket art by Cly Wallace for *Glass Slippers Give You Blisters* (1989)

jacket art by Jean Harris for *A Sudden Change of Family* (1990)

was discovered in a pile of unsolicited manuscripts. "It was quite amazing," Auch recalls, "because I had just read Russell Freedman's *Holiday House: The First Fifty Years* and was thinking, 'Here is a house I would like to work with,' when Margery called about publishing my manuscript."

In reviewing her career, Auch says, "Writing is a lot of revising. The first book I actually wrote, *Glass Slippers Give You Blisters*, received encouraging comments from Natalie Babbitt, who taught a seminar I'd attended. However, when it came to getting it published, I rewrote the whole thing, and when finished, only one scene from the first writing was still intact. And I remember submitting *A Sudden Change of Family* to Margery, who said that she liked the beginning and the end but had trouble with the middle. 'How much of the middle?' I asked. 'Well, actually,' she said, 'everything from after the first scene to the very last one.' We really had a laugh, but I rolled up my sleeves and rebuilt the 'middle' until finally it worked."

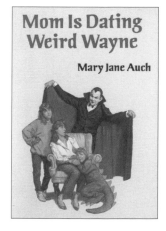

jacket art by Richard Williams for *Mom Is Dating Weird Wayne* (1988)

jacket art by Richard Lauter for *Kidnapping Kevin Kowalski* (1990)

CHAPTER

15

"What a different path my career would have taken—I'd still be teaching at Portland State!" This remark by Eric A. Kimmel was prompted by his remembering that he almost threw out a letter from Holiday House, about which he knew little, offering to publish *Hershel and the Hanukkah Goblins.*

Kimmel's arrival at the house is a story of twists and turns. It began not with his first book published but with *Hershel.* "This funny little story," Kimmel relates, "was something that I seemingly couldn't give away, and I had relegated it to my dead file. Then, in 1984, Marianne Carus from *Cricket* magazine called me, saying she needed a Hanukkah piece right away for the December issue. I told her I would send a story I had and she could use it, but that if she didn't like it, I would try to do something in a hurry. Luckily she liked it, and it appeared in the December issue with decorative drawings by Trina Schart Hyman. At the time it was published, Margery, who was in the hospital having a baby, read *Cricket* and also liked the story. And, as they say, the rest is history. All my stars came together in one story. I owe the beginning to

art by Trina Schart Hyman from *Hershel and the Hanukkah Goblins* (1989)

art by Janet Stevens from *Anansi and the Moss-Covered Rock* (1988)

Cricket, because Marianne had been a supporter for years when no one else wanted my work."

"If it weren't for Marianne and her magazine," notes Briggs, "we may not have published Eric or several illustrators on our list, so you can imagine how indebted *we* are to her."

Hershel and the Hanukkah Goblins, with illustrations by Trina Schart Hyman, was a Caldecott Honor Book. "Rarely are author and illustrator so in tune," noted *Kirkus*.

About preparing the illustrations for *Hershel*, Hyman says, "I had to start over from scratch; the ones I did for the magazine were small and in black and white. The book, of course, was to have a different trim size, and the illustrations were to be in full color. Actually, it was good that I needed to redo the pictures, as I was able to incorporate some new ideas I had for the goblins."

In the meantime, Cuyler had asked Kimmel if he had any animal stories, because she admired the work of a wonderful artist on the list, Janet Stevens, who could draw animals so well. "So I sent her *Anansi and the Moss-Covered Rock*," says Kimmel, "which Janet did so magnificently and which came out before *Hershel*. That was the beginning. For years I had thought that I couldn't do anything right, and suddenly I couldn't do anything wrong."

art by Janet Stevens from *Anansi Goes Fishing* (1992)

art by Janet Stevens from *Anansi and the Talking Melon* (1994)

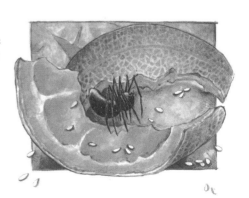

art by Janet Stevens from *Coyote Steals the Blanket* (1993)

art by Janet Stevens from *The Dog Who Had Kittens* (1991)

art by Janet Stevens from *From Pictures to Words* (1995)

Janet Stevens had come to the list years before. "Psychologically," she says, "*The Tortoise and the Hare* (1984) was my breakthrough book, because for the first time I was able to inject the kind of movement I wanted in the drawings. Hare, for example, jumps across the spread on his way to the finishing line, and I felt free to use larger, exaggerated images to enhance the humor, which emotionally the story clearly calls for." In response to how this came about, Stevens replied, "While attending a drawing seminar, I was asked by Ed Young why I kept drawing the same way. This simple question at first took me by surprise, but it broke through my artistic reserve, and I've felt freer to experiment ever since—sometimes in subtle, sometimes in more rash ways. Most importantly, it has allowed me to respond to the story rather than have the story just be a showcase for my art. After all, the integration of art and text is what picture book making is all about."

As to her most popular book? "Teachers," Stevens says, "seem to like the Anansi books the best, but this is partially dependent on the part of the country they live in. For instance, in the Southwest, *Coyote Steals the Blanket* is definitely the preferred choice. As for children, *The Dog Who Had Kittens* by Polly Robertus wins hands down."

According to Cuyler, Steven Kroll is "an author who is gifted with the ability to tell a story that leaves spaces for visual images. *Looking for Daniela* had an interesting background. Anita Lobel had sketched

art by Anita Lobel from *Looking for Daniela* (1988)

art by Janet Stevens from *The Big Bunny and the Magic Show* (1986)

art by Jeni Bassett from *The Squirrels' Thanksgiving* (1991)

out a long, involved *commedia dell'arte* tale that wasn't working, and she showed it to Steven, who was a close friend. He volunteered to rewrite the story, cutting it down to picture-book length, and then brought it to me. I liked it—it was such a romantic tale, and there weren't many around. Then, of course, we asked Anita to illustrate it, which she did in her wonderfully fluid and colorful style. It received stars in both *Booklist* and *School Library Journal*."

Before her death in 1991, Margot Tomes provided artwork for John Warren Stewig's two Grimm retellings, *The Fisherman and His Wife* and *Stone Soup*. In reflecting on their collaboration, Stewig remarked: "In *Stone Soup*, Margot took a subdued yet sophisticated color palette and used it to evoke a sense of 'otherness' in the setting, and gave a charming gawkiness to the heroine that appeals to me." Stewig, a professor of children's literature at the University of Wisconsin-Milwaukee, went on to say, "Tomes treated texts with great care. She was able to identify places in the story that merited visual interpretation—some that I wouldn't have necessarily thought about. She saw herself as a vehicle to extend the text, not to call attention to herself or her work." Stewig's next retelling, *King Midas*, was complemented by "the grace, intelligence, and wit of the [Omar Rayyan] artwork," noted *School Library Journal* in a starred review.

art by Lillian Hoban from *Will You Be My Valentine?* (1993)

art by Margot Tomes from *The Fisherman and His Wife* (1988)

art by Margot Tomes from *Stone Soup* (1991)

art by Omar Rayyan from *King Midas* (1999)

art by Patience Brewster from
Bear and Mrs. Duck (1988)

art by Patience Brewster from
Bear's Christmas Surprise (1991)

art by Patience Brewster from
Bear and Roly-Poly (1996)

jacket art by Ronald
Himler for *West Against
the Wind* (1987)

jacket art by Stephen
Marchesi for *Twelve
Days in August* (1993)

Elizabeth Winthrop returned to the picture book scene with *Bear and Mrs. Duck*, which features an understanding baby-sitter, Mrs. Duck, and Bear, a reluctant "sittee," who is eventually won over through games, story time, and lots of love. When her daughter was four, Winthrop overheard her saying, "Bear, I am going out. You will stay with Mrs. Duck. Don't cry. I'll be home soon." Intrigued by her daughter's words, Winthrop wrote them down and deposited them in an 'idea box' that she keeps on her desk. It wasn't until some fourteen years later that she rediscovered those sentences and turned them into a story, which was followed by two more books featuring the beguiling Bear.

In 1987, Liza Ketchum Murrow joined the list with her first novel, *West Against the Wind*, which received a starred review from *School Library Journal*; and in 1990, veteran Bruce McMillan came onboard with *One Sun: A Book of Terse Verse*, which was an ALA Notable Book.

Elvira Woodruff's first book was *Awfully Short for the Fourth Grade*, a fantasy about a boy and a miniature-making toy machine. She says, "Miniatures are something I am well acquainted with. Having two sons, we had hundreds of 'little guys' around our home, a situation that activated this story into being." This Pennsylvania author has found a direct line to children's preferences, capturing state awards in Arkansas, Florida, Minnesota, and Maryland.

jacket photo by Bruce
McMillan for *Mouse Views*
(1993)

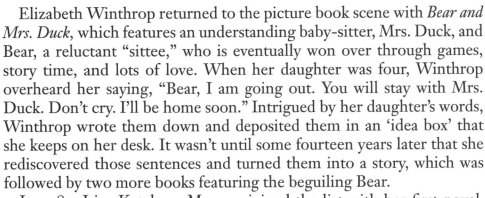

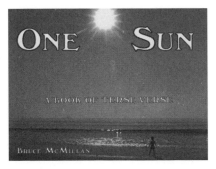

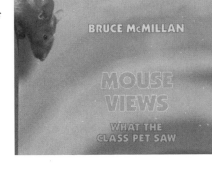

jacket photo by
Bruce McMillan for
One Sun (1990)

jacket art by Will
Hillenbrand for *Awfully
Short for the Fourth Grade*
(1989)

jacket art by
Katherine Coville for
*The Summer I Shrank
My Grandmother*
(1990)

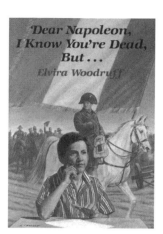

jacket art by Robert Barrett
for *Dear Napoleon, I Know
You're Dead, But...*(1992)

Awfully Short for the Fourth Grade was also the debut of a remarkable young illustrator, Will Hillenbrand. A native of Ohio, Will began his art career in advertising but changed direction after a three-week seminar with Ken Marantz, an art education professor at Ohio State University. Will found a niche in picture book illustration and compiled a portfolio. Having arranged interviews with four publishers, he drove east and had what he thought of as a classic New York experience. After a series of misadventures with wrong and delayed trains, Will was accosted by tough characters on a city street and found himself two twenty-dollar bills poorer. Late for his first interview, he said, "I felt unfocused and discouraged when I arrived. The formal corporate atmosphere there only increased my gnawing despondency, but I stoically endured the experience."

art by Jacqueline Garrick
from *Thomas Jefferson*
(1987)

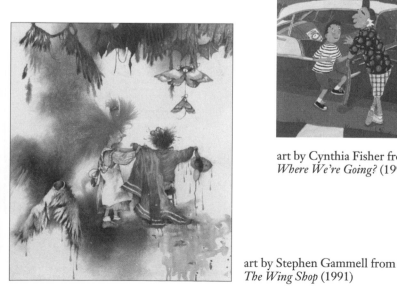

art by Cynthia Fisher from *Can You Guess
Where We're Going?* (1998)

art by Robert Casilla from
Jackie Robinson (1989)

art by Stephen Gammell from
The Wing Shop (1991)

art by Glen Rounds from *Charlie Drives the Stage* (1989)

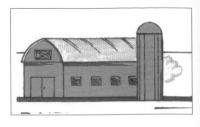

art by Gail Gibbons from *Farming* (1988)

art by Glen Rounds from *Four Dollars and Fifty Cents* (1990)

art by Stephen Gammell from *Halloween Poems* (1989)

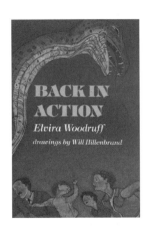

jacket art by Will Hillenbrand for *Back in Action* (1991)

Will's second appointment was at Holiday House. He felt his spirits lift as he entered an office comfortably full of clamor and awash with books. He remembers those first moments well. "I told the receptionist that I had an appointment with Margery Cuyler, only to be informed that she was not in due to a train strike. Feeling desperate, I asked if I could show my portfolio to someone. Kate Briggs, overhearing the conversation, introduced herself. She said 'You're from Ohio, aren't you? I grew up in Cleveland. Welcome to Holiday House.' I couldn't help but feel an instant connection with Kate. After all, she had lived in Ohio. She carefully examined my portfolio and suggested a meeting with Margery the next day. Kate then phoned Margery to check her schedule, made an appointment, and set up a lunch as well.

"The next day both Margery and I managed to arrive at Holiday without mishap. After reviewing a few pages of my portfolio, she disappeared into a back room for a moment. When she returned, she announced that Holiday House wanted to be the first publisher to put my work into print. That phrase brought such a thrill; it still rings with delight in my head. Then we did have that lunch at a Chinese restaurant, where my fortune cookie predicted continued good luck. Certainly my relationship with Holiday House has made the prediction true."

art by Will Hillenbrand from *I'm the Best!* (1991)

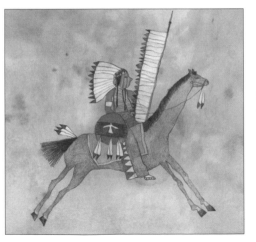

art by Stephen Gammell from *Dancing Teepees* (1989)

This relationship began with the cover art and line drawings for *Awfully Short for the Fourth Grade*, which was followed by its sequel, *Back in Action.* The next two manuscripts were for picture books: *I'm the Best!* by Marjorie Weinman Sharmat and *The Magic Rocket* by Steven Kroll.

Having written five novels with Native American themes for Holiday House in the 1970s, Virginia Driving Hawk Sneve returned in 1989 with *Dancing Teepees: Poems of American Indian Youth*, with illustrations by Stephen Gammell. "Together she and Gammell have created a collection that could well be read and re-read with pleasure and thoughtfulness by adults as well as children," reported *School Library Journal* in a starred review.

Michael McCurdy wrote and illustrated *Hannah's Farm: The Seasons on an Early American Homestead.* He then published his first book with full-color wood engravings, Louisa May Alcott's *An Old-Fashioned Thanksgiving.*

jacket art by Michael McCurdy for *An Old-Fashioned Thanksgiving* (1989)

jacket art by Michael McCurdy for *Hannah's Farm* (1988)

As the picture book market flourished in the rising economy of the late 1980s, Holiday House offered a wide variety of books to a wide variety of readers. As always, however, it was the dedication to books that would please children that lay at the heart of the house's ventures.

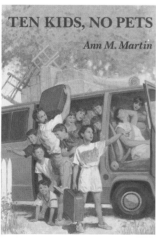

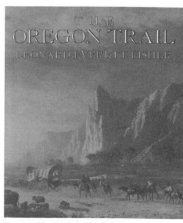

jacket art by Richard Williams for *Ten Kids, No Pets* (1988)

jacket art by Stephen Mancusi for *With You and Without You* (1986)

Monticello (1988)

The Oregon Trail (1990) jacket art by Albert Bierstadt

CHAPTER

16

The beginning of a new decade brought some fundamental changes to the firm. In January 1990, it moved to an open, airy full floor with windows on all four sides in a building at 40 East 49th Street. (The address of the building was changed to 425 Madison Avenue shortly thereafter.) Later that year, Judy Ang, "who is as good at her job as she is nice," says Briggs, joined the house as controller. And Barbara Walsh was appointed vice president.

Barbara Walsh came to Holiday House as a temp in 1974 and gradually assumed numerous responsibilities. Currently, those include selling all the house accounts, communicating with approximately thirty-five sales representatives, and getting books into direct mail catalogs, as well as advertising, some editing, and some subsidiary rights. "And she performs them all expertly," says Briggs. "Her contribution cannot be overstated."

David Rogers retired in 1991 as vice president of design and production. Tere LoPrete, who had been assisting David for several years as a

art by Gail Gibbons from
*Weather Words and What
They Mean* (1990)

art by Gail Gibbons from
From Seed to Plant (1991)

art by Tomie dePaola from *Little Grunt and the Big Egg* (1990)

art by Leonard Everett Fisher from *Cyclops* (1991)

art by Lisl Weil from *Wolferel* (1991)

freelancer, took over in what amounted to a seamless transition. That same year Diane Bailey (later Foote) arrived to help Kate expand the efforts of the marketing department.

Her arrival happened in a roundabout way. Says Foote, "I had been working as an assistant at William Morrow for almost two years, when I noticed an ad in *Publishers Weekly* for a marketing assistant at Holiday House. I was happy at Morrow, so I did nothing about it. But shortly thereafter, I sought to get involved beyond the assistant level, and I applied for an author-appearance coordinator position at Penguin with Mimi Kayden. She told me that job had been filled, and I thought back to the ad I'd seen earlier in the year, wishing I had responded. Unbeknownst to me, Mimi knew the opportunity to work with Kate was open again and forwarded my resume to her. A year after first noticing the ad, I had been given a second chance! I was wary of working at a small company at first, but when I got here and saw the president [John Briggs] working the mail machine and Kate [Briggs] stuffing envelopes, I knew I'd found the place where I'd be able to get involved the way I wanted to, with lots of hands-on work."

Her responsibilities depend on what needs to be done, she says, "but I was hired to take care of author appearances—we have about 200 a year—submit books for the major awards, and handle, with Kate, the conventions. I also write targeted press releases and promotional

art by Giora Carmi from *The Chanukkah Guest* (1990)

art by Kenn Compton from *Jack the Giant Chaser* (1993)

art by Glen Rounds from *Three Billy Goats Gruff* (1993)

art by Glen Rounds from *Three Little Pigs and the Big Bad Wolf* (1992)

pieces." Now director of marketing, her enthusiasm bubbles quickly to the surface as she talks about authors and illustrators and the books she helps to promote. "We try to promote our books in inventive ways; there is always the pull between finding each book's individual niche— its own personality, so to speak—and promoting the list as a whole through exhibits and getting books to reviewers."

Kate Briggs adds, "We are always looking for new ways to tell people about our books and our authors and illustrators. It's what we are all about—publishing and promoting good books."

"I always thought Rose Vallario exemplified the conscience of Holiday House," says John Briggs. "Anyone who worked with her was better for it. As you can imagine, she performed any number of tasks during the fifty years she was here before retiring in 1992, and eight years later she is still missed."

The new decade brought Diane Hoyt-Goldsmith, who, with photographer Lawrence Migdale, has celebrated and documented the culture of many different ethnic groups in the United States. Their story of finding Holiday House, still their only trade publisher after ten years, is unusual. "I have a background in children's book design," Hoyt-Goldsmith relates, "but I never imagined I would become an author. I had been interested in totem poles and the art of the Pacific Northwest Coast Indians for years. When I met a Tsimshian carver and his young son, I had the idea that a children's book about native culture told from the point of view of an individual child would be very exciting and different. When I talked it over with Lawrence, I discovered that he was just as excited by the idea as I was."

Together Hoyt-Goldsmith and Migdale created a photo-essay about totem poles and the people who make them. Then Hoyt-Goldsmith put together a book package, combining the photos and text with a compelling design. "We sent out sixty-five query letters to tell publishers about our book. We had positive responses from eight, and planned a

jacket photo by Lawrence Migdale
for *Totem Pole* (1990)

jacket photo by Lawrence Migdale
for *Pueblo Storyteller* (1991)

jacket photo by Lawrence Migdale for
Celebrating Chinese New Year (1998)

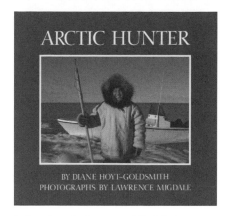

jacket photo by Lawrence Migdale for
Celebrating Kwanzaa (1993)

jacket photo by Lawrence Migdale for
Arctic Hunter (1992)

weeklong trip to New York to present our project. At the end of the week, our last appointment was with Margery Cuyler of Holiday House. When we went into that meeting, we had offers from two other publishers. However, Margery was enthusiastic and said she wanted to make us an offer. 'Go downstairs and have a cup of coffee,' she said. 'I want to talk with John. Come back in half an hour and I'll give you our answer.' After we came back, she did make us a great offer, but what really sold us on Holiday House was Margery's tremendous enthusiasm. After all these years with Holiday House, we have never been sorry."

As to their most exciting project? Migdale claims, "It was our trip to Alaska and our book *Arctic Hunter*. We went to Kotzebue, Alaska, north of the Arctic Circle, and spent several weeks with an Inupiat family at their fishing and hunting camp." The result is a richly illustrated book that documents a culture in which subsistence hunting is still a way of life. "It was incredibly interesting to be a part of a way of life that is so rare," he continued. Hoyt-Goldsmith and Migdale describe their approach as journalistic. Migdale says, "We don't create the story—we find it."

A brilliant artist who continued to work with Holiday House before his death in 1993 was Charles Mikolaycak. According to Pratt Institute

jacket art by
Charles Mikolaycak
for *A Gift from
Saint Nicholas*
(1988)

art by Charles
Mikolaycak from
*The Legend of the
Christmas Rose*
(1990)

art by Charles Mikolaycak from *Bearhead* (1991)

art by Charles Mikolaycak from *The Hero of Bremen* (1993)

art by Charles Mikolaycak from *Exodus* (1987)

of Art classmate Tomie dePaola, "Chuck was one of the best figure-drawing illustrators in the business. His control of line and ability to depict the body were phenomenal." The books Mikolaycak illustrated were often religious in nature, such as *He Is Risen: The Easter Story* (1985) and *Exodus.* Christmas was a favorite subject: *A Child Is Born: The Christmas Story* (1983); *Babushka: An Old Russian Folktale* (1984); *The Legend of the Christmas Rose;* and *A Gift from Saint Nicholas.* Although he retold *Babushka* from his own childhood memories, he preferred to illustrate the texts of other authors, distinguishing the books of his wife, Carole Kismaric, Miriam Chaikin, Eric A. Kimmel, and Elizabeth Winthrop with a keen sense of page harmony and a knowing balance of art and text.

"We published Chuck's last book, *The Hero of Bremen* by Margaret Hodges," says John Briggs. "There was no one like him."

As the face of America continued to change, books with multicultural themes continued to be published. Tom Birdseye wrote *A Song of Stars: An Asian Legend,* which Ju-Hong Chen illustrated. The artist, who was born in Shanghai and now lives in Beaverton, Oregon, also provided the pictures for *The Fourth Question: A Chinese Folktale, The Jade Stone,* and *The Tale of Aladdin and the Wonderful Lamp.*

art by Ju-Hong Chen from *The Tale of Aladdin and the Wonderful Lamp* (1992)

art by Ju-Hong Chen from *A Song of Stars* (1990)

art by Ju-Hong Chen from *The Fourth Question* (1991)

art by Ju-Hong Chen from *The Jade Stone* (1992)

art by Samuel Byrd
from *Dancing with
the Indians* (1991)

art by Terea Shaffer
from *The Singing Man*
(1994)

"Also," Cuyler remembers, "stories by Angela Shelf Medearis, who came to Holiday House by way of an unsolicited submission titled *Dancing with the Indians*, were matched with the artwork of African-American illustrators Sterling Brown, Samuel Byrd, James Ransome, Terea Shaffer and John Ward." Medearis's *The Singing Man*, an adaptation of a West African folktale with illustrations by Terea Shaffer, won a Coretta Scott King Honor Award for Illustration. James Ransome did the artwork for Medearis's *Rum-a-Tum-Tum*, a lyrical celebration of New Orleans in the early 1900s.

Ransome had first met Cuyler when he came to Holiday House for a portfolio review. Sometime later, the two saw each other again when they were both doing presentations at a high school in New Jersey. "Afterward," Ransome says, "Margery contacted me, hoping we might work together. She suggested I take a look at James Weldon Johnson's *God's Trombones: Seven Negro Sermons in Verse*, a collection of poetic sermons that captures the rhythm and character of the southern black country preachers of the 1800s—an idea I liked, which eventually resulted in *The Creation*. Its biggest challenge was how to show God, and if so, what sex, what color, what image should be presented? I didn't

jacket art by James E. Ransome
for *Rum-a-Tum-Tum* (1997)

art by Sterling Brown
from *Tailypo* (1996)

art by John Ward from
Poppa's New Pants (1995)

art by James E. Ransome from *The Creation* (1994)

art by Gersom Griffith from *Journey to Freedom* (1994)

art by Gershom Griffith from *Jumping the Broom* (1994)

art by Gershom Griffith from *Wagon Train* (1995)

want to show God at all. Margery suggested I keep re-reading the material. Finally, I worked out a different way to tell the story—a preacher talking to a group of children under a tree—giving the sermon a storyteller's perspective. I placed the story at a church picnic with a preacher telling how the world was created, interspersed with double-page spreads showing God's magnificent work. I ended up illustrating it in an entirely different way because of Margery and my ongoing conversations and our close working relationship." *The Creation* won the Coretta Scott King Illustrator Award.

Courtni C. Wright joined the list with three picture books based on historical events concerning the African-American experience. They feature richly colored illustrations by Gershom Griffith.

In 1993, John Briggs invited Virginia Driving Hawk Sneve to write, and Ronald Himler to illustrate, books about various Native Americans, which resulted in a nine-book series titled *The First Americans*. Covering the Apaches, Cherokees, Cheyennes, Hopis, Iroquois, Navajos, Nez Perce, Seminoles, and Sioux, the books discuss each group's history, customs, and current status.

art by Ronald Himler from *The Sioux* (1993)

art by Ronald Himler from *The Iroquois* (1995)

art by Ronald Himler from *The Navajos* (1993)

art by Ronald Himler from *The Cheyennes* (1996)

The illustrations were, Himler said, "an easy move from my gallery work" that features Native Americans, which he has been producing in Tucson for the last twenty years. "I had done a lot of research and reading over the years for my fine art," he remarked, "and so I felt comfortable creating the pictures for this series."

Highly lauded, the books filled a void, as noted in *The Bulletin of the Center for Children's Books:* "The very commitment of each book to a particular people will help dispel the amorphous lumping together of 'Indians' that tends to dominate elementary school units on U.S. history."

Eric A. Kimmel's continuing repertoire of stories from many cultures allowed the firm to match his texts with many of the finest illustrators in the field.

art by Megan Lloyd from *Baba Yaga* (1991)

art by Kimberly Bulcken Root from *Boots and His Brothers* (1992)

art by Robert Rayevsky from *Three Sacks of Truth* (1993)

art by Leonard Everett Fisher from *The Three Princes* (1994)

In 1992, Mary Jane Auch, who had won recognition as a funny contemporary novelist for middle graders, took her career into a new dimension and began writing and illustrating picture books. Her deadpan humor seems to derive from offbeat connections to eggs and chickens, which surfaced in her first picture book effort, *The Easter Egg Farm.*

art by Mary Jane Auch from *The Easter Egg Farm* (1992)

art by Mary Jane Auch from *Peeping Beauty* (1993)

art by Mary Jane Auch from
Hen Lake (1995)

art by Mary Jane Auch from
Bantam of the Opera (1997)

art by Mary Jane Auch from
The Nutquacker (1999)

art by Mary Jane
Auch from *Eggs
Mark the Spot* (1996)

"I had always wanted to do picture books," Auch says. "I was an art major in college and had created illustrations for a newspaper before I got into children's books. In fact I had asked about doing the jacket art for my first book, *Cry Uncle!*, and even did a sample. Margery felt that the art wasn't quite right but thought the chickens I had used in the background were wonderful. So eventually I wrote *The Easter Egg Farm* and did the artwork as well."

The fun followed with *Peeping Beauty, Hen Lake, Eggs Mark the Spot, Bantam of the Opera*, and *The Nutquacker*. "It's gotten to be," Auch says, "that I'm called 'the chicken lady.' My husband has suggested I write a scary book and call it *Poultrygeist*." A resident of upstate New York, Auch says that she used to raise chickens and that her grandmother once had a chicken farm, so "I guess the stories come naturally."

Gillian Cross, whose books originate with Ron Heapy at Oxford University Press, continued to contribute to the list. "Her books are consistently well received," says Briggs, who notes that *The Great American Elephant Chase* garnered four starred reviews. "She is a consummate writer, and it has been our good fortune to be able to publish ten of her novels."

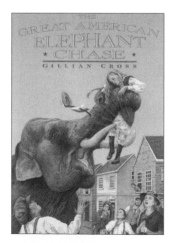

jacket art by Jennifer Webb
for *The Great American
Elephant Chase* (1993)

jacket art by Mike Allport
for *Wolf* (1991)

jacket art by Greg Spalenka for
Tightrope (1999)

jacket art by Slatter-Anderson for *Pictures in the Dark* (1996)

jacket art by Donald Teskey for *Under the Hawthorn Tree* (1990)

jacket art by Donald Teskey for *Wildflower Girl* (1992)

jacket art by Donald Teskey for *Fields of Home* (1997)

jacket art by Stephen T. Johnson for *October Moon* (1994)

jacket art by Jeff Fisher for *Gemini Game* (1994)

As Barbara Walsh points out, "Gillian adds distinction to the list. Her books always receive superb reviews."

A trip to Ireland by the Briggses resulted in the publishing of a trilogy by Marita Conlon-McKenna. Her first novel—and the first in the trilogy which begins with the Irish famine of the 1840s—was *Under the Hawthorn Tree*, a winner of the International Reading Association Young Adult Book Award. The author got her first look at the United States when she came to receive the award—in Las Vegas!

A subsequent trip to Ireland brought another opportunity, this time to publish *October Moon* and *The Gemini Game* by Michael Scott.

Dorothy Hinshaw Patent is an author who brings a scholarly touch to her nonfiction. She writes about topics far from her landlocked Montana home (dolphins, whales, and sea lions) as well as subjects found in

Looking at Dolphins and Porpoises (1989) jacket photo by Alisa Schulman

jacket photo by William Muñoz for *Draft Horses* (1986)

African Elephants (1991) jacket photo by Oria Douglas-Hamilton

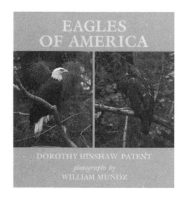

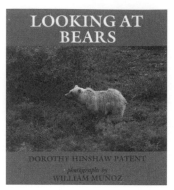

jacket photo by William Muñoz for *Prairies* (1996)

jacket photo by William Muñoz for *Looking at Bears* (1994)

jacket photo by William Muñoz for *Eagles of America* (1995)

her own backyard, so to speak (horses and eagles). Patent, a zoology professor who began writing for Holiday House in 1973, has continued to demonstrate her writing skills with wide-ranging topics—everything from elephants to ants. And when her texts are matched with the camera work of William Muñoz, as in *Eagles of America*, *Prairies*, and *Looking at Bears*, for example, readers are treated in both graphics and writing to top-quality explorations of the natural world.

Steven Kroll penned his first nonfiction for the firm in 1994. "I suggested to John that I write some historical pieces for Holiday House," says Kroll. "The informational-book genre was blossoming and a need was there. He agreed, and I came to him with a list of topics. We decided on *Lewis and Clark: Explorers of the American West*, which was followed by *Ellis Island: Doorway to Freedom*; *The Boston Tea Party*; *Robert Fulton: From Submarine to Steamboat*; and *William Penn: Founder of Pennsylvania*. At Holiday House, there is such a sense of home, of continuity, of being nurtured through the whole creative process."

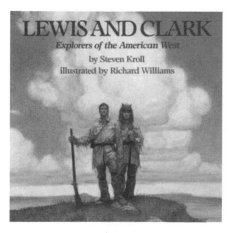

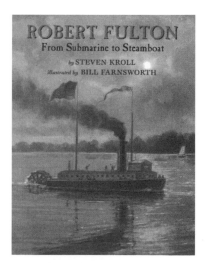

jacket art by Richard Williams for *Lewis and Clark* (1994)

jacket art by Peter Fiore for *The Boston Tea Party* (1998)

jacket art by Bill Farnsworth for *Robert Fulton* (1999)

jacket art by John and Alexandra Wallner for *A Picture Book of Louis Braille* (1997)

jacket art by John and Alexandra Wallner for *A Picture Book of Helen Keller* (1990)

art by Alexandra Wallner from *Laura Ingalls Wilder* (1997)

art by Alexandra Wallner from *Betsy Ross* (1994)

Alexandra Wallner—who, with her husband, John, has illustrated thirteen of the *Picture Book Biography* titles by David A. Adler—contributed *Betsy Ross*, the first of five distinguished titles she has both written and illustrated.

Loreen Leedy recalls, "Margery suggested that math books for young children were scarce and I should try making one." The result was *Fraction Action*, which has become one of Leedy's most popular titles and led to its sequel, *Mission: Addition*, as well as *2 × 2 = BOO!: A Set of Spooky Multiplication Stories*.

"The math idea was perfect for me, because I love finding a neglected area in children's books—there aren't many—and then creating a book on that topic. *Messages in the Mailbox: How to Write a Letter; Postcards from Pluto: A Tour of the Solar System;* and *The Edible Pyramid: Good Eating Every Day* are additional examples. I feel so fortunate to be making picture books, because they are a unique art form. Each one is a little

art by Loreen Leedy from *Fraction Action* (1994)

art by Loreen Leedy from *Mission: Addition* (1997)

jacket art by Loreen Leedy for *2 x 2 = BOO!* (1995)

art by Loreen Leedy from *Messages in the Mailbox* (1991)

art by Loreen Leedy from *Postcards from Pluto* (1993)

art by Loreen Leedy from *The Edible Pyramid* (1994)

art by Loreen Leedy from *How Humans Make Friends* (1996)

art by Loreen Leedy from *Celebrate the 50 States!* (1999)

world created with words and pictures where characters can have fun, get into trouble, and learn a thing or two. It is a truly satisfying career for me."

Kay Chorao's entrée into Holiday House links back to her deliciously scary illustrations for *Monster Poems* (1976). Following that, she went on to create the artwork for books by Marjorie Weinman Sharmat and Steven Kroll. She also wrote and illustrated her own story, *Lemon Moon* (1983), a tale in which shapes on a patchwork quilt come alive and lead a boy on a fanciful nocturnal adventure.

"That story was based," Chorao says, "on a nighttime incident involving my son, and it was a very special book for me." After a several-year hiatus from Holiday House due to heavy commitments with other publishers, Chorao was, she said, "pleased to return in 1995 with *Number One Number Fun*. I've now worked with Regina Griffin on *The Christmas Story*, a simple retelling of the nativity story [a Book-of-the-Month Club selection], and on *The Cats Kids*, a trio of seasonal tales featuring three feline children. One of the things that is great about Holiday House is that they keep books in print a long time. It was nice to know that, even when I wasn't doing anything new for them, *I'm Terrific* (1977) and *Monster Poems*, both published in the seventies, were still available."

Will Hillenbrand's career continued to flourish as well. His breakthrough book was *Wicked Jack* by Connie Nordhielm Wooldridge. This decidedly offbeat story about an old blacksmith so mean that, when he dies, neither St. Peter nor the devil wants him, drew three starred reviews. *Kirkus* called the artwork "stunning" with "a knack for being eerie without being scary."

art by Kay Chorao from *Number One Number Fun* (1995)

art by Kay Chorao from *The Christmas Story* (1996)

art by Kay Chorao from *The Cats Kids* (1998)

art by Will Hillenbrand from
Wicked Jack (1995)

Hillenbrand had always been partial to folktales, but this one was a challenge. "Despite its odd theme," he says, "my first reaction to the story was strong. It reminded me of the kind of quirky plot that I would have loved as a child. When I began the illustrations, however, the big question set in: how do you show someone who is downright mean yet not make him off-putting? What I did from the very beginning, even on the book jacket, was to show Jack in partial profile so that I could give a gleam to his eye and an upturned lip on his face. The sideways glance seems to suggest a shared secret and draws the reader into the story. I also put a slingshot in his back pocket and gave Jack a sidekick—a pig. These are never mentioned in the text, but convey a subtle humor that I wanted to underlie the story. The pig is a great foil for Jack and hopefully induces belly laughs, a lighter touch that the story needs to make it really work."

Another example of Hillenbrand's subtlety is found on the cover, where he forms the word *Mom* from the blacksmith's anvils hanging on his worktable. "This old codger," the illustrator says with a small knowing smile, "is really a Mama's boy." Hillenbrand's details create small stories within the large story and support his theory that a picture book is like a suite of pictures that captures both the overarching continuity and great diversity of a story.

On occasion Holiday House brings one of its books back into print, or one that was originally published elsewhere. "One of the latter," Briggs says, "was *How Six Found Christmas* by Trina Schart Hyman, originally published by Little, Brown in 1969. I bless Trina for so much (including calling me 'Boss'), in this case for giving us the opportunity

jacket art by Trina Schart Hyman
for *How Six Found Christmas*
(1991)

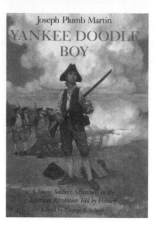

jacket art by Richard Williams
for *Yankee Doodle Boy* (1995)

to reissue one of her treasures, which we also sold to the Book-of-the-Month Club and to a Japanese publisher."

Then, in 1995, the firm brought out *Yankee Doodle Boy*, an eyewitness account of the Revolutionary War as seen through the eyes of a young soldier named Joseph Plumb Martin, which was edited by George F. Scheer and originally published by William R. Scott in 1964.

"George was always ever-so patient and tolerant," says Briggs, "from the day I arrived here in '65. In the early '90s, he offered us the book and got a 'no thank you' in reply. Then in '94 he gave us another crack at it, and we accepted with pleasure. It's had two printings and was sold to a paperback book club. Some of George's reassuring and self-effacing nature, as well as his gentle humor, is reflected in a conversation we had after he spent a summer vacation in Maine. I asked George what he did there, and he replied—almost as a confession—that there was a very expensive model boat in a store that he knew he shouldn't buy but finally did. 'I was nothing but a fool,' he said. I protested with 'No, you're not' in an effort to bolster his spirits, and added *'I'm* the fool. I not only spend too much on a boat, I do it every year.' Without hesitation, back came, 'Yeah, John, but you can get *on* yours.'" George Scheer died in 1996.

Historian David Lavender, a two-time Pulitzer nominee, finally joined the list in 1995 with *The Santa Fe Trail*. He had been Briggs's English teacher at The Thacher School in Ojai, California, and they had talked about doing a book together for years. When Briggs told him that he was wary about editing his teacher, Lavender replied, "How do you think I like the idea of being edited by one of my students?" Actually, Barbara Walsh co-edited the book, as well as *Snowbound: The*

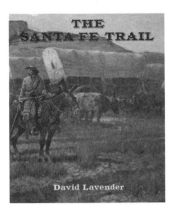

The Santa Fe Trail (1995)
jacket art by Nick Eggenhofer

Snowbound (1996) jacket photo by
Stephen Trimble

Mother Earth, Father Sky (1998)

Tragic Story of the Donner Party. Mother Earth, Father Sky: The Pueblo Indians of the American Southwest was edited by Mary Cash. All received recognition worthy of the author's reputation. "Publishing David has been an especially gratifying experience," notes Briggs.

Holiday House continued to support the beginning author. In 1995, novels appeared by then first-timers Lucy Jane Bledsoe, Lucy Frank, Linda Oatman High, D. Anne Love, Jo Ann Muchmore, and Malka Penn.

jacket art by Sterling
Brown for *The Big Bike
Race* (1995)

jacket art by Barbara J.
Roman for *I Am an
Artichoke* (1995)

jacket art by Ronald Himler
for *Maizie* (1995)

jacket art by
Ronald Himler
for *Bess's Log
Cabin Quilt*
(1995)

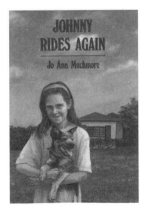

jacket art by
Emma Witmer
for *Johnny Rides
Again* (1995)

jacket art by
Trina Schart
Hyman for
*The Hanukkah
Ghosts* (1995)

art by Tomie dePaola from
An Early American Christmas (1987)

art by Tomie dePaola
from *The Miracles of
Jesus* (1987)

art by Tomie dePaola from
The Parables of Jesus (1987)

Tomie dePaola, a major contributor to the list since 1971, continued to be a mainstay of the firm. The fall 1987 list was graced with *An Early American Christmas*, *The Miracles of Jesus*, and *The Parables of Jesus*. The latter two reflect dePaola's longtime spiritual interest. Having entered a monastery (twice) early in his life, but finding it wasn't the right vocation for him, the author-illustrator has continued to explore spiritual subjects in a variety of ways. By writing about Jesus' miracles and parables, dePaola says he "wanted to extend children's understanding of the Holy Family." These two books not only fit naturally into dePaola's oeuvre but also represent the kind of out-of-the-mainstream publication that, for the late 1980s, Cuyler felt comfortable doing.

"Both of us were interested," Cuyler says, "in doing these stories in a classical manner—the way they are in the Bible—and yet simplifying the text to make them approachable to children."

DePaola reiterated this shared feeling, saying that these books "came about because of Margery's and my shared interest in spirituality. Our conversations began back when I wrote and illustrated *The Lady of Guadalupe* (1980) and *Francis: The Poor Man of Assisi* (1982). Margery wanted me to continue in this vein, yet she wanted something different than what other mainstream publishers were doing. We didn't want books that were sentimental or full of candy-box art. A lot of discussion ensued, and *The Miracles of Jesus* and *The Parables of Jesus* were the result. Following that was my last book for Holiday House, *Mary: The Mother of Jesus*, which, for many reasons, was a very special book for me."

"And it was a very special book for us," noted Barbara Walsh, "so we put it on the cover of our fall 1995 catalog."

DePaola's formal relationship with Holiday House ended when he signed an exclusive agreement with G. P. Putnam's Sons. "Given the personal as well as the professional satisfaction that has come from publishing thirty-two of Tomie's books over a twenty-four-year period, I can't help but remain hopeful there will be another opportunity to work with him," says John Briggs.

"I loved working with Holiday House," dePaola claims. "There is something special about working with a small house. Besides, Kate gives some of the best parties ever!"

art by Tomie dePaola from *Mary: The Mother of Jesus* (1995)

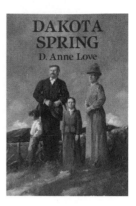

art by Leonard Everett Fisher
from *Moses* (1995)

art by Glen Rounds from
Sod Houses on the Great Plains (1995)

jacket art by Ronald Himler
for *Dakota Spring* (1995)

"In November 1995, Margery told Kate and me that she was leaving to go to Henry Holt," recalls Briggs. "We were stunned. We had worked with her for twenty-one years and couldn't imagine Holiday House without her. We tried to understand that she could want to undertake new challenges and that adversity just might possibly create opportunity for us, but those thoughts were of little consolation during a long, sleepless night. If ever there was a call to action, that was it, so I sent a letter out the next day to the authors and illustrators."

> I deeply regret having to announce that Margery will be leaving Holiday House the end of next month to join Henry Holt as vice president and associate publisher. It's been a joy to work with her, so the loss is just as personal as it is professional, and that's saying something. As you know, Margery has been the guiding light of our list for twenty-one years. Her record speaks for itself.
>
> The search for a successor begins this morning. We will be looking for someone with superior editorial skills who will also be caring, nurturing and supportive of your efforts.

CHAPTER

17

It is a pleasure to announce that Regina Griffin will be joining Holiday House as vice president and editor-in-chief on Thursday, February 1st.

For the past ten years Regina has been at Scholastic where she has acquired reprint rights, been Senior Editor and, most recently, Executive Editor of Scholastic Hardcover. In a letter shortly after our first meeting she wrote: "I have always admired both the Holiday House list and the company's way of doing business. The number of titles I purchased from Margery for reprint and book club rights is proof of the first statement; I think everyone in children's books agrees with the second. . . . It's clear to me that there is no possible reason you would want to change the direction of the list . . . it pleases both critics and children, and that's the real job of any children's book publisher."

You can see why we welcome Regina with unqualified enthusiasm, and why we are confident you will receive the support and attention that we have always tried to provide for those we have had the honor of publishing.

This letter was sent to the authors and illustrators on January 2, 1996. "Regina's acceptance brought relief, joy, and excitement," recalls Briggs.

jacket art by Nancy Poydar
for *Second-Grade Pig Pals*
(1994)

jacket art by Nancy Poydar
for *Cody and Quinn, Sitting
in a Tree* (1996)

"February first couldn't come soon enough. She had a tough act to follow, and she came through with flying colors."

One reaction to the changeover came from Eric Kimmel: "Margery's leaving Holiday House hit me like an earthquake. She was more than an editor; she had become—and still is—a close friend. She had been at Holiday House for twenty-one years, and I fully expected her to be there for twenty-one years more. I was numb when she called me to say she was leaving.

"I knew we would be working together on other projects. But Holiday House was my base. All my best books were there. Kate, John, Barbara, and Diane were my friends; they had always been exceptionally kind to me. What was going to happen? Who would be the new editor? Would she like me? Would I like her? All the publishing horror tales of botched projects and incompetent and tyrannical editors came to mind. It was such a relief to come to New York and meet Regina. She has the

art by Megan Lloyd from
Seven at One Blow (1998)

same quirky sense of humor Margery does, I thought. She likes kung fu movies. She knows good wine. We can work together! We can have fun! And we have. Regina is exceptional, and so is Mary Cash. The change, traumatic as it was at the time, turned out for the best. Before, I knew one terrific editor. Now I knew three. Good career move, I might say, even though I had nothing to do with it."

Although Griffin had specialized in books for older readers, she liked "the idea of a small place, and John proved very persuasive." Her mission, she says, is to "keep the list stable, bring in both older and younger level titles, and update the look of the list in general." She wants the list to be broad-based and plans that it will stay at fifty to sixty titles a year. "What I like about Holiday House," she says, "is that when they say they think about the authors and illustrators first, they really mean it. John and Kate are devoted to the people who create the books and have a long-term commitment to their careers."

Griffin wasted no time in signing up *Hey Dad, Get a Life!* by Todd Strasser ("a compassionate and accessible tale of a family's adjustment to loss"—*Booklist*) and *A Shooting Star: A Novel about Annie Oakley* by Shcila Solomon Klass ("This tale hits the mark."—*Publishers Weekly*). The latter was followed by *The Uncivil War* ("funny and credible"—*The Bulletin of the Center for Children's Books*).

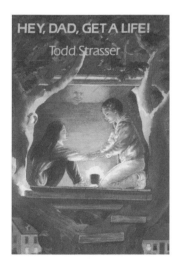

jacket art by Jan Palmer for
Hey Dad, Get a Life! (1996)

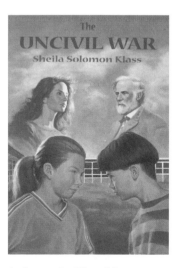

jacket art by Tony Meers
for *The Uncivil War* (1997)

jacket art by Ronald Himler for
A Shooting Star (1996)

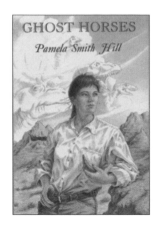

jacket art by Jonathan and
Lisa Hunt for *Ghost Horses*
(1996)

art by Katya Arnold from
Onions and Garlic (1996)

The year 1996 also saw new novels by Gillian Cross, Eileen Dunlop,
Lucy Frank, Linda Oatman High, Kirby Larson, and D. Anne Love, as
well as Pamela Smith Hill's first book, *Ghost Horses*. Also, Katya Arnold
and Katya Krenina joined the list with *Onions and Garlic* and *The Magic
Dreidels: A Hanukkah Story*.

That same year *The Golem*, retold by Barbara Rogasky with haunting
illustrations by Trina Schart Hyman, was published. It went on to win a
1997 National Jewish Book Award.

For the older reader, Russell Freedman's continued interest in Native
Americans manifested itself in *The Life and Death of Crazy Horse*, the
heroic saga of the Oglala Sioux warrior who triumphed at the Battle of
the Little Bighorn.

"When I wrote *Indian Chiefs*," Freedman remarked, "I wanted to
include six different tribal groups and six different leaders, men who had

art by Katya Krenina from
The Magic Dreidels (1996)

art by Trina
Schart Hyman
from *The Golem*
(1996)

jacket art by Ronald Himler for *The Life and Death of Crazy Horse* (1996)

dealt with the European threat each in his own way. Sitting Bull, an Oglala Sioux, was one of my subjects. Later I decided that Crazy Horse, who was also an Oglala Sioux, deserved his own book. He was one of the greatest of all Indian leaders. His integrity, courage, and refusal to budge from his ideals all stand out."

Initially, the illustrations for the book on Crazy Horse loomed as a problem. "There are no authentic photos of Crazy Horse," Freedman recalled. "He refused to have them taken. And I had already used so many nineteenth-century photos from the Smithsonian and other sources in *Indian Chiefs* that I would have had to repeat myself, which I was reluctant to do. Then, when I visited the Little Bighorn Battlefield National Monument, the curator asked me if I had seen the Oglala Sioux pictographs. 'What pictographs?' I asked. He showed me the ones created by Amos Bad Heart Bull, who was not only a Sioux historian but also a cousin of Crazy Horse. I was overjoyed. This gave me the chance to include more than fifty of those historic pictographs in my Crazy Horse biography. It was a great example of serendipity, which has blessed me so many times in my writing career."

Festivals by Myra Cohn Livingston with illustrations by Leonard Everett Fisher, a companion to their *Celebrations* (1985), was published

art by Leonard Everett Fisher from *Festivals* (1996)

in the spring of 1996. It was Livingston's last book for Holiday House before her death that summer. She was a winner of both the Excellence in Poetry Award given by the National Council of Teachers of English and the Kerlan Award from the University of Minnesota, and her death was a loss to the house and the children's literature world in general.

Since the list was growing, Griffin and Briggs had had several conversations about adding depth to the editorial department. Their idea was to hire an experienced associate editor who was ready to become a full editor, and they advertised accordingly. "But to our surprise and delight," says Griffin, "we ended up with someone who was as long on talent as her title, namely, Mary Cash, who was Editorial Director of Hardcover Books, Bantam Doubleday Dell Books for Young Readers. She joined us as executive editor in August 1996."

"I came to Holiday House," says Cash, "because I wanted to get back to a family-run independent publisher. I began at Farrar, Straus and Giroux when it was still owned by the Straus family. I've worked with some brilliant people at larger, more corporate companies and learned things from them that I would never have learned at a smaller house. However, ever since I left FSG, I was nostalgic for the smaller scale, the less formal environment, the lack of bureaucracy, and, most of all, the focus on the books themselves. Unfortunately, by the mid '90s, there were very few independent publishers left.

"When I found out that Holiday House was looking for an editor, I realized that this was a rare opportunity that comes along, let's face it, once every decade or two. I called Regina Griffin and took a very direct approach. I told her, 'I've read your ad and realize you're looking for someone with less experience, but are you sure you can't use me?'

jacket art by Robert Casilla for
A Picture Book of Thurgood Marshall
(1997)

art by Gail Gibbons from
Gulls...Gulls...Gulls... (1997)

"Soon after I arrived, I had a manuscript I wanted to acquire. So I amassed all the ammunition an editor needs to make an acquisition at a large, corporate publishing house: the author's sales figures, reviews of the author's previous titles, a list of books that could be viewed as competition to this one, copies of the author's books, and a biography of the author. I made a list of marketing points describing the audience for this title and giving a myriad of reasons why a publisher should take it on. When Regina and I sat down with John to discuss the title, I launched right into my sales pitch. John looked more and more puzzled as I went on. Finally, he stopped me and asked, 'Well, Mary, what about the *book*?' I must have looked a little stunned myself, because it was the first time in years that someone in a business meeting wanted to know about an actual book. After I recovered, I realized that I had definitely taken a job at the right place."

"After Margery left," says Diane Hoyt-Goldsmith, "Mary Cash became our new editor. She has been tremendous to work with. Lawrence [Migdale] and I look forward to each new book, because working with Mary and everyone else at Holiday House has been so rewarding. It's an experience unique in publishing these days." They have published seventeen books with Holiday House.

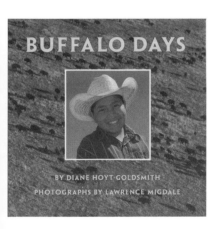

jacket photo by Lawrence Migdale
for *Buffalo Days* (1997)

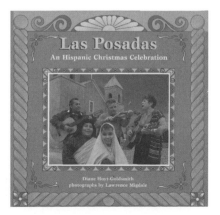

jacket photo by Lawrence Migdale
for *Las Posadas* (1999)

jacket photo by Lawrence Migdale
for *Celebrating Passover* (2000)

art by Will Hillenbrand
from *The Tale of Ali Baba
and the Forty Thieves* (1996)

Will Hillenbrand's relationship with the firm has continued through his collaborations with Regina and Mary. He recalls the support that Regina provided when he needed to take some artistic license in capturing the more gruesome scenes in Eric Kimmel's *The Tale of Ali Baba and the Forty Thieves*. "I experimented quite a bit with how to record the stitching of the corpse, and Regina responded with confidence and encouragement on a subject that might have been thought touchy. She provided just the right balance of guidance and freedom." Will recalls working with Mary on *The Golden Sandal* and sending her his artwork through overnight mail, only to have it returned almost immediately with insightful and stimulating suggestions. Always he has felt that his conversations at Holiday House have revolved around the integrity and quality of the book, creating relationships centered on a shared love for a good story rendered well.

Glen Rounds, who all along had been contributing books that were welcomed with starred reviews, revised and provided full-color illustrations for *Once We Had a Horse*, which was originally published in 1971. The result was "a delightful blend of Rounds's dry, witty storytelling

art by Will Hillenbrand from
The Golden Sandal (1998)

art by Glen Rounds from
Once We Had a Horse (1996)

with illustrations that capture the humor," according to *School Library Journal* in a starred review. The same publication starred *The Children of Topaz: The Story of a Japanese-American Internment Camp Based on a Classroom Diary* by Michael O. Tunnell and George W. Chilcoat, "a vital purchase for all collections."

Leonard Everett Fisher, the 1989 winner of *The Washington Post/Children's Book Guild Nonfiction Award*, provided *Niagara Falls*. Tom and Debbie Birdseye collaborated on *What I Believe: Kids Talk About Faith*, which was followed by *Under Our Skin: Kids Talk About Race*.

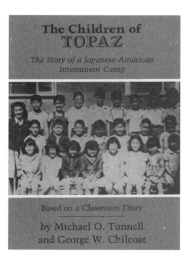

The Children of Topaz
(1996)

jacket photo by Robert
Crum for *What I Believe*
(1996)

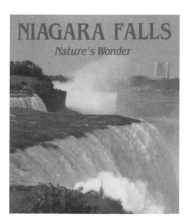

jacket photo by Leonard
Everett Fisher for *Niagara
Falls* (1996)

jacket photo by Robert Crum
for *Under Our Skin* (1997)

art by Kimberly Bulcken Root from
Gulliver in Lilliput (1995)

art by Omar Rayyan from *Ramadan* (1996)

Margaret Hodges thought Jonathan Swift should be introduced to young audiences and wrote *Gulliver in Lilliput*, which was illustrated by Kimberly Bulcken Root and named a *School Library Journal* Best Book of the Year. The author and artist collaborated again two years later to create *The True Tale of Johnny Appleseed*.

Newcomers welcomed to the list included Suhaib Hamid Ghazi, whose book *Ramadan* filled an important need, and Ellen Howard, whose *The Log Cabin Quilt* won the Christopher Award. Linda White's *Too*

art by Kimberly Bulcken Root from
The True Tale of Johnny Appleseed (1997)

art by Ronald Himler from *The Log Cabin Quilt* (1996)

art by Megan Lloyd from *Too Many Pumpkins* (1996)

Many Pumpkins told the story of an unusually lucky gardener and proved to be enormously popular. The hilarious illustrations in it were painted by Megan Lloyd, whose warm and humorous watercolors had worked so well previously with tales by Kimmel and Birdseye.

art by Megan Lloyd from *The Gingerbread Man* (1993)

art by Megan Lloyd from
A Regular Flood of Mishap
(1994)

CHAPTER
18

The spring of 1997 brought new evidence of Griffin's far-reaching contacts. From Australia came John Winch's "rich and humorous" *(Booklist)* *The Old Woman Who Loved to Read* and Wendy Orr's *Peeling the Onion*, an ALA Best Book for Young Adults.

Mary Cash was enthusiastic about launching *Holiday House Readers*, a new line of books for children who have just learned to read on their own. The first two titles were *Turtle Dreams* by Marion Dane Bauer, illustrated by Diane Dawson Hearn, and *The Biggest Pest on Eighth Avenue* by Laurie Lawlor with illustrations by Cynthia Fisher, who also created the *Holiday House Reader* logo. Talented author-illustrators Kathy Caple, Karen Gray Ruelle, and Martha Weston have also contributed to the line.

174

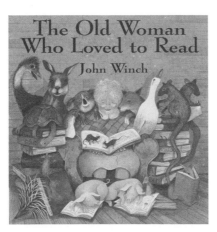

jacket art by John Winch for *The Old Woman Who Loved to Read* (1997)

jacket photo by Jacqui Henshaw for *Peeling the Onion* (1997)

jacket art by Diane Dawson Hearn for *Turtle Dreams* (1997)

jacket art by Cynthia Fisher for *The Biggest Pest on Eighth Avenue* (1997)

jacket art by Diane Dawson Hearn for *Christmas in the Forest* (1998)

jacket art by Diane Dawson Hearn for *Bear's Hiccups* (1998)

jacket art by Cynthia Fisher for *The Worst Kid Who Ever Lived on Eighth Avenue* (1998)

jacket art by Karen Gray Ruelle for *The Thanksgiving Beast Feast* (1999)

jacket art by Karen Gray Ruelle for *The Monster in Harry's Backyard* (1999)

jacket art by Martha Weston for *Cats Are Like That* (1999)

jacket art by Kathy Caple for *The Friendship Tree* (2000)

jacket art by Martha Weston for *Space Guys!* (2000)

art by Edward Miller from *Cross a Bridge* (1998)

art by Edward Miller from *Into the Sky* (1998)

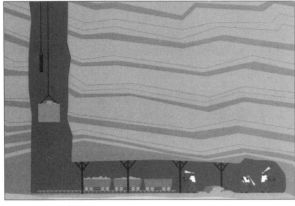

art by Edward Miller from *Take Off!* (2000)

art by Edward Miller from *Dig a Tunnel* (1999)

Along with the new editors came a host of authors and illustrators either new to the list or new to children's books. Pamela D. Greenwood and Elizabeth G. Macalaster collaborated on four books about engineering under the name Ryan Ann Hunter. All were illustrated by Edward Miller, who already had a reputation as an innovative children's book designer.

Judy Cox wrote two spirited chapter books, *Third Grade Pet* and *Mean, Mean Maureen Green*, both illustrated by Cynthia Fisher, as well as a picture book, *Now We Can Have a Wedding!*, which brought illustra-

jacket art by Cynthia Fisher for *Third Grade Pet* (1998)

jacket art by Cynthia Fisher for *Mean, Mean Maureen Green* (1999)

art by DyAnne DiSalvo-Ryan from
Now We Can Have a Wedding! (1998)

art by DyAnne
DiSalvo-Ryan from
A Dog Like Jack
(1999)

tor DyAnne DiSalvo-Ryan to the list. "I have always wanted to be published by Holiday House," DiSalvo-Ryan declared during her first visit to the office. *A Dog Like Jack*, which she wrote and illustrated, followed in spring of 1999 and received a starred review in *Publishers Weekly*.

Other new faces included Bob Barner, whose crisp paper-cutout style had already gained him renown; Martha Freeman, an author of comic novels; Amy Lowry Poole, a fine artist whose time in China influenced her unique style and techniques; and Vera Rosenberry, an author and

art by Bob Barner from *Which Way
to the Revolution?* (1998)

jacket art by Eric Brace for
*The Year My Parents Ruined
My Life* (1997)

art by Amy Lowry Poole from *How
the Rooster Got His Crown* (1999)

art by Vera Rosenberry
from *Run ♦ Jump ♦
Whiz ♦ Splash* (1999)

art by Dorothy Donohue
from *Frozen Noses* (1999)

art by Paul Meisel from
A Cake All for Me! (1998)

art by Robert Bender
from *The Chizzywink and
the Alamagoozlum* (1998)

art by Robert Bender
from *Swine Divine* (1999)

skilled watercolor painter. Stories by Karen Magnuson Beil, Jan Carr, and Tony Johnston were illustrated by Paul Meisel, Dorothy Donohue, and Robert Bender.

Artists already on the list expanded their range. Nancy Poydar, who had illustrated chapter books and Ann Martin's picture book, *Rachel Parker, Kindergarten Show-off*, wrote and illustrated her own school-based picture books, *Snip, Snip . . . Snow!* and *First Day, Hooray!* First-time author Teresa Bateman began her career with *The Ring of Truth*, illustrated by Omar Rayyan, "a well-crafted tale with a storyteller's touch" *(School Library Journal)*. Cat Bowman Smith, who had illustrated

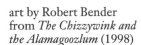

art by Nancy Poydar from *Rachel Parker,
Kindergarten Show-off* (1992)

art by Nancy Poydar from
First Day, Hooray! (1999)

art by Omar Rayyan from
The Ring of Truth (1997)

art by Nancy Poydar from
Snip, Snip…Snow! (1997)

art by Cat Bowman Smith
from *Bedtime!* (1999)

art by Andrew Glass from
A Right Fine Life (1997)

art by Andrew Glass from *Grizz!* (2000)

chapter books, began to illustrate full-color picture books, starting with Ruth Freeman Swain's *Bedtime!*

    Andrew Glass both wrote and illustrated his first picture book for the house, *A Right Fine Life: Kit Carson on the Santa Fe Trail*, a work of historical fiction that explores the relationships between tall tales, legend, and fact. His humorous paintings also enlivened Eric Kimmel's tale of a lovesick cowboy in *Grizz!* Lucy Jane Bledsoe's second novel, *Tracks in the Snow*, was a nominee for six state awards; and Mary Jane Auch came out with *I Was a Third Grade Science Project*, a hilarious short chapter book illustrated with drawings by her husband, Herm.

    Other familiar faces were paired with new ones as Ronald Himler illustrated Katherine Kirkpatrick's *Redcoats and Petticoats*, Teresa Bateman's

jacket art by Lawrence
Schwinger for *Tracks in the
Snow* (1997)

jacket art by Herm Auch
for *I Was a Third Grade
Science Project* (1998)

art by Ronald Himler from
Redcoats and Petticoats (1999)

art by Rosanne Litzinger from
Leprechaun Gold (1998)

art by Jacqueline Rogers from
There Goes Lowell's Party! (1998)

Leprechaun Gold was illustrated by Rosanne Litzinger, and Jacqueline Rogers illustrated *There Goes Lowell's Party!* by Esther Hershenhorn.

Nonfiction flourished during this time as distinguished authors joined the list. The team of Patricia C. and Fredrick L. McKissack wrote *Young, Black, and Determined: A Biography of Lorraine Hansberry*, which was named an ALA Best Book for Young Adults. Ellen Levine's *Darkness over Denmark: The Danish Resistance and the Rescue of the Jews* and Susan Goldman Rubin's *Fireflies in the Dark: The Story of Friedl Dicker-Brandeis and the Children of Terezin* added distinction to the Holocaust studies list.

Other authors expanded the range of American history titles, including Richard Ferrie with *The World Turned Upside Down: George Washington and the Battle of Yorktown*, Charlotte Jones with *Yukon Gold: The Story of the Klondike Gold Rush*, Laurie Lawlor with *Window on the West: The Frontier Photography of William Henry Jackson*, and Judith St. George with *In the Line of Fire: Presidents' Lives at Stake*.

Young, Black, and Determined (1998) jacket photo by Robert Nemiroff

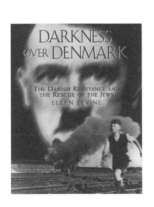

Darkness over Denmark (2000)

Fireflies in the Dark (2000) jacket illustration by Margit Koretzová

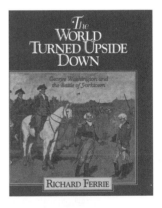

The World Turned Upside Down (1999) jacket illustration by Howard Pyle

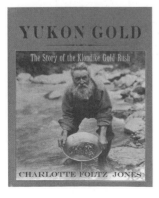

Yukon Gold (1999)

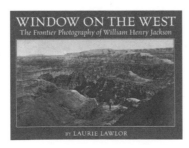

Window on the West (1999) jacket photo by William Henry Jackson

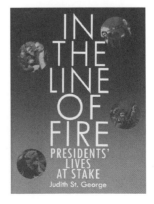

In the Line of Fire (1999)

jacket art by Joan Holub for
*If That Breathes Fire, We're
Toast!* (1999)

jacket art by Elizabeth
Sayles for *November
Ever After* (1999)

jacket art by Linda Kelen
for *DogBreath Victorious*
(1999)

Michael Tunnell's first novel was *School Spirits*. "Regina was a god-send for me," Tunnell says. "I was lucky to hook up with someone who has the same vision and can take you where you want to go. She has been willing to work with me on longer fiction, which is really what I have wanted to do."

Holiday House has always been known for publishing new writers and artists. So Griffin spent many weekends in the fall of 1997 at writers' conferences in the West, looking for new talent. These trips resulted in a number of first books, including Jennifer J. Stewart's funny middle-grade novel, *If That Breathes Fire, We're Toast!*; Laura Torres's poignant young adult story, *November Ever After*; and Chad Henry's hilarious *DogBreath Victorious*. Many more first novels were signed up and are scheduled for the coming years.

Tere LoPrete, vice president and director of design and production, retired in August 1998. "Some idea of her contribution," says John Briggs, "is apparent when one considers that it took two very able people to replace her."

Kinderlager (1998)

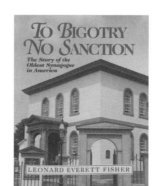

jacket photo by Leonard Everett
Fisher for *To Bigotry No Sanction*
(1998)

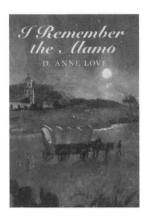

jacket art by Peter Fiore
for *I Remember the Alamo*
(1999)

jacket art by
Sue Truesdell
for *A Fairy
Called Hilary*
(1999)

One of those was Virginia Weinstein, who joined the firm as director of production. She gained her experience, she says, "by working for large houses such as Simon & Schuster, Random House, and Penguin Putnam. It was a true schooling. But when the opportunity came up to work at a small house—one which was successful, established, and where the owner was so hands on—I couldn't resist." Weinstein continued, "I feel that my work, which begins with pre-press and ends with the printing and binding, is the 'final' story in the making of a book. Knowing how much time and effort has gone into the writing, illustrating, editing, and pre-production makes me want to ensure that the books turn out the way everyone *expects* them to turn out. There is great satisfaction there."

The time had come to have a full-time art director. Claire Counihan, who had been art director at Scholastic (and a Pratt classmate of Diane Hoyt-Goldsmith), helped in the search by suggesting a number of possible candidates to her longtime friend, Regina Griffin. "Then," she says, "somewhat to my own surprise, I decided to take the job myself. I knew Regina and I would work together easily, and here everyone is very respectful of everyone else's skills. I like that. When they offered

art by Michael Letzig from
Trick or Treat Countdown (1999)

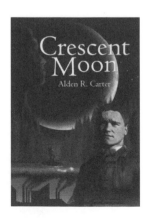

jacket art by Joseph Guillette
for *Crescent Moon* (1999)

jacket art by Eric Brace for
Fourth Grade Weirdo (1999)

me the position, I began mentally designing the new books even before I had accepted the job!"

Says Trina Schart Hyman, "She's the best in the business."

Much of Counihan's day as director of art and design includes sitting in front of a computer, where she scans in jacket art, selects typefaces, and lays out each book. "Flexibility is a real boon to a designer," Counihan says. "For example, different typefaces can be viewed simply and quickly on the computer. And you get a far better book, because your options are as infinite as your patience. However, we still do mechanicals for our illustrators who don't work on the computer, such as Gail Gibbons. Here I work closely with John and Barbara to ensure we get the look that Gail and they are after."

Although *Beaver*, Glen Rounds's latest title, was published sixty-three years after his first book, it demonstrates that the master has neither slowed down nor softened his acerbic wit and wry charm. Rounds's laconic but personable text recounts a day in the life of a single beaver. The illustrations, which alternate between full-color images on one side, and black-and-white line work on the other, capture the energy, strength, and playfulness of the animal. "He brings an extraordinary intimacy and authenticity to his subject," noted *The Horn Book* in a starred review.

According to Griffin, the making of this book "demanded all of Rounds's own energy, strength, and playfulness. After slipping while delivering the dummy to a rural North Carolina post office during a blizzard, Rounds confessed that he was slightly injured. His slight injury turned out to be a broken back! That didn't stop him. After spending what he considered too long recovering, the self-described 'tough old character' was back working within the year and published *Beaver* to starred reviews. It earned a slot in The Original Art exhibition in New York."

art by Glen Rounds
from *Beaver* (1999)

art by Gail Gibbons
from *Penguins!* (1998)

art by Gail Gibbons
from *Pigs* (1999)

Gail Gibbons says that her Holiday House books "are aimed at the very youngest reader." She asserts, "I enjoy the whole bookmaking process, from getting an idea, which frequently comes from Barbara, to completing the research, to the writing and illustrating and designing of the book. My husband, Kent [Ancliffe], helps me with the research; in fact, for my book *Penguins!*, he found himself on the floor of the New England Aquarium. While he was trying to take photographs of little fairy penguins, they kept pulling on his jacket. It was really funny."

Pigs was Gibbons's one-hundredth book, her fortieth for Holiday House, and "one of her most satisfying" *(Booklist)*. It came out in the spring of 1999. "All of her books have been most satisfying," says Briggs. "Gail is so talented and so easy to work with."

Bats and *The Pumpkin Book* were published that fall and *Rabbits, Rabbits & More Rabbits!* the following spring. Gibbons says, "I have been writing and illustrating books for Holiday House for about twenty years. During this time, I have deeply appreciated the editorial and emotional support from my editor, John Briggs, and my co-editor, Barbara Walsh. I treasure my working relationship with them and the time and care Holiday House has given to each and every one of my books."

art by Gail Gibbons from *Bats* (1999)

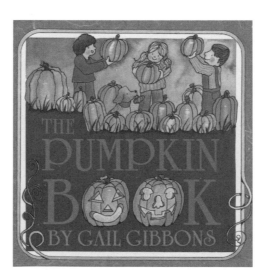

jacket art by Gail Gibbons for
The Pumpkin Book (1999)

art by Gail Gibbons from
*Rabbits, Rabbits & More
Rabbits!* (2000)

art by YongSheng Xuan from
The Rooster's Antlers (1999)

art by YongSheng Xuan
from *Ten Suns* (1998)

The fall 1999 list further demonstrates the editors' desire to blend the work of veteran Holiday House writers and artists with that of newcomers. *The Rooster's Antlers: A Story of the Chinese Zodiac* combines Eric Kimmel's lively text explaining the origins of the Chinese zodiac with the remarkable paper cutouts of YongSheng Xuan.

Several years earlier, Kate Briggs had been struck by Xuan's traditional paper cutouts while paging through an issue of *Cricket* magazine. Griffin contacted the Chinese-born artist, asking to see samples of his work and expecting to receive color xeroxes or perhaps some transparencies. One day an enormous and beaten portfolio was rolled into the office, after having spent some time in the limbo of customs. Absolutely bursting with original art of astonishing technical skill and variety, the portfolio contained everything from traditional watercolors and intricate paper cutouts to powerful oils and very modern air-brushed images. The artist also enclosed photographs of his tiles and sculptures. It was an embarrassment of riches. The entire office was wowed—but what to do next?

Eric Kimmel dashed to the rescue with a Chinese folktale entitled *Ten Suns: A Chinese Legend*, which marked the first collaboration between the two. Yet Xuan felt that the story would be better served by paintings than by the paper cutouts that had first brought him to the house's attention. It was not until his third book, *The Rooster's Antlers*, that Xuan found the right story for his amazing cutouts.

During the work on his first book, Xuan's daughter, Faye, had translated the letters and faxes between the office and the artist. Then, to Griffin's horror, Faye, a member of the Canadian navy, was called to duty. Griffin called in friends and relatives of friends to help translate the letters and faxes. One morning, controller Judy Ang picked up a fax from Xuan and brought it to Griffin, commenting on something he had written. From that moment on, Ang served not only as controller extraordinaire, but chief translator as well!

Margaret Hodges provided another artist the opportunity to use a different medium. Her deceptively simple yet powerful story, *Joan of Arc: The Lily Maid*, inspired Robert Rayevsky to employ etchings, something he had been longing to do for many years.

After receiving the manuscript, Rayevsky wrote to Griffin, "What a coincidence! I was looking for a project to use hand-colored etchings. (I have an etching press in my studio.) *Joan of Arc* seems to be ideal for it. After all, etching is a medieval-looking technique." He continued, "I would use the technique to suit children and give the book an authentic medieval look. However, I wouldn't just copy the medieval style; I would do the pictures for today's children." Apparently his use of two different printmaking styles—dry point and etching—has succeeded in drawing both adults and children to this work, which "is also very successful in its design . . . The pictures are full of action and naive charm, and they have the same strong simplicity as the text," noted *Booklist* in one of the title's starred reviews.

After more than forty years in the industry, Leonard Everett Fisher manages to retain the majesty and power for which his art is renowned, while constantly reinventing his work. In *Gods and Goddesses of the Ancient Maya*, the artist captures the awe and terror of these gods by using old traditional Mayan art styles coupled with intense and vivid

art by Leonard Everett Fisher from *Gods and Goddesses of the Ancient Maya* (1999)

art by Robert Rayevsky from *Joan of Arc* (1999)

art by Leonard Everett
Fisher from *The Gods and
Goddesses of Ancient Egypt*
(1997)

colors. Fisher did not mix colors while preparing the illustrations for
this book. Instead, he says, "They came straight from the tube—all
pure, nothing mixed. I started this with *The Gods and Goddesses of Ancient
Egypt* and wanted to see where it would take me. And where it took
me—I like it fine." Always open to new ideas and techniques, Fisher has
spent time with Counihan learning what the computer is able to do for
the design and layout of his latest books.

Opportunity knocked "loudly and clearly," says Briggs, when the
chance to reissue *A Child's Calendar* by John Updike (Knopf 1965)
arose. The text was immediately offered to Trina Schart Hyman, and it
proved to be an ideal match. Hyman was taken by the "evocative and
charming poems," and Updike ended up "stunned at the warmth and
wit" of the illustrations. It became Trina's third Caldecott Honor Book.
While the two were at a signing, an observer was overheard to remark
about Updike, "Isn't it curious that he has the same name as the novelist, and even looks like him, too!"

"All of my most important books," says Hyman, "the ones I'm most
emotionally attached to, have been my books at Holiday House. The
people there are the reason I'm still illustrating books at all. I was at a

art by Trina Schart Hyman from
A Child's Calendar (1999)

art by Trina Schart Hyman from *Cat Poems* (1987)

jacket art by Trina Schart Hyman for *The Water of Life* (1986)

crossroad, or maybe a turning point, in my career when I first met John and Kate in the '70s at a book fest in Portsmouth, New Hampshire. I was cresting on an incredible peak of creativity combined with artistic ambition and a real love for children's books. John and Kate shared my views and always seemed to be interested in my work and its growth, and my well-being both as an artist and a human being. They understood that both of those things go together, which is something approaching miraculous from any artist's viewpoint.

"I think it's unusual for authors and illustrators to feel the kind of intense loyalty most of us have for Holiday House. Sure, you get attached to an editor or art director, and God knows you want to have good feelings toward your publisher. After all, they're supposed to be mom and pop, in a way. But they never are, particularly now when almost every publisher in the world is owned by General Electric or Dow Chemical or Megabucks.com.

"When you walk into the Holiday House office, you immediately feel you're in a place where things get done, where people respect each other, and where there is no hierarchy, no corporate power, no b.s. To an old feminist like me, this is where I want my books to be published and where I want to be."

art by Trina Schart Hyman from *The Kitchen Knight* (1990)

art by Trina Schart Hyman from *Comus* (1996)

art by Colin Bootman from
The Music in Derrick's Heart (2000)

art by Bob Barner from *Fish Wish* (2000)

Spring 2000 brought a host of wonderful books by new and familiar authors and artists. Gwendolyn Battle-Lavert's *The Music in Derrick's Heart*, a story about one generation nurturing the next's talents, was poignantly illustrated by Colin Bootman ("charming, uplifting," reported *Booklist* in a starred review). Bob Barner explored a coral reef in *Fish Wish*. Eric Kimmel turned his attention to Mexico with *Montezuma and the Fall of the Aztecs*, with pictures by Daniel San Souci, and *The Two Mountains: An Aztec Legend*, illustrated by Leonard Everett Fisher. Paul

art by Daniel San Souci from
*Montezuma and the Fall of the
Aztecs* (2000)

art by Leonard Everett Fisher from
The Two Mountains (2000)

art by Paul Brett Johnson
from *Bearhide and Crow* (2000)

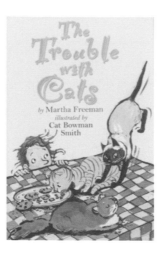

art by Cat Bowman Smith from
The Trouble with Cats (2000)

art by Katya Arnold from *Me Too!* (2000)

Brett Johnson provided *Bearhide and Crow*, a hilarious Appalachian tale about giving a trickster a taste of his own medicine. And there was *The Trouble with Cats* by Martha Freeman, a chapter book with drawings by Cat Bowman Smith. Also, Katya Arnold made her third appearance as both author and illustrator with *Me Too!*

There were books for older readers as well by Mary Amato, Sharon Heisel, Tom Lalicki, D. Anne Love, Virginia Frances Schwartz, and John B. Severance.

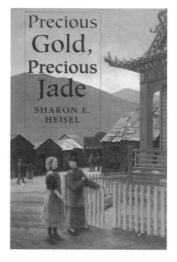

jacket art by Nicholas Debon for
Precious Gold, Precious Jade (2000)

jacket art by Christopher Ryniak
for *The Word Eater* (2000)

Spellbinder (2000)

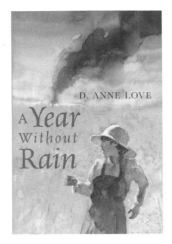

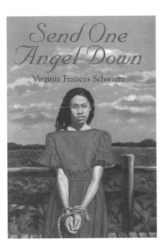

jacket art by Peter Fiore for
A Year Without Rain (2000)

jacket art by Colin Bootman for
Send One Angel Down (2000)

Skyscrapers (2000)

Walter Dean Myers's *The Blues of Flats Brown* came about because of Myers's and Griffin's shared love of the blues. According to Griffin, "It wasn't easy finding the right illustrator—how many artists have just the right touch for a story about the blues playingest dogs you've ever heard? Not many. One day an agent came in with an artist. This artist's previous work included a story of a dog who goes off alone at night, a sort of Sam Spade–ish story about an iguana, and a hilarious account of modern art starring Pigasso and Mootise. Not only that, she could play blues guitar! Within minutes, Nina Laden walked off with an offer to do *Flats Brown*, and that, as they say, was the start of a beautiful relationship."

art by Nina Laden from
The Blues of Flats Brown (2000)

A new undertaking for veteran author Russell Freedman is *Give Me Liberty!: The Story of the Declaration of Independence*—an idea suggested by Griffin and scheduled for fall 2000. "Regina asked if I'd be interested in writing about an important American document, and I jumped at the chance to explore the Declaration of Independence," says Freedman. "I wanted to look at the reasons that prominent men such as George Washington and Thomas Jefferson felt compelled to risk their necks and commit treason. Why did they feel so strong about the issues of their time? And what would have happened to them if the colonists' cause had been lost?" While researching the book, the author says he found these men "marvelously articulate in comparison to so many members of Congress today; to have read their speeches and then to have listened, for example, to speeches given during the impeachment hearings against Clinton was depressing and discouraging. And I was impressed how politically involved those revolutionary leaders were and what rich personal lives they lived."

Griffin notes, "It is a joy to work with Russell. His documentation and research are there, but it is the human interest he explores that makes his books special. I love it that he typed the book on the Fourth of July (for good luck, he said) and delivered it on the fifth, after which we had lunch at the New York restaurant An American Place."

John Briggs says, "While you have to keep your eye on the times, we plan to continue in our traditional way of publishing good books for children." Fifteen years ago, the house expected to continue to publish thirty to forty new titles a year. Now the plan is to publish fifty to sixty.

The firm has changed over the years, sometimes by design and sometimes not. And it will continue to evolve and adapt. Yet in many ways it remains the same old place: relatively small, very independent, and completely devoted to its authors and illustrators.

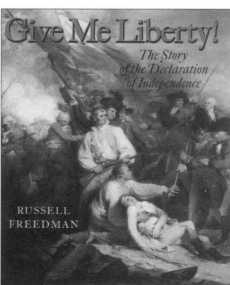

Give Me Liberty!
(2000) jacket art
by John Trumbull

catalog cover art by Synthia Saint James
from *To Dinner, for Dinner* (2000)

LIST OF PUBLICATIONS

The following represents sixty-five years of publishing, beginning with the fall 1935 list and ending with the spring 2000 list

The names in the AUTHOR column, listed alphabetically by year, include retellers, adapters, and editors where indicated. Exceptions are Anonymous and the various sources which are identified.

"P" to the left of a title indicates that the edition is paperback.

"R" to the left of a title indicates that an edition of the book had been published previously and was either reissued in the same format, with a different binding, with additional or revised text, and/or with additional or new illustrations.

"S" to the left of a title indicates that the edition is in Spanish.

If a space in the ILLUSTRATOR column is blank, the book was not illustrated.

AUTHOR	TITLE	ILLUSTRATOR
1935 (FALL LIST)		
Hans Christian Andersen	THE LITTLE MERMAID	*Pamela Bianco*
anonymous	JACK AND THE BEANSTALK (a stocking book)	*Arvilla Parker*
anonymous	JAUFRY THE KNIGHT AND THE FAIR BRUNISSENDE	*John Atherton*
Mother Goose	COCK ROBIN (a stocking book)	*Anne Heyneman*
Mother Goose	HEY! DIDDLE, DIDDLE (a broadside)	*Valenti Angelo*
Mother Goose	I SAW A SHIP A-SAILING (a broadside)	*Valenti Angelo*
Mother Goose	OLD KING COLE (a broadside)	*Valenti Angelo*
Caroline Singer & Cyrus LeRoy Baldridge	BOOMBA LIVES IN AFRICA	*Cyrus LeRoy Baldridge*

AUTHOR	TITLE	ILLUSTRATOR
1936		
anonymous	AUCASSIN AND NICOLETTE	*Maxwell Simpson*
anonymous	THE OLD WOMAN AND HER PIG *and* TITTY MOUSE, TATTY MOUSE *(a stocking book)*	*Jack Tinker*
George MacDonald	THE FAIRY FLEET	*Stuyvesant Van Veen*
Mother Goose	A WAS AN ARCHER *(a broadside)*	*Valenti Angelo*
Mother Goose	ONE, TWO, BUCKLE MY SHOE *(a broadside)*	*Valenti Angelo*
Charles Perrault	PUSS IN BOOTS *(a stocking book)*	*Fritz Eichenberg*
Glen Rounds	OL' PAUL, THE MIGHTY LOGGER	*Glen Rounds*
Percival Stutters	HOW PERCIVAL CAUGHT THE TIGER	*Percival Stutters*
1937		
anonymous	DICK WHITTINGTON AND HIS CAT *(a stocking book)*	*Fritz Eichenberg*
Irmengarde Eberle	HOP, SKIP, AND FLY	*Else Bostelmann*
Irmengarde Eberle	SEA-HORSE ADVENTURE	*Else Bostelmann*
Selden M. Loring	MIGHTY MAGIC	*Clara Skinner*
Clement Moore	THE NIGHT BEFORE CHRISTMAS *(a stocking book)*	*Ilse Bischoff*
Mother Goose	LITTLE JACK HORNER *(a broadside)*	*Philip Reed*
Mother Goose	THERE WAS AN OLD WOMAN WHO LIVED IN A SHOE *(a broadside)*	*Anne Heyneman*
Glen Rounds	LUMBERCAMP	*Glen Rounds*
Caroline Singer	ALI LIVES IN IRAN	*Cyrus LeRoy Baldridge*
Percival Stutters	HOW PERCIVAL CAUGHT THE PYTHON	*Percival Stutters*
1938		
Irma Simonton Black	HAMLET: A Cocker Spaniel	*Kurt Wiese*
Nora Burglon	STICKS ACROSS THE CHIMNEY	*Fritz Eichenberg*
William Allen Butler	TOM TWIST	*Anne Heyneman*
Kenneth Grahame	THE RELUCTANT DRAGON	*Ernest H. Shepard*
Charles Perrault	CINDERELLA *(a stocking book)*	*Hilda Scott*
Glen Rounds	PAY DIRT	*Glen Rounds*
1939		
The Arabian Nights	THE SEVEN VOYAGES OF SINDBAD THE SAILOR	*Philip Reed*
Irma Simonton Black	KIP: A Young Rooster	*Kurt Wiese*
Robert Davis	PADRE PORKO: The Gentlemanly Pig	*Fritz Eichenberg*

AUTHOR	TITLE	ILLUSTRATOR
Irmengarde Eberle	A FAMILY TO RAISE	*Else Bostelmann*
Rosalys Hall	ANIMALS TO AFRICA	*Fritz Eichenberg*
Joe Lederer	FAFAN IN CHINA	*William Sanderson*
Mother Goose	MOTHER GOOSE	*Ruth Ives*
Charles Perrault	THE HISTORY OF TOM THUMB *and* THUMBELINA *(stocking books, boxed set)*	*Hilda Scott*
Lt. Robert A. Winston, U.S.N.	DIVE BOMBER	*Walter I. Dothard*
wordless	CLOTH BOOK 1 *(familiar objects)*	*Leonard Weisgard*
wordless	SECOND CLOTH BOOK *(zoo animals)*	*Glen Rounds*

1940

Irma Simonton Black	FLIPPER: A SEA-LION	*Glen Rounds*
Irmengarde Eberle	SPICE ON THE WIND	*Richard Jones*
Alexander Finta	MY BROTHERS AND I	*Alexander Finta*
Helen Laughlin Marshall	A NEW MEXICAN BOY	*Olive Rush*
Margaret W. Nelson	PINKY FINDS A HOME	*Anne Heyneman*
Glen Rounds	THE FARMER'S FRIENDS	*Glen Rounds*
Ellen Simon	THE CRITTER BOOK	*Ellen Simon*
Nora S. Unwin	ROUND THE YEAR	*Nora S. Unwin*
wordless	CLOTH BOOK 3 *(vehicles)*	*Leonard Weisgard*
wordless	CLOTH BOOK 4 *(food)*	*Glen Rounds*

1941

Dorothy W. Baruch	FOUR AIRPLANES	*Lee Maril*
Robert Davis	PEPPERFOOT OF THURSDAY MARKET	*Cyrus LeRoy Baldridge*
Charles Dickens	A CHRISTMAS CAROL	*Philip Reed*
Jim Kjelgaard	FOREST PATROL	*Tony Palazzo*
Geraldine Pederson-Krag	THE MELFORTS GO TO SEA	*Gregor Duncan*
Glen Rounds	THE BLIND COLT	*Glen Rounds*
Lt. Robert A. Winston, U. S. N.	ACES WILD	*Grant Powers*
wordless	CLOTH BOOK 5 *(familiar scenes)*	*Leonard Weisgard*

1942

Elizabeth Barrett Browning	SONNETS FROM THE PORTUGUESE	
Rafaello Busoni	AUSTRALIA *(a Lands and Peoples book)*	*Rafaello Busoni*
Rafaello Busoni	MEXICO AND THE INCA LANDS *(a Lands and Peoples book)*	*Rafaello Busoni*
Robert Davis	HUDSON BAY EXPRESS	*Henry C. Pitz*
Irmengarde Eberle	OUR OLDEST FRIENDS	*Marguerite Kirmse*
Quail Hawkins	WHO WANTS AN APPLE?	*Lolita & David Granahan*

AUTHOR	TITLE	ILLUSTRATOR
Betty Holdridge	ISLAND BOY	*Paul Lantz*
Saint Matthew	THE SERMON ON THE MOUNT	
Caroline R. Stone	INGA OF PORCUPINE MINE	*Ellen Simon*
wordless	CLOTH BOOK 6 (*farm animals*)	*Kurt Wiese*

1943

Nora Burglon	SHARK HOLES	*Cyrus LeRoy Baldridge*
Cateau De Leeuw	THE DUTCH EAST INDIES AND THE PHILIPPINES (*a Lands and Peoples book*)	*Rafaello Busoni*
Quail Hawkins	A PUPPY FOR KEEPS	*Kurt Wiese*
Eleanor Hoffman	MISCHIEF IN FEZ	*Fritz Eichenberg*
Vernon Ives	RUSSIA (*a Lands and Peoples book*)	*Rafaello Busoni*
Jim Kjelgaard	REBEL SIEGE	*Charles Banks Wilson*

1944

Don Aspden	BARNEY'S BARGES	*Henry C. Pitz*
Hilda W. Boulter	INDIA (*a Lands and Peoples book*)	*Rafaello Busoni*
David Greenhood	DOWN TO EARTH: Mapping for Everybody	*Ralph Graeter*
Quail Hawkins	DON'T RUN, APPLE!	*Phyllis Coté*
Cornelia Spencer	CHINA (*a Lands and Peoples book*)	*Rafaello Busoni*

1945

Charles Borden	OCEANIA (*a Lands and Peoples book*)	*Rafaello Busoni*
Robert Davis	GID GRANGER	*Charles Banks Wilson*
Vernon Ives	TURKEY (*a Lands and Peoples book*)	*Rafaello Busoni*
Jim Kjelgaard	BIG RED	*Bob Kuhn*
Louise A. Neyhart	HENRY'S LINCOLN	*Charles Banks Wilson*

1946

Barbara Chapin, ed.		HOLIDAY CHEER (*pamphlet*)	*Philip Reed*
Paul Falkenberg		PALESTINE (*a Lands and Peoples book*)	*Rafaello Busoni*
Quail Hawkins		TOO MANY DOGS	*Kurt Wiese*
Eleanor Hoffmann		LION OF BARBARY	*Jack Coggins*
Clement Moore	R	THE NIGHT BEFORE CHRISTMAS (*pamphlet*)	*Ilse Bischoff*
William Sloane		THE BRITISH ISLES (*a Lands and Peoples book*)	*Rafaello Busoni*
Cmdr. Robert A. Winston, U.S.N.		FIGHTING SQUADRON	*photos*

AUTHOR		TITLE	ILLUSTRATOR

1947

Mary S. Brittain		ARAB LANDS *(a Lands and Peoples book)*	*Rafaello Busoni*
Robert Davis		FRANCE *(a Lands and Peoples book)*	*Rafaello Busoni*
Robert Davis		PARTNERS OF POWDER HOLE	*Marshall Davis*
Quail Hawkins		MARK, MARK, SHUT THE DOOR!	*Rafaello Busoni*
Phyllis Wynn Jackson		VICTORIAN CINDERELLA: The Story of Harriett Beecher Stowe	*Elliott Means*
Jim Kjelgaard		BUCKSKIN BRIGADE	*Ralph Ray, Jr.*
Marion McCook Moodey		HERE COMES THE PEDDLER!	*Kyra Markham*
Wheaton P. Webb		UNCLE SWITHIN'S INVENTIONS	*Glen Rounds*

1948

Irma Simonton Black		TOBY: A Curious Cat	*Zhenya Gay*
Robert Davis	R	PADRE PORKO: The Gentlemanly Pig	*Fritz Eichenberg*
Robert Davis		THAT GIRL OF PIERRE'S	*Lloyd Lózes Goff*
Charles Dickens	R	A CHRISTMAS CAROL	*Philip Reed*
Edwin B. Evans		SCANDINAVIA *(a Lands and Peoples book)*	*Rafaello Busoni*
Jim Kjelgaard		SNOW DOG	*Jacob Landau*
Stanley Rogers		IT TOOK COURAGE	
Glen Rounds		STOLEN PONY	*Glen Rounds*
Cornelia Spencer		JAPAN *(a Lands and Peoples book)*	*Rafaello Busoni*
Eugenia Stone		SECRET OF THE BOG	*Christine Price*

1949

Irma Simonton Black		MAGGIE: A Mischievous Magpie	*Barbara Latham*
Phyllis Wynn Jackson		GOLDEN FOOTLIGHTS: The Merry-Making Career of Lotta Crabtree	*Lloyd Lózes Goff*
Jim Kjelgaard		KALAK OF THE ICE	*Bob Kuhn*
Jim Kjelgaard		A NOSE FOR TROUBLE	
Glen Rounds	R	OL' PAUL, THE MIGHTY LOGGER	*Glen Rounds*
Glen Rounds		RODEO: Bulls, Broncs and Buckaroos	*Glen Rounds*
Cornelia Spencer		THE LOW COUNTRIES *(a Lands and Peoples book)*	*Rafaello Busoni*
Virginia F. Voight		APPLE TREE COTTAGE	*Eloise Wilkin*

1950

Zachary Ball		JOE PANTHER	*Elliott Means*
Irma Simonton Black		DUSTY AND HIS FRIENDS	*Barbara Latham*
Rafaello Busoni		ITALY *(a Lands and Peoples book)*	*Rafaello Busoni*
Dale Collins		SHIPMATES DOWN UNDER	*Rafaello Busoni*
Philip Harkins		KNOCKOUT	

AUTHOR		TITLE	ILLUSTRATOR
Philip Harkins		SON OF THE COACH	
Jim Kjelgaard		CHIP, THE DAM BUILDER	Ralph Ray
Jim Kjelgaard		WILD TREK	

1951

Mary Adrian		GARDEN SPIDER (a Life-Cycle book)	Ralph Ray
Elsa R. Berner		GERMANY (a Lands and Peoples book)	Rafaello Busoni
Irmengarde Eberle	R	HOP, SKIP, AND FLY	Else Bostelmann
Martha Goldberg		LUNCH BOX STORY	Beatrice Tobias
David Greenhood	R	DOWN TO EARTH: Mapping for Everybody	Ralph Graeter
Philip Harkins		DOUBLE PLAY	
Jim Kjelgaard		FIRE-HUNTER	Ralph Ray
Jim Kjelgaard		IRISH RED: Son of Big Red	
Glen Rounds		HUNTED HORSES	Glen Rounds
Glen Rounds		WHITEY AND THE RUSTLERS	Glen Rounds
Virginia F. Voight		THE HOUSE IN ROBIN LANE	Jean Martinez
Manly Wade Wellman		THE HAUNTS OF DROWNING CREEK	

1952

Mary Adrian		HONEYBEE (a Life-Cycle book)	Barbara Latham
Marian E. Baer		SOUND: An Experiment Book	Jean Martinez
Zachary Ball		SWAMP CHIEF	
Jean Fiedler		THE GREEN THUMB STORY	Barbara Latham
Martha Goldberg		WAIT FOR THE RAIN	Christine Price
Philip Harkins		CENTER ICE	
George Kish		YUGOSLAVIA (a Lands and Peoples book)	Rafaello Busoni
Jim Kjelgaard		TRAILING TROUBLE	
Robert Patterson, Mildred Mebel, Lawrence Hill, eds.		ON OUR WAY: Young Pages from American Autobiography	Robert Patterson
Glen Rounds		BUFFALO HARVEST	Glen Rounds
Glen Rounds		WHITEY AND THE BLIZZARD	Glen Rounds
Manly Wade Wellman		WILD DOGS OF DROWNING CREEK	

1953

Mary Adrian		FIDDLER CRAB (a Life-Cycle book)	Jean Martinez
Irma Simonton Black		PUDGE: A Summertime Mixup	Peggy Bacon
Ruth Jaeger Buntain		THE BIRTHDAY STORY	Eloise Wilkin
Jean Fiedler		BIG BROTHER DANNY	Harold Fiedler
Kenneth Grahame	R	THE RELUCTANT DRAGON	Ernest H. Shepard

AUTHOR	TITLE	ILLUSTRATOR
Jim Kjelgaard	Outlaw Red	
Jim Kjelgaard	Rebel Siege: The Story of a Frontier Riflemaker's Son	Charles Banks Wilson
Glen Rounds	Lone Muskrat	Glen Rounds
Paul McCutcheon Sears	Downy Woodpecker (a Life-Cycle book)	Barbara Latham
Alice Taylor	Egypt (a Lands and Peoples book)	Rafaello Busoni
Virginia F. Voight	Zeke and the Fisher-Cat	
Manly Wade Wellman	The Last Mammoth	Lee J. Ames

1954

Irma Simonton Black	Pete the Parrakeet	Kurt Werth
Martha Goldberg	The Twirly Skirt	Helen Stone
Leonard S. Kenworthy	Brazil (a Lands and Peoples book)	Rafaello Busoni
Jim Kjelgaard	Haunt Fox	Glen Rounds
Marion W. Marcher	Monarch Butterfly (a Life-Cycle book)	Barbara Latham
Glen Rounds	Whitey Takes a Trip	Glen Rounds
Paul McCutcheon Sears	Tree Frog (a Life-Cycle book)	Barbara Latham
Alice Taylor	South Africa (a Lands and Peoples book)	Rafaello Busoni
Manly Wade Wellman	Rebel Mail Runner	Stuyvesant Van Veen

1955

Mary Adrian	Gray Squirrel (a Life-Cycle book)	Walter Ferguson
Zachary Ball	Bar Pilot	
James W. English	Tailbone Patrol	Peter Wells
Jim Kjelgaard	Lion Hound	Jacob Landau
Dorothy Koch	I Play at the Beach	Feodor Rojankovsky
Lydia Perera	Frisky	Oscar Liebman
Paul McCutcheon Sears	Barn Swallow (a Life-Cycle book)	Walter Ferguson
Alice Taylor	Iran (a Lands and Peoples book)	Rafaello Busoni
Virginia F. Voight	Lions in the Barn	Kurt Wiese

1956

Jane and Paul Annixter	The Runner	
Zachary Ball	Skin Diver	
Margaret Embry	The Blue-Nosed Witch	Carl Rose
Jim Kjelgaard R	Big Red	Bob Kuhn
Jim Kjelgaard	Desert Dog	
Dorothy Koch	Gone Is My Goose	Doris Lee

AUTHOR		TITLE	ILLUSTRATOR
Thomas Liggett		PIGEON, FLY HOME!	Marc Simont
Glen Rounds		WHITEY ROPES AND RIDES	Glen Rounds
Paul McCutcheon Sears		FIREFLY (a Life-Cycle book)	Glen Rounds
Virginia F. Voight		ROLLING SHOW	Kurt Wiese
Manly Wade Wellman		TO UNKNOWN LANDS	Leonard Everett Fisher

1957

Howard Baer		NOW THIS, NOW THAT: Playing with Points of View	Howard Baer
Alex W. Bealer, III		THE PICTURE-SKIN STORY	Alex W. Bealer III
Irma Simonton Black		NIGHT CAT	Paul Galdone
Quail Hawkins	R	WHO WANTS AN APPLE?	Lolita & David Granahan
Jim Kjelgaard		WILDLIFE CAMERAMAN	
Jim Kjelgaard		WOLF BROTHER	
Elizabeth & Charles Schwartz		COTTONTAIL RABBIT (a Life-Cycle book)	Charles Schwartz
Alice Taylor	R	INDIA (a Lands and Peoples book)	Rafaello Busoni

1958

Jane & Paul Annixter		BUFFALO CHIEF	
Zachary Ball		YOUNG MIKE FINK	
Irma Simonton Black		BUSY WATER	Jane Castle
Gladys Conklin		I LIKE CATERPILLARS	Barbara Latham
Margaret Embry		KID SISTER	Don Freeman
Quail Hawkins		THE AUNT-SITTER	Brinton Turkle
Dorothy Koch		WHEN THE COWS GOT OUT	Paul Lantz
Thomas Liggett		THE HOLLOW	
Louise A. Neyhart	R	HENRY'S LINCOLN	Charles Banks Wilson
Glen Rounds		WHITEY AND THE WILD HORSE	Glen Rounds

1959

Pauline Arnold & Percival White		FOOD: America's Biggest Business	Tom Funk
Gladys Baker Bond		BLUE CHIMNEY	Leonard Shortall
Jane Castle		PEEP-LO	Jane Castle
Jim Kjelgaard		STORMY	
Dorothy Koch		LET IT RAIN!	Helen Stone
Lois Baker Muehl		MY NAME IS ———	Aldren Watson
Barbara & Russell Peterson		WHITEFOOT MOUSE (a Life-Cycle book)	Russell Peterson

AUTHOR		TITLE	ILLUSTRATOR
Glen Rounds	R	WHISTLE PUNK OF CAMP 15 (*originally* LUMBERCAMP)	*Glen Rounds*
Elizabeth & Charles Schwartz		BOBWHITE (*a Life-Cycle book*)	*Charles Schwartz*

1960

Jane & Paul Annixter		HORNS OF PLENTY	
Pauline Arnold & Percival White		HOMES: America's Building Business	*Tom Funk*
Zachary Ball		NORTH TO ABILENE	
Irma Simonton Black		BIG PUPPY, LITTLE PUPPY	*Theresa Sherman*
Gladys Conklin		I LIKE BUTTERFLIES	*Barbara Latham*
Jim Kjelgaard		BOOMERANG HUNTER	*W. T. Mars*
Charles Paul May		BOX TURTLE (*a Life-Cycle book*)	*Jane Castle*
Glen Rounds	R	THE BLIND COLT	*Glen Rounds*
Glen Rounds		WHITEY'S FIRST ROUNDUP	*Glen Rounds*
Samuel Selden		SHAKESPEARE: A Player's Handbook of Short Scenes	
Arnold Spilka		WHOM SHALL I MARRY?	*Arnold Spilka*

1961

Pauline Arnold & Percival White		CLOTHES AND CLOTH: America's Apparel Business	*Paul Davis*
Zachary Ball		KEP	
Zachary Ball		SALVAGE DIVER	
Russell Freedman		TEENAGERS WHO MADE HISTORY	*Arthur Shilstone*
David Greenhood		WATCH THE TIDES	*Jane Castle*
Lincoln & Jean LaPaz		SPACE NOMADS: Meteorites in Sky, Field, and Laboratory	*photos & illustrations*
Lois Baker Muehl		WORST ROOM IN THE SCHOOL	*Don Freeman*
Glen Rounds		WILD ORPHAN	*Glen Rounds*
Vivian L. Thompson		CAMP-IN-THE-YARD	*Brinton Turkle*

1962

Oren Arnold		WHITE DANGER	
Pauline Arnold & Percival White		MONEY: Make It, Spend It, Save It	*Tom Funk*
Zachary Ball		BRISTLE FACE	
Gladys Conklin		WE LIKE BUGS	*Artur Marokvia*
Tom Funk		I READ SIGNS	*Tom Funk*
Jim Kjelgaard		HIDDEN TRAIL	

AUTHOR	TITLE	ILLUSTRATOR
Dorothy Koch	MONKEYS ARE FUNNY THAT WAY	*Don Freeman*
Robin McKown	THE FABULOUS ISOTOPES: What They Are and What They Do	*photos; drawings by Isadore Steinberg*
Glen Rounds	WHITEY AND THE COLT-KILLER	*Glen Rounds*
Vivian L. Thompson	SAD DAY, GLAD DAY	*Lilian Obligado*

1963

Jane & Paul Annixter	WINDIGO	
Pauline Arnold & Percival White	THE AUTOMATION AGE	*photos & illustrations*
Zachary Ball	SPUTTERS	
Irma Simonton Black	CASTLE, ABBEY, AND TOWN: How People Lived in the Middle Ages	*W. T. Mars*
Jane Castle	WHOSE TREE HOUSE?	*Jane Castle*
Margaret Embry	MR. BLUE	*Brinton Turkle*
Russell Freedman	2000 YEARS OF SPACE TRAVEL	*photos & illustrations*
Glen Rounds	WHITEY'S NEW SADDLE	*Glen Rounds*
Vivian L. Thompson	FARAWAY FRIENDS	*Marion Greenwood*

1964

Zachary Ball		TENT SHOW	
Brian Burland		SAINT NICHOLAS AND THE TUB	*Joseph Low*
Dorothy Koch		UP THE BIG MOUNTAIN	*Lucy & John Hawkinson*
Selden M. Loring	R	MIGHTY MAGIC	*Brinton Turkle*
Julian Scheer		RAIN MAKES APPLESAUCE	*Marvin Bileck*
Elizabeth & Charles Schwartz		WHEN ANIMALS ARE BABIES	*Charles Schwartz*

1965

Andy Adams		TRAIL DRIVE	*Glen Rounds*
Jane & Paul Annixter		WAGON SCOUT	
Gladys Conklin		IF I WERE A BIRD	*Artur Marokvia*
Russell Freedman		JULES VERNE: Portrait of a Prophet	*photos & illustrations*
Daniel S. Halacy, Jr.		BIONICS: The Science of "Living" Machines	*photos; drawings by David Michael Steinberg*
Charles Paul May		WHEN ANIMALS CHANGE CLOTHES	*Walter Ferguson*
Julian May		THEY TURNED TO STONE	*Jean Zallinger*
Robert Patterson, Mildred Mebel & Lawrence Hill, eds.	R	ON OUR WAY: Young Pages from American Autobiography	*Robert Patterson*
Anico Surany		THE BURNING MOUNTAIN	*Leonard Everett Fisher*

AUTHOR	TITLE	ILLUSTRATOR
1966		
Jane & Paul Annixter	THE GREAT WHITE	
Paul Annixter	THE CAT THAT CLUMPED	*Brinton Turkle*
Gladys Conklin	THE BUG CLUB BOOK: A Handbook for Young Bug Collectors	*Girard Goodenow*
Margaret Embry	PEG-LEG WILLY	*Ann Grifalconi*
Daniel S. Halacy, Jr.	RADIATION, MAGNETISM, AND LIVING THINGS	*photos & illustrations*
Frank Jupo	COUNT CARROT	*Frank Jupo*
Herbert Kondo	ADVENTURES IN SPACE AND TIME	*George Solonevich*
Vladimir & Nada Kovalik	THE OCEAN WORLD	*photos & illustrations*
Charles Paul May	HIGH-NOON ROCKET	*Brinton Turkle*
George Frederick Ruxton	MOUNTAIN MEN	*Glen Rounds*
Anico Surany	KATI AND KORMOS	*Leonard Everett Fisher*
Vivian L. Thompson	HAWAIIAN MYTHS OF EARTH, SEA, AND SKY	*Leonard Weisgard*
John M. Youngpeter	WINTER SCIENCE ACTIVITIES	*Gardner J. Ryan*
1967		
Zachary Ball	SKY DIVER	
Marianne Besser	THE CAT BOOK	*Shannon Stirnweis*
Gladys Conklin	I CAUGHT A LIZARD	*Artur Marokvia*
Donna E. DeSeyn	TERMITE *(a Life-Cycle book)*	*Juan Barberis*
Russell Freedman	SCOUTING WITH BADEN-POWELL	*photos & illustrations*
Johanna Johnston	SUPPOSINGS	*Rudy Sayers*
Ryerson Johnson	LET'S WALK UP THE WALL	*Eva Cellini*
Frank Jupo	ATU, THE SILENT ONE	*Frank Jupo*
Julian May	THEY LIVED IN THE ICE AGE	*Jean Zallinger*
Lois Baker Muehl	THE HIDDEN YEAR OF DEVLIN BATES	*John Martinez*
Glen Rounds	THE TREELESS PLAINS	*Glen Rounds*
Michael Sage	CAREFUL CARLOS	*Arnold Spilka*
Anico Surany	THE COVERED BRIDGE	*Leonard Everett Fisher*
Barbara & John Waters	SALT-WATER AQUARIUMS	*photos; drawings by Robert Candy*
1968		
Pauline Arnold & Percival White	FOOD FACTS FOR YOUNG PEOPLE	*Gilbert Etheredge*
Irma Simonton Black	BUSY WINDS	*Robert Quackenbush*
Gladys Conklin	LUCKY LADYBUGS	*Glen Rounds*
Hal Hellman	LIGHT AND ELECTRICITY IN THE ATMOSPHERE	*Nancy & Gilbert Etheredge*

AUTHOR	TITLE	ILLUSTRATOR
Julian May	THE FIRST MEN	*Lorence F. Bjorklund*
Julian May	HORSES: How They Came To Be	*Lorence F. Bjorklund*
Oliver Postgate	THE ICE DRAGON	*Peter Firmin*
Oliver Postgate	KING OF THE NOGS	*Peter Firmin*
Glen Rounds	THE PRAIRIE SCHOONERS	*Glen Rounds*
George F. Scheer, ed.	CHEROKEE ANIMAL TALES	*Robert Frankenberg*
Julian Scheer	UPSIDE DOWN DAY	*Kelly Oechsli*
William M. Stephens	SOUTHERN SEASHORES: A World of Animals and Plants	*photos by William M. Stephens*
William M. & Peggy Stephens	OCTOPUS *(a Life-Cycle book)*	*Anthony D'Attilio*
Anico Surany	MALACHY'S GOLD	*Leonard Everett Fisher*

1969

Jane & Paul Annixter	VIKAN THE MIGHTY	
Gladys Conklin	HOW INSECTS GROW	*Girard Goodenow*
Gladys Conklin	WHEN INSECTS ARE BABIES	*Artur Marokvia*
Frank Francis	TIMIMOTO'S GREAT ADVENTURE	*Frank Francis*
Russell Freedman & James E. Morriss	HOW ANIMALS LEARN	*photos; drawings by John Morris*
Daniel S. Halacy, Jr.	X RAYS AND GAMMA RAYS	*photos & illustrations*
Marie M. Jenkins	MOON JELLY *(a Life-Cycle book)*	*René Martin*
Julian May	BEFORE THE INDIANS	*Symeon Shimin*
Julian May	WHY THE EARTH QUAKES	*Leonard Everett Fisher*
Glen Rounds R	STOLEN PONY	*Glen Rounds*
Glen Rounds	WILD HORSES OF THE RED DESERT	*Glen Rounds*
William M. & Peggy Stephens	HERMIT CRAB *(a Life-Cycle book)*	*Christine Sapieha*
William M. & Peggy Stephens	SEA HORSE *(a Life-Cycle book)*	*Anthony D'Attilio*
Anico Surany	ÉTIENNE-HENRI AND GRI-GRI	*Sylvie Selig*
Vivian L. Thompson	HAWAIIAN LEGENDS OF TRICKSTERS AND RIDDLERS	*Sylvie Selig*

1970

Jane & Paul Annixter	AHMEEK	*Robert Frankenberg*
Irma Simonton Black	BUSY SEEDS	*Robert Quackenbush*
Gladys Conklin	CHIMPANZEE *(a Life-Cycle book)*	*Matthew Kalmenoff*
Gladys Conklin	LITTLE APES	*Joseph Cellini*
Margaret Embry	MY NAME IS LION	*Ned Glattauer*
Russell Freedman & James E. Morriss	ANIMAL INSTINCTS	*photos; drawings by John Morris*
Helen Griffiths	MOSHIE CAT	*Shirley Hughes*
Paul W. Hodge	THE REVOLUTION IN ASTRONOMY	*photos & illustrations*
Marie M. Jenkins	ANIMALS WITHOUT PARENTS	*photos & illustrations*

AUTHOR	TITLE	ILLUSTRATOR
Julian May	THE FIRST LIVING THINGS	Howard Berelson
Julian May	WHY BIRDS MIGRATE	Chet Reneson
George Maxim Ross	WHAT DID THE ROCK SAY?	George Maxim Ross
Elizabeth & Charles Schwartz	WHEN WATER ANIMALS ARE BABIES	Charles Schwartz

1971

AUTHOR	TITLE	ILLUSTRATOR
Jane & Paul Annixter	WHITE SHELL HORSE	
Philip S. Callahan	INSECTS AND HOW THEY FUNCTION	photos & drawings by Philip S. Callahan
Gladys Conklin	GIRAFFE (a Life-Cycle book)	Matthew Kalmenoff
Margaret Embry	SHÁDÍ	
Sam & Beryl Epstein	PICK IT UP	Tomie dePaola
Russell Freedman	ANIMAL ARCHITECTS	Matthew Kalmenoff
Mehlli Gobhai	THE LEGEND OF THE ORANGE PRINCESS	Mehlli Gobhai
Florence Parry Heide	THE SHRINKING OF TREEHORN	Edward Gorey
Ann Larris	PEOPLE ARE LIKE LOLLIPOPS	Ann Larris
Julian May	BLUE RIVER	Robert Quackenbush
Julian May	THE LAND BENEATH THE SEA	Leonard Everett Fisher
Julian May	WHY PEOPLE ARE DIFFERENT COLORS	Symeon Shimin
Edna Miller	DUCK DUCK	Edna Miller
Glen Rounds	ONCE WE HAD A HORSE	Glen Rounds
William M. & Peggy Stephens	KILLER WHALE (a Life-Cycle book)	Lydia Rosier
William M. & Peggy Stephens	SEA TURTLE (a Life-Cycle book)	René Martin
Vivian L. Thompson	HAWAIIAN TALES OF HEROES AND CHAMPIONS	Herbert Kawainui Kane

1972

AUTHOR	TITLE	ILLUSTRATOR
Jane & Paul Annixter	SEA OTTER	John Hamberger
Philip S. Callahan	THE EVOLUTION OF INSECTS	photos & illustrations
Ruth Chew	THE WEDNESDAY WITCH	Ruth Chew
Gladys Conklin	ELEPHANTS OF AFRICA	Joseph Cellini
Gladys Conklin	INSECTS BUILD THEIR HOMES	Jean Zallinger
Gladys Conklin	TARANTULA: The Giant Spider	Glen Rounds
Beryl Epstein & Dorritt Davis	TWO SISTERS AND SOME HORNETS	Rosemary Wells
Russell Freedman & James E. Morriss	THE BRAINS OF ANIMALS AND MAN	photos; drawings by James Caraway
Marie M. Jenkins	THE CURIOUS MOLLUSKS	photos & illustrations
Julian May	PLANKTON: Drifting Life of the Waters	Jean Zallinger
Glen Rounds	THE COWBOY TRADE	Glen Rounds
Mary Francis Shura	THE SEVEN STONE	Dale Payson
Mary Francis Shura	TOPCAT OF TAM	Charles Robinson
Seymour Simon	SCIENCE PROJECTS IN ECOLOGY	Charles Jakubowski

AUTHOR	TITLE	ILLUSTRATOR
Seymour Simon	SCIENCE PROJECTS IN POLLUTION	Charles Jakubowski
Virginia Driving Hawk Sneve	HIGH ELK'S TREASURE	Oren Lyons
Virginia Driving Hawk Sneve	JIMMY YELLOW HAWK	Oren Lyons
William M. & Peggy Stephens	FLAMINGO (a Life-Cycle book)	Matthew Kalmenoff

1973

Jane & Paul Annixter	TRUMPETER: The Story of a Swan	Gilbert Riswold
Val Biro	THE HONEST THIEF	Val Biro
Gladys Conklin	FAIRY RINGS AND OTHER MUSHROOMS	Howard Berelson
Gladys Conklin	THE LION FAMILY	Joseph Cellini
Sam & Beryl Epstein	HOLD EVERYTHING	Tomie dePaola
Sam & Beryl Epstein	LOOK IN THE MIRROR	Tomie dePaola
Mehlli Gobhai	TO YOUR GOOD HEALTH	Mehlli Gobhai
Helen Griffiths	RUSSIAN BLUE	Victor Ambrus
Marilyn Hirsh	BEN GOES INTO BUSINESS	Marilyn Hirsh
Dahlov Ipcar	A FLOOD OF CREATURES	Dahlov Ipcar
Oren Lyons	DOG STORY	Oren Lyons
Julian May	WILD TURKEYS	John Hamberger
Dorothy Hinshaw Patent	WEASELS, OTTERS, SKUNKS, AND THEIR FAMILY	Matthew Kalmenoff
Glen Rounds	THE DAY THE CIRCUS CAME TO LONE TREE	Glen Rounds
Elizabeth & Charles Schwartz	WHEN FLYING ANIMALS ARE BABIES	Charles Schwartz
Marjorie Weinman Sharmat	MORRIS BROOKSIDE, A DOG	Ronald Himler
Seymour Simon	A BUILDING ON YOUR STREET (a Science-on-Your-Street book)	Leonard Shortall
Seymour Simon	A TREE ON YOUR STREET (a Science-on-Your-Street book)	Betty Fraser

1974

Joan Arehart-Treichel	TRACE ELEMENTS: How They Help and Harm Us	photos
Philip S. Callahan	THE MAGNIFICENT BIRDS OF PREY	photos & illustrations
Gladys Conklin	JOURNEY OF THE GRAY WHALES	Leonard Everett Fisher
Russell Freedman	THE FIRST DAYS OF LIFE	Joseph Cellini
Philip Goldstein	ANIMALS AND PLANTS THAT TRAP	photos; drawings by Matthew Kalmenoff
Marilyn Hirsh	COULD ANYTHING BE WORSE?	Marilyn Hirsh
Irving Howe & Eliezer Greenberg, eds.	YIDDISH STORIES OLD AND NEW	
Richard B. Lyttle	PAINTS, INKS, AND DYES	photos & illustrations
Julian May	HOW THE ANIMALS CAME TO NORTH AMERICA	Lorence F. Bjorklund

AUTHOR		TITLE	ILLUSTRATOR
Dorothy Hinshaw Patent		MICROSCOPIC ANIMALS AND PLANTS	photos & illustrations
Glen Rounds	R	WILDLIFE AT YOUR DOORSTEP	Glen Rounds
Marjorie Weinman Sharmat		MORRIS BROOKSIDE IS MISSING	Ronald Himler
Seymour Simon		BIRDS ON YOUR STREET (a Science-on-Your-Street book)	Jean Zallinger
Seymour Simon		WATER ON YOUR STREET (a Science-on-Your-Street book)	Sonia O. Lisker
Virginia Driving Hawk Sneve		BETRAYED	
Virginia Driving Hawk Sneve		WHEN THUNDERS SPOKE	Oren Lyons
William M. Stephens		ISLANDS	Lydia Rosier

1975

T. Ernesto Bethancourt		NEW YORK CITY TOO FAR FROM TAMPA BLUES	
Gladys Conklin		I LIKE BEETLES	Jean Zallinger
Gladys Conklin		THE LLAMAS OF SOUTH AMERICA	Lorence F. Bjorklund
Tomie dePaola		THE CLOUD BOOK	Tomie dePaola
Russell Freedman		GROWING UP WILD: How Young Animals Survive	Leslie Morrill
Helen Griffiths		JUST A DOG	Victor Ambrus
Helen Griffiths		THE MYSTERIOUS APPEARANCE OF AGNES	Victor Ambrus
Dahlov Ipcar		BUG CITY	Dahlov Ipcar
Marie M. Jenkins		EMBRYOS AND HOW THEY DEVELOP	photos & illustrations
Marie M. Jenkins		KANGAROOS, OPOSSUMS, AND OTHER MARSUPIALS	Matthew Kalmenoff
Steven Kroll		IS MILTON MISSING?	Dick Gackenbach
Dorothy Hinshaw Patent		FROGS, TOADS, SALAMANDERS, AND HOW THEY REPRODUCE	Matthew Kalmenoff
Dorothy Hinshaw Patent		HOW INSECTS COMMUNICATE	photos & illustrations
Robert Newton Peck		WILD CAT	Hal Frenck
Marjorie Weinman Sharmat		BURTON AND DUDLEY	Barbara Cooney
Marjorie Weinman Sharmat		WALTER THE WOLF	Kelly Oechsli
Virginia Driving Hawk Sneve		THE CHICHI HOOHOO BOGEYMAN	Nadema Agard
Lisl Weil		THE CANDY EGG BUNNY	Lisl Weil

1976

Joan Arehart-Treichel		IMMUNITY: How Our Bodies Resist Disease	photos & illustrations
Joan Arehart-Treichel		POISONS AND TOXINS	photos & illustrations
T. Ernesto Bethancourt		THE DOG DAYS OF ARTHUR CANE	
Gladys Conklin		CHEETAHS, THE SWIFT HUNTERS	Charles Robinson

AUTHOR		TITLE	ILLUSTRATOR
Tomie dePaola		WHEN EVERYONE WAS FAST ASLEEP	Tomie dePaola
Russell Freedman		ANIMAL FATHERS	Joseph Cellini
Russell Freedman		ANIMAL GAMES	St. Tamara
Dianne Glaser		THE DIARY OF TRILBY FROST	
Philip & Margaret Goldstein		HOW PARASITES LIVE	photos & illustrations
Marilyn Hirsh		CAPTAIN JIRI AND RABBI JACOB	Marilyn Hirsh
Marilyn Hirsh		THE RABBI AND THE TWENTY-NINE WITCHES: A Talmudic Legend	Marilyn Hirsh
Richard Kennedy		THE BLUE STONE	Ronald Himler
Steven Kroll		THE TYRANNOSAURUS GAME	Tomie dePaola
Dorothy Hinshaw Patent		FISH AND HOW THEY REPRODUCE	Matthew Kalmenoff
Dorothy Hinshaw Patent		PLANTS AND INSECTS TOGETHER	Matthew Kalmenoff
Glen Rounds		THE BEAVER: How He Works	Glen Rounds
Glen Rounds		MR. YOWDER AND THE LION ROAR CAPSULES	Glen Rounds
Glen Rounds	R	OL' PAUL, THE MIGHTY LOGGER	Glen Rounds
Daisy Wallace, ed.		MONSTER POEMS	Kay Chorao
Daisy Wallace, ed.		WITCH POEMS	Trina Schart Hyman

1977

AUTHOR	TITLE	ILLUSTRATOR
Betty Bates	BUGS IN YOUR EARS	
T. Ernesto Bethancourt	THE MORTAL INSTRUMENTS	
Robert Censoni	COWGIRL KATE	Robert Censoni
Robert Censoni	THE SHOPPING-BAG LADY	Robert Censoni
Gladys Conklin	I WATCH FLIES	Jean Zallinger
Gladys Conklin	THE OCTOPUS AND OTHER CEPHALOPODS	photos
Anne Eliot Crompton	THE RAIN-CLOUD PONY	Paul Frame
Tomie dePaola	THE QUICKSAND BOOK	Tomie dePaola
Russell Freedman	HANGING ON: How Animals Carry Their Young	photos
Russell Freedman	HOW BIRDS FLY	Lorence F. Bjorklund
Dianne Glaser	SUMMER SECRETS	
Helen Griffiths	RUNNING WILD	Victor Ambrus
Jane E. Hartman	LIVING TOGETHER IN NATURE: How Symbiosis Works	Lorence F. Bjorklund
Marilyn Hirsh	HANNIBAL AND HIS 37 ELEPHANTS	Marilyn Hirsh
Dorothy Childs Hogner	WATER PLANTS	photos & illustrations
Steven Kroll	GOBBLEDYGOOK	Kelly Oechsli
Steven Kroll	SANTA'S CRASH-BANG CHRISTMAS	Tomie dePaola
Dorothy Hinshaw Patent	EVOLUTION GOES ON EVERYDAY	Matthew Kalmenoff
Dorothy Hinshaw Patent	REPTILES AND HOW THEY REPRODUCE	Matthew Kalmenoff
Glen Rounds	MR. YOWDER AND THE STEAMBOAT	Glen Rounds

AUTHOR	TITLE	ILLUSTRATOR
Marjorie Weinman Sharmat	I'M TERRIFIC	Kay Chorao
Elizabeth Winthrop	POTBELLIED POSSUMS	Barbara McClintock
Elizabeth Winthrop	THAT'S MINE	Emily McCully

1978

Betty Bates	THE UPS AND DOWNS OF JORIE JENKINS	
T. Ernesto Bethancourt	DR. DOOM: SUPERSTAR	
T. Ernesto Bethancourt	TUNE IN YESTERDAY	
Gladys Conklin	PRAYING MANTIS: The Garden Dinosaur	Glen Rounds
Anne Eliot Crompton	THE LIFTING STONE	Marcia Sewall
Tomie dePaola	THE POPCORN BOOK	Tomie dePaola
Malka Drucker with Tom Seaver	TOM SEAVER: Portrait of a Pitcher	photos
Russell Freedman	GETTING BORN	photos; drawings by Corbett Jones
Dianne Glaser	THE CASE OF THE MISSING SIX	David K. Stone
Helen Griffiths	GRIP, A DOG STORY	Douglas Hall
Jane E. Hartman	LOOKING AT LIZARDS	photos & illustrations
Florence Parry Heide	BANANA TWIST	
Marilyn Hirsh	DEBORAH THE DYBBUK: A Ghost Story	Marilyn Hirsh
Alice L. Hopf	ANIMAL AND PLANT LIFE SPANS	photos
Marie M. Jenkins	GOATS, SHEEP, AND HOW THEY LIVE	Matthew Kalmenoff
Richard Kennedy	THE DARK PRINCESS	Donna Diamond
Steven Kroll	FAT MAGIC	Tomie dePaola
Steven Kroll	T. J. FOLGER, THIEF	Bill Morrison
Julian May	THE WARM-BLOODED DINOSAURS	Lorence F. Bjorklund
Dorothy Hinshaw Patent	ANIMAL AND PLANT MIMICRY	photos & illustrations
Dorothy Hinshaw Patent	THE WORLD OF WORMS	photos & illustrations
Dorothy Hinshaw Patent & Paul C. Schroeder	BEETLES AND HOW THEY LIVE	photos & illustrations
Glen Rounds	MR. YOWDER AND THE GIANT BULL SNAKE	Glen Rounds
Marjorie Weinman Sharmat	THORNTON THE WORRIER	Kay Chorao
Geraldine Sherman	ANIMALS WITH POUCHES— THE MARSUPIALS	Lorence F. Bjorklund
Daisy Wallace, ed.	GIANT POEMS	Margot Tomes
Elizabeth Winthrop	KNOCK, KNOCK, WHO'S THERE?	

AUTHOR	TITLE	ILLUSTRATOR
1979		
Betty Bates	MY MOM, THE MONEY NUT	
T. Ernesto Bethancourt	INSTRUMENTS OF DARKNESS	
T. Ernesto Bethancourt	NIGHTMARE TOWN	
Philip S. Callahan	BIRDS AND HOW THEY FUNCTION	photos & illustrations
Lewis Carroll (words), Don Harper (music)	SONGS FROM ALICE (also on cassette)	Charles Folkard
Gladys Conklin	BLACK WIDOW SPIDER—DANGER!	Leslie Morrill
Tomie dePaola	THE KIDS' CAT BOOK	Tomie dePaola
Tomie dePaola	SONGS OF THE FOG MAIDEN	Tomie dePaola
Malka Drucker with George Foster	THE GEORGE FOSTER STORY	photos
Leonard Everett Fisher	THE FACTORIES (a Nineteenth Century America book)	Leonard Everett Fisher
Leonard Everett Fisher	THE RAILROADS (a Nineteenth Century America book)	Leonard Everett Fisher
Helen Griffiths	THE LAST SUMMER	Victor Ambrus
Jane E. Hartman	ANIMALS THAT LIVE IN GROUPS	photos
Marilyn Hirsh	ONE LITTLE GOAT: A Passover Song	Marilyn Hirsh
Marilyn Hirsh	THE SECRET DINOSAUR	Marilyn Hirsh
Alice L. Hopf	ANIMALS THAT EAT NECTAR AND HONEY	Matthew Kalmenoff
Alice L. Hopf	PIGS WILD AND TAME	photos & illustrations
Marie M. Jenkins	DEER, MOOSE, ELK, AND THEIR FAMILY	Matthew Kalmenoff
Steven Kroll	THE CANDY WITCH	Marylin Hafner
Steven Kroll	SPACE CATS	Friso Henstra
Lady McCrady	MISS KISS AND THE NASTY BEAST	Lady McCrady
Evaline Ness	MARCELLA'S GUARDIAN ANGEL	Evaline Ness
Dorothy Hinshaw Patent	BUTTERFLIES AND MOTHS: How They Function	photos & illustrations
Dorothy Hinshaw Patent	RACCOONS, COATIMUNDIS, AND THEIR FAMILY	photos
Dorothy Hinshaw Patent	SIZES AND SHAPES IN NATURE— WHAT THEY MEAN	photos & illustrations
Marjorie Weinman Sharmat	SAY HELLO, VANESSA	Lillian Hoban
Daisy Wallace, ed.	GHOST POEMS	Tomie dePaola
Elizabeth Winthrop	JOURNEY TO THE BRIGHT KINGDOM	Charles Mikolaycak
Elizabeth Winthrop	MARATHON MIRANDA	
1980		
Betty Bates	LOVE IS LIKE PEANUTS	
T. Ernesto Bethancourt	DORIS FEIN: QUARTZ BOYAR	

AUTHOR		TITLE	ILLUSTRATOR
T. Ernesto Bethancourt		Doris Fein: Superspy	
Tomie dePaola		The Family Christmas Tree Book	Tomie dePaola
Tomie dePaola		The Lady of Guadalupe	Tomie dePaola
Tomie dePaola	p	The Lady of Guadalupe	Tomie dePaola
Tomie dePaola	s	Nuestra Señora de Guadalupe	Tomie dePaola
Tomie dePaola	s, p	Nuestra Señora de Guadalupe	Tomie dePaola
Donna Diamond		Swan Lake	Donna Diamond
Malka Drucker		Hanukkah: Eight Nights, Eight Lights (a Jewish Holidays book)	photos; drawings by Brom Hoban
Leonard Everett Fisher		The Hospitals (a Nineteenth Century America book)	Leonard Everett Fisher
Leonard Everett Fisher		The Sports (a Nineteenth Century America book)	Leonard Everett Fisher
Russell Freedman		They Lived with the Dinosaurs	photos
Russell Freedman		Tooth and Claw: A Look at Animal Weapons	photos
Helen Griffiths		Blackface Stallion	Victor Ambrus
Jane E. Hartman		Armadillos, Anteaters, and Sloths: How They Live	photos
Jane E. Hartman		How Animals Care for Their Young	photos
Steven Kroll		Amanda and the Giggling Ghost	Dick Gackenbach
Steven Kroll		Monster Birthday	Dennis Kendrick
Lady McCrady		Junior's Tune	Lady McCrady
Lady McCrady		Mildred and the Mummy	Lady McCrady
Clement Moore		The Night Before Christmas	Tomie dePaola
Clement Moore	p	The Night Before Christmas	Tomie dePaola
Evaline Ness		Fierce the Lion	Evaline Ness
Dorothy Hinshaw Patent		Bacteria: How They Affect Other Living Things	photos & illustrations
Dorothy Hinshaw Patent		Bears of the World	photos
Dorothy Hinshaw Patent		The Lives of Spiders	photos & illustrations
Glen Rounds		Blind Outlaw	Glen Rounds
Glen Rounds		Mr. Yowder, the Peripatetic Sign Painter	Glen Rounds
Marjorie Weinman Sharmat		Grumley the Grouch	Kay Chorao
Marjorie Weinman Sharmat		Taking Care of Melvin	Victoria Chess
Bill Wallace		A Dog Called Kitty	
Daisy Wallace, ed.		Fairy Poems	Trina Schart Hyman
Elizabeth Winthrop		Miranda in the Middle	

AUTHOR		TITLE	ILLUSTRATOR
1981			
David A. Adler		A PICTURE BOOK OF JEWISH HOLIDAYS	Linda Heller
anonymous		ANIMAL FAIR	Janet Stevens
Betty Bates		PICKING UP THE PIECES	
T. Ernesto Bethancourt		DORIS FEIN: THE MAD SAMURAI	
T. Ernesto Bethancourt		DORIS FEIN: PHANTOM OF THE CASINO	
Ruth Chew		SECONDHAND MAGIC	Ruth Chew
Tomie dePaola		FIN M'COUL: The Giant of Knockmany Hill	Tomie dePaola
Tomie dePaola	P	FIN M'COUL: The Giant of Knockmany Hill	Tomie dePaola
Tomie dePaola		THE HUNTER AND THE ANIMALS	Tomie dePaola
Tomie dePaola	P	THE HUNTER AND THE ANIMALS	Tomie dePaola
Donna Diamond		THE PIED PIPER OF HAMELIN	Donna Diamond
Malka Drucker		PASSOVER: A Season Of Freedom (a Jewish Holidays book)	photos; drawings by Brom Hoban
Malka Drucker		ROSH HASHANAH AND YOM KIPPUR: Sweet Beginnings (a Jewish Holidays book)	photos; drawings by Brom Hoban
Leonard Everett Fisher		THE NEWSPAPERS (a Nineteenth Century America book)	Leonard Everett Fisher
Leonard Everett Fisher		THE SEVEN DAYS OF CREATION	Leonard Everett Fisher
Russell Freedman		FARM BABIES	photos
Florence Parry Heide		TREEHORN'S TREASURE	Edward Gorey
Marilyn Hirsh	R	THE RABBI AND THE TWENTY-NINE WITCHES	Marilyn Hirsh
Marilyn Hirsh		THE TOWER OF BABEL	Marilyn Hirsh
Steven Kroll		FRIDAY THE 13TH	Dick Gackenbach
Steven Kroll		GIANT JOURNEY	Kay Chorao
Mother Goose/Lisl Weil		MOTHER GOOSE PICTURE RIDDLES: A Book of Rebuses	Lisl Weil
Dorothy Hinshaw Patent		HORSES AND THEIR WILD RELATIVES	photos & illustrations
Dorothy Hinshaw Patent		HORSES OF AMERICA	photos
Dorothy Hinshaw Patent		THE HUNTERS AND THE HUNTED	photos
Glen Rounds		MR. YOWDER AND THE TRAIN ROBBERS	Glen Rounds
Marjorie Weinman Sharmat		LUCRETIA THE UNBEARABLE	Janet Stevens
Marjorie Weinman Sharmat		TWITCHELL THE WISHFUL	Janet Stevens
Betty Ren Wright		GETTING RID OF MARJORIE	

AUTHOR	TITLE	ILLUSTRATOR
1982		
David A. Adler	A PICTURE BOOK OF HANUKKAH	Linda Heller
David A. Adler	A PICTURE BOOK OF PASSOVER	Linda Heller
Hans Christian Andersen, retold by Janet Stevens	THE PRINCESS AND THE PEA	Janet Stevens
Betty Bates	IT MUST'VE BEEN THE FISH STICKS	
Betty Bates	THAT'S WHAT T. J. SAYS	
Joyce Becker	BIBLE CRAFTS	Joyce Becker
Joyce Becker P	BIBLE CRAFTS	Joyce Becker
T. Ernesto Bethancourt	DORIS FEIN: DEADLY APHRODITE	
T. Ernesto Bethancourt	DORIS FEIN: MURDER IS NO JOKE	
Victoria Chess	POOR ESMÉ	Victoria Chess
Ruth Chew	MOSTLY MAGIC	Ruth Chew
Maggie S. Davis	THE BEST WAY TO RIPTON	Stephen Gammell
Maggie S. Davis	GRANDMA'S SECRET LETTER	John Wallner
Tomie dePaola	FRANCIS: THE POOR MAN OF ASSISI	Tomie dePaola
Malka Drucker	SUKKOT: A Time to Rejoice (a Jewish Holidays book)	photos; drawings by Brom Hoban
Leonard Everett Fisher	THE UNIONS (a Nineteenth Century America book)	Leonard Everett Fisher
Russell Freedman	KILLER FISH	photos
Russell Freedman	KILLER SNAKES	photos
Ann O'Neal García	SPIRIT ON THE WALL	
Gail Gibbons	CHRISTMAS TIME	Gail Gibbons
Gail Gibbons	TOOL BOOK	Gail Gibbons
Helen Griffiths	DANCING HORSES	
The Brothers Grimm, retold by Barbara Rogasky	RAPUNZEL	Trina Schart Hyman
Florence Parry Heide	TIME'S UP!	Marylin Hafner
Florence Parry Heide	THE WENDY PUZZLE	
Steven Kroll	THE BIG BUNNY AND THE EASTER EGGS	Janet Stevens
Steven Kroll	ONE TOUGH TURKEY: A Thanksgiving Story	John Wallner
Edward Lear; Myra Cohn Livingston, ed.	HOW PLEASANT TO KNOW MR. LEAR!	Edward Lear
Myra Cohn Livingston	A CIRCLE OF SEASONS	Leonard Everett Fisher
Ann McGovern	NICHOLAS BENTLEY STONINGPOT III	Tomie dePaola
Judith Whitelock McInerney	JUDGE BENJAMIN: SUPERDOG	Leslie Morrill
Dorothy Hinshaw Patent	ARABIAN HORSES	photos
Dorothy Hinshaw Patent	A PICTURE BOOK OF COWS	photos by William Muñoz
Dorothy Hinshaw Patent	SPIDER MAGIC	photos

AUTHOR	TITLE	ILLUSTRATOR
Marjorie Weinman Sharmat	THE BEST VALENTINE IN THE WORLD	*Lilian Obligado*
Betty Ren Wright	THE SECRET WINDOW	

1983

David A. Adler	THE CARSICK ZEBRA AND OTHER ANIMAL RIDDLES	*Tomie dePaola*
Betty Bates	CALL ME FRIDAY THE THIRTEENTH	*Linda Strauss Edwards*
T. Ernesto Bethancourt	DORIS FEIN: DEAD HEAT AT LONG BEACH	
T. Ernesto Bethancourt	T.H.U.M.B.B.	
Kay Chorao	LEMON MOON	*Kay Chorao*
Tomie dePaola	MARIANNA MAY AND NURSEY	*Tomie dePaola*
Charles Dickens	A CHRISTMAS CAROL	*Trina Schart Hyman*
Malka Drucker	SHABBAT: A Peaceful Island *(a Jewish Holidays book)*	*photos; drawings by Brom Hoban*
Leonard Everett Fisher	THE SCHOOLS *(a Nineteenth Century America book)*	*Leonard Everett Fisher*
Leonard Everett Fisher	STAR SIGNS	*Leonard Everett Fisher*
Russell Freedman	DINOSAURS AND THEIR YOUNG	*Leslie Morrill*
Gail Gibbons	BOAT BOOK	*Gail Gibbons*
Gail Gibbons	THANKSGIVING DAY	*Gail Gibbons*
Helen Griffiths	RAFA'S DOG	
The Brothers Grimm, retold by Donna Diamond	RUMPELSTILTSKIN	*Donna Diamond*
The Brothers Grimm, retold by Trina Schart Hyman	LITTLE RED RIDING HOOD	*Trina Schart Hyman*
Florence Parry Heide	BANANA BLITZ	
Steven Kroll	THE HAND-ME-DOWN DOLL	*Evaline Ness*
Steven Kroll	TOOT! TOOT!	*Anne Rockwell*
Edward Lear	THE OWL AND THE PUSSYCAT	*Janet Stevens*
Ann M. Martin	BUMMER SUMMER	
Judith Whitelock McInerney	JUDGE BENJAMIN: THE SUPERDOG SECRET	*Leslie Morrill*
Ann Nevins	SUPER STITCHES: A Book of Superstitions	*Dan Nevins*
Dorothy Hinshaw Patent	GERMS!	*photos*
Dorothy Hinshaw Patent	A PICTURE BOOK OF PONIES	*photos by William Muñoz*
Glen Rounds	MR. YOWDER AND THE WINDWAGON	*Glen Rounds*
Glen Rounds	WILD APPALOOSA	*Glen Rounds*
Marjorie Weinman Sharmat	FRIZZY THE FEARFUL	*John Wallner*
Elizabeth Winthrop	A CHILD IS BORN: The Christmas Story	*Charles Mikolaycak*
Betty Ren Wright	THE DOLLHOUSE MURDERS	

AUTHOR		TITLE	ILLUSTRATOR
1984			
David A. Adler		A PICTURE BOOK OF ISRAEL	photos
Aesop, adapted by Janet Stevens		THE TORTOISE AND THE HARE	Janet Stevens
Betty Bates		SAY CHEESE	Jim Spence
T. Ernesto Bethancourt		DORIS FEIN: LEGACY OF TERROR	
T. Ernesto Bethancourt		THE TOMORROW CONNECTION	
Gillian Cross		BORN OF THE SUN	Mark Edwards
Maggie S. Davis		RICKETY WITCH	Kay Chorao
Tomie dePaola	P	THE CLOUD BOOK	Tomie dePaola
Tomie dePaola	P	THE FAMILY CHRISTMAS TREE BOOK	Tomie dePaola
Tomie dePaola	P	THE KIDS' CAT BOOK	Tomie dePaola
Tomie dePaola	P	THE POPCORN BOOK	Tomie dePaola
Tomie dePaola	P	THE QUICKSAND BOOK	Tomie dePaola
Malka Drucker		CELEBRATING LIFE: Jewish Rites of Passage	photos
Olivier Dunrea		RAVENA	Olivier Dunrea
Leonard Everett Fisher		THE OLYMPIANS: Great Gods and Goddesses of Ancient Greece	Leonard Everett Fisher
Russell Freedman		RATTLESNAKES	photos
Gail Gibbons		HALLOWEEN	Gail Gibbons
Gail Gibbons		TUNNELS	Gail Gibbons
Helen Griffiths		THE DOG AT THE WINDOW	
Sarah Josepha Hale		MARY HAD A LITTLE LAMB	Tomie dePaola
Sarah Josepha Hale	P	MARY HAD A LITTLE LAMB	Tomie dePaola
Florence Parry Heide		TIME FLIES!	Marylin Hafner
Florence Parry Heide		TREEHORN'S WISH	Edward Gorey
Marilyn Hirsh		I LOVE HANUKKAH	Marilyn Hirsh
Steven Kroll		THE BIGGEST PUMPKIN EVER	Jeni Bassett
Steven Kroll		LOOSE TOOTH	Tricia Tusa
Myra Cohn Livingston, ed.		CHRISTMAS POEMS	Trina Schart Hyman
Myra Cohn Livingston		SKY SONGS	Leonard Everett Fisher
Ann M. Martin		INSIDE OUT	
Ann M. Martin		STAGE FRIGHT	Blanche Sims
Judith Whitelock McInerney		JUDGE BENJAMIN: THE SUPERDOG RESCUE	Leslie Morrill
Charles Mikolaycak		BABUSHKA: An Old Russian Folktale	Charles Mikolaycak
Dorothy Hinshaw Patent		FARM ANIMALS	photos by William Muñoz
Dorothy Hinshaw Patent		WHALES: Giants of the Deep	photos & illustrations
Glen Rounds		THE MORNING THE SUN REFUSED TO RISE	Glen Rounds
Marjorie Weinman Sharmat		SASHA THE SILLY	Janet Stevens
Mary Ann Sullivan		CHILD OF WAR	
Tricia Tusa		LIBBY'S NEW GLASSES	Tricia Tusa

AUTHOR		TITLE	ILLUSTRATOR
Bill Wallace		Trapped in Death Cave	
Betty Ren Wright		Ghosts Beneath Our Feet	

1985

AUTHOR		TITLE	ILLUSTRATOR
David A. Adler		My Dog and the Knock Knock Mystery	*Marsha Winborn*
David A. Adler	P	A Picture Book of Hanukkah	*Linda Heller*
David A. Adler		The Twisted Witch and Other Spooky Riddles	*Victoria Chess*
Aesop, adapted by Janet Stevens	P	The Tortoise and the Hare	*Janet Stevens*
Hans Christian Andersen, adapted by Janet Stevens		The Emperor's New Clothes	*Janet Stevens*
Betty Bates		Thatcher Payne-in-the-Neck	*Linda Strauss Edwards*
Gillian Cross		On the Edge	
Olivier Dunrea		Fergus and Bridey	*Olivier Dunrea*
Olivier Dunrea		Mogwogs on the March!	*Olivier Dunrea*
Kenneth E. Ethridge		Toothpick	
Leonard Everett Fisher		The Statue of Liberty	*photos & illustrations*
Russell Freedman		Holiday House: The First Fifty Years	*illustrations*
Russell Freedman		Sharks	*photos*
Gail Gibbons	P	Christmas Time	*Gail Gibbons*
Gail Gibbons	P	Halloween	*Gail Gibbons*
Gail Gibbons		Playgrounds	*Gail Gibbons*
Gail Gibbons	P	Thanksgiving Day	*Gail Gibbons*
Marilyn Hirsh		I Love Passover	*Marilyn Hirsh*
Steven Kroll		Happy Mother's Day	*Marylin Hafner*
Steven Kroll		Mrs. Claus's Crazy Christmas	*John Wallner*
Oretta Leigh		The Merry-Go-Round	*Kathryn E. Shoemaker*
Loreen Leedy		A Number of Dragons	*Loreen Leedy*
Myra Cohn Livingston		Celebrations	*Leonard Everett Fisher*
Myra Cohn Livingston, ed.		Easter Poems	*John Wallner*
Myra Cohn Livingston, ed.		Thanksgiving Poems	*Stephen Gammell*
Ann M. Martin		Me and Katie (The Pest)	*Blanche Sims*
Judith Whitelock McInerney		Judge Benjamin: The Superdog Surprise	*Leslie Morrill*
Mother Goose		The House that Jack Built	*Janet Stevens*
Dorothy Hinshaw Patent		Thoroughbred Horses	*photos by William Muñoz*
Dorothy Hinshaw Patent		Quarter Horses	*photos by William Muñoz*
Ann Rinaldi		But in the Fall I'm Leaving	
Glen Rounds		Washday on Noah's Ark	*Glen Rounds*
Marjorie Weinman Sharmat		Attila the Angry	*Lillian Hoban*
Marjorie Weinman Sharmat		One Terrific Thanksgiving	*Lilian Obligado*

AUTHOR		TITLE	ILLUSTRATOR
Robert Swindells		BROTHER IN THE LAND	
Dylan Thomas		A CHILD'S CHRISTMAS IN WALES	Trina Schart Hyman
Bill Wallace		SHADOW ON THE SNOW	
Elizabeth Winthrop		THE CASTLE IN THE ATTIC	Trina Schart Hyman
Elizabeth Winthrop		HE IS RISEN: The Easter Story	Charles Mikolaycak
Betty Ren Wright		CHRISTINA'S GHOST	

1986

AUTHOR		TITLE	ILLUSTRATOR
David A. Adler		MARTIN LUTHER KING, JR.: Free at Last	Robert Casilla
David A. Adler	P	MARTIN LUTHER KING, JR.: Free at Last	Robert Casilla
David A. Adler		MY DOG AND THE GREEN SOCK MYSTERY	Dick Gackenbach
David A. Adler	P	A PICTURE BOOK OF PASSOVER	Linda Heller
David A. Adler		THE PURPLE TURKEY AND OTHER THANKSGIVING RIDDLES	Marylin Hafner
Betty Bates		THE GREAT MALE CONSPIRACY	
Tom Birdseye		I'M GOING TO BE FAMOUS	
Edward Boyer		RIVER AND CANAL	Edward Boyer
Tomie dePaola	P	MARIANNA MAY AND NURSEY	Tomie dePaola
Olivier Dunrea		SKARA BRAE: The Story of a Prehistoric Village	Olivier Dunrea
Hazel Edwards		THERE'S A HIPPOPOTAMUS ON OUR ROOF EATING CAKE	Deborah Niland
Leonard Everett Fisher		ELLIS ISLAND: Gateway to the New World	photos and illustrations
Dick Gackenbach		TIMID TIMOTHY'S TONGUE TWISTERS	Dick Gackenbach
Gail Gibbons		FLYING	Gail Gibbons
Gail Gibbons		HAPPY BIRTHDAY!	Gail Gibbons
Gail Gibbons		VALENTINE'S DAY	Gail Gibbons
The Brothers Grimm, retold by Barbara Rogasky		THE WATER OF LIFE	Trina Schart Hyman
Brett Harvey		MY PRAIRIE YEAR	Deborah Kogan Ray
Marilyn Hirsh	P	I LOVE HANUKKAH	Marilyn Hirsh
Steven Kroll		ANNIE'S FOUR GRANNIES	Eileen Christelow
Steven Kroll		THE BIG BUNNY AND THE MAGIC SHOW	Janet Stevens
Steven Kroll	P	SANTA'S CRASH-BANG CHRISTMAS	Tomie dePaola
Steven Kroll	P	THE TYRANNOSAURUS GAME	Tomie dePaola
Michel Laroche		THE SNOW ROSE	Sandra Laroche
Loreen Leedy		THE DRAGON ABC HUNT	Loreen Leedy

AUTHOR	TITLE	ILLUSTRATOR
Loreen Leedy	THE DRAGON HALLOWEEN PARTY	Loreen Leedy
Myra Cohn Livingston	EARTH SONGS	Leonard Everett Fisher
Myra Cohn Livingston, ed.	POEMS FOR JEWISH HOLIDAYS	Lloyd Bloom
Myra Cohn Livingston	SEA SONGS	Leonard Everett Fisher
Ann M. Martin	MISSING SINCE MONDAY	
Ann M. Martin	WITH YOU AND WITHOUT YOU	
Christobel Mattingley	THE ANGEL WITH A MOUTH-ORGAN	Astra Lacis
Judith Whitelock McInerney	JUDGE BENJAMIN: THE SUPERDOG GIFT	Leslie Morrill
James Nichols	BOUNDARY WATERS	
Pat O'Shea	THE HOUNDS OF THE MORRIGAN	
Dorothy Hinshaw Patent	DRAFT HORSES	photos by William Muñoz
Dorothy Hinshaw Patent	MOSQUITOES	photos
Ann Rinaldi	TIME ENOUGH FOR DRUMS	
Marjorie Weinman Sharmat	HOORAY FOR MOTHER'S DAY!	John Wallner
Janet Stevens	GOLDILOCKS AND THE THREE BEARS	Janet Stevens
Bill Wallace	FERRET IN THE BEDROOM, LIZARDS IN THE FRIDGE	
Betty Ren Wright	THE SUMMER OF MRS. MACGREGOR	
Thomas Yeomans	FOR EVERY CHILD A STAR: A Christmas Story	Tomie dePaola

1987

David A. Adler	MY DOG AND THE BIRTHDAY MYSTERY	Dick Gackenbach
David A. Adler	REMEMBER BETSY FLOSS AND OTHER COLONIAL AMERICAN RIDDLES	John Wallner
David A. Adler	THOMAS JEFFERSON: Father of Our Democracy	Jacqueline Garrick
Aesop, adapted by Janet Stevens	THE TOWN MOUSE AND THE COUNTRY MOUSE	Janet Stevens
Mary Jane Auch	CRY UNCLE!	
Betty Bates	ASK ME TOMORROW	
Miriam Chaikin	EXODUS	Charles Mikolaycak
Gillian Cross	CHARTBREAKER	
Gillian Cross	ROSCOE'S LEAP	
Tomie dePaola	AN EARLY AMERICAN CHRISTMAS	Tomie dePaola
Tomie dePaola	THE MIRACLES OF JESUS	Tomie dePaola
Tomie dePaola	THE PARABLES OF JESUS	Tomie dePaola
Eileen Dunlop	CLEMENTINA	
Eileen Dunlop	THE HOUSE ON THE HILL	
Leonard Everett Fisher	THE ALAMO	photos & illustrations
Russell Freedman	INDIAN CHIEFS	photos & illustrations

AUTHOR		TITLE	ILLUSTRATOR
Gail Gibbons		DINOSAURS	Gail Gibbons
Gail Gibbons		TRAINS	Gail Gibbons
Gail Gibbons	P	TUNNELS	Gail Gibbons
The Brothers Grimm, retold by Trina Schart Hyman	P	LITTLE RED RIDING HOOD	Trina Schart Hyman
The Brothers Grimm, retold by Barbara Rogasky	P	RAPUNZEL	Trina Schart Hyman
Brett Harvey		IMMIGRANT GIRL: Becky of Eldridge Street	Deborah Kogan Ray
Marilyn Hirsh	P	COULD ANYTHING BE WORSE?	Marilyn Hirsh
Steven Kroll		I LOVE SPRING!	Kathryn E. Shoemaker
Steven Kroll		IT'S GROUNDHOG'S DAY!	Jeni Bassett
Loreen Leedy		BIG, SMALL, SHORT, TALL	Loreen Leedy
Myra Cohn Livingston, ed.		CAT POEMS	Trina Schart Hyman
Myra Cohn Livingston	P	CELEBRATIONS	Leonard Everett Fisher
Myra Cohn Livingston, ed.		NEW YEAR'S POEMS	Margot Tomes
Myra Cohn Livingston, ed.		VALENTINE POEMS	Patience Brewster
Ann M. Martin		JUST A SUMMER ROMANCE	
Ann M. Martin		SLAM BOOK	
Liza Ketchum Murrow		WEST AGAINST THE WIND	
Pat O'Shea		FINN MAC COOL AND THE SMALL MEN OF DEEDS	Stephen Lavis
Dorothy Hinshaw Patent		ALL ABOUT WHALES	photos
Dorothy Hinshaw Patent		DOLPHINS AND PORPOISES	photos
Ken Radford		HOUSE IN THE SHADOWS	
Deborah Kogan Ray		MY DOG, TRIP	Deborah Kogan Ray
Ann Rinaldi		THE GOOD SIDE OF MY HEART	
Marjorie Weinman Sharmat		HOORAY FOR FATHER'S DAY!	John Wallner
Bill Wallace		RED DOG	
Lisl Weil		SANTA CLAUS AROUND THE WORLD	Lisl Weil
Elizabeth Winthrop		MAGGIE AND THE MONSTER	Tomie dePaola
Betty Ren Wright		A GHOST IN THE WINDOW	

1988

David A. Adler		THE DINOSAUR PRINCESS AND OTHER PREHISTORIC RIDDLES	Loreen Leedy
David A. Adler		GEORGE WASHNGTON: Father of Our Country	Jacqueline Garrick
David A. Adler	P	MY DOG AND THE BIRTHDAY MYSTERY	Dick Gackenbach
David A. Adler		WILD PILL HICKOK AND OTHER OLD WEST RIDDLES	Glen Rounds

AUTHOR		TITLE	ILLUSTRATOR
Hans Christian Andersen, adapted by Janet Stevens		IT'S PERFECTLY TRUE!	Janet Stevens
Frank Asch		OATS AND WILD APPLES	Frank Asch
Mary Jane Auch		MOM IS DATING WEIRD WAYNE	
Mary Jane Auch		PICK OF THE LITTER	
Betty Bates		TOUGH BEANS	Leslie Morrill
Tom Birdseye		AIRMAIL TO THE MOON	Stephen Gammell
Leonard Everett Fisher		MONTICELLO	photos & illustrations
Leonard Everett Fisher		THESEUS AND THE MINOTAUR	Leonard Everett Fisher
Russell Freedman		BUFFALO HUNT	paintings & drawings
Dick Gackenbach	P	TIMID TIMOTHY'S TONGUE TWISTERS	Dick Gackenbach
Gail Gibbons	P	BOAT BOOK	Gail Gibbons
Gail Gibbons	P	DINOSAURS	Gail Gibbons
Gail Gibbons		FARMING	Gail Gibbons
Gail Gibbons		PREHISTORIC ANIMALS	Gail Gibbons
Gail Gibbons	P	TOOL BOOK	Gail Gibbons
Gail Gibbons	P	TRAINS	Gail Gibbons
The Brothers Grimm, retold by John Warren Stewig		THE FISHERMAN AND HIS WIFE	Margot Tomes
Brett Harvey		CASSIE'S JOURNEY: Going West in the 1860s	Deborah Kogan Ray
Frances Hendry		QUEST FOR A KELPIE	
Marilyn Hirsh	P	I LOVE PASSOVER	Marylin Hirsh
Caryll Houselander		PETOOK: An Easter Story	Tomie dePaola
Eric A. Kimmel		ANANSI AND THE MOSS-COVERED ROCK	Janet Stevens
Eric A. Kimmel		THE CHANUKKAH TREE	Giora Carmi
Steven Kroll		HAPPY FATHER'S DAY	Marylin Hafner
Steven Kroll		LOOKING FOR DANIELA: A Romantic Adventure	Anita Lobel
Loreen Leedy		A DRAGON CHRISTMAS: Things to Make and Do	Loreen Leedy
Loreen Leedy		THE BUNNY PLAY	Loreen Leedy
Myra Cohn Livingston	P	A CIRCLE OF SEASONS	Leonard Everett Fisher
Myra Cohn Livingston, ed.		POEMS FOR MOTHERS	Deborah Kogan Ray
Myra Cohn Livingston		SPACE SONGS	Leonard Everett Fisher
Ann M. Martin		TEN KIDS, NO PETS	
Ann M. Martin		YOURS TURLY, SHIRLEY	
Michael McCurdy		HANNAH'S FARM: The Seasons on an Early American Homestead	Michael McCurdy
Charles Mikolaycak	P	BABUSHKA: An Old Russian Folktale	Charles Mikolaycak
Dorothy Hinshaw Patent		APPALOOSA HORSES	photos by William Muñoz
Dorothy Hinshaw Patent		BABIES!	photos
Ken Radford		HAUNTING AT MILL LANE	

AUTHOR		TITLE	ILLUSTRATOR
Ann Rinaldi		THE LAST SILK DRESS	
Barbara Rogasky		SMOKE AND ASHES: The Story of the Holocaust	photos
Glen Rounds	P	OL' PAUL, THE MIGHTY LOGGER	Glen Rounds
Carolyn Sloan		THE SEA CHILD	
Felix Timmermans, adapted by Carole Kismaric		A GIFT FROM SAINT NICHOLAS	Charles Mikolaycak
Bill Wallace		BEAUTY	
Lisl Weil		LET'S GO TO THE CIRCUS	Lisl Weil
Elizabeth Winthrop		BEAR AND MRS. DUCK	Patience Brewster
Elizabeth Winthrop	P	MAGGIE AND THE MONSTER	Tomie dePaola
Betty Ren Wright		THE PIKE RIVER PHANTOM	

1989

AUTHOR		TITLE	ILLUSTRATOR
David A. Adler		JACKIE ROBINSON: He Was the First	Robert Casilla
David A. Adler	P	A PICTURE BOOK OF JEWISH HOLIDAYS	Linda Heller
David A. Adler		A PICTURE BOOK OF ABRAHAM LINCOLN	John & Alexandra Wallner
David A. Adler		A PICTURE BOOK OF GEORGE WASHINGTON	John & Alexandra Wallner
David A. Adler		A PICTURE BOOK OF MARTIN LUTHER KING, JR.	Robert Casilla
David A. Adler		A TEACHER ON ROLLER SKATES AND OTHER SCHOOL RIDDLES	John Wallner
Aesop, adapted by Janet Stevens	P	THE TOWN MOUSE AND THE COUNTRY MOUSE	Janet Stevens
Aesop, adapted by Janet Stevens		ANDROCLES AND THE LION	Janet Stevens
Louisa May Alcott		AN OLD-FASHIONED THANKSGIVING	Michael McCurdy
Hans Christian Andersen, adapted by Janet Stevens	P	THE PRINCESS AND THE PEA	Janet Stevens
Frank Asch		BABY IN THE BOX	Frank Asch
Frank Asch		JOURNEY TO TEREZOR	
Frank Asch	P	OATS AND WILD APPLES	Frank Asch
Mary Jane Auch		GLASS SLIPPERS GIVE YOU BLISTERS	
Tom Birdseye	P	AIRMAIL TO THE MOON	Stephen Gammell
Gillian Cross		A MAP OF NOWHERE	
Eileen Dunlop		THE VALLEY OF DEER	
Kenneth E. Ethridge		VIOLA, FURGY, BOBBI, AND ME	
Leonard Everett Fisher	P	THE OLYMPIANS	Leonard Everett Fisher
Leonard Everett Fisher	P	THE SEVEN DAYS OF CREATION	Leonard Everett Fisher
Leonard Everett Fisher		THE WHITE HOUSE	photos & illustrations

AUTHOR		TITLE	ILLUSTRATOR
Susan Gates		THE BURNHOPE WHEEL	
Gail Gibbons		EASTER	Gail Gibbons
Gail Gibbons		MONARCH BUTTERFLY	Gail Gibbons
Libby Gleeson		I AM SUSANNAH	
Kenneth Grahame	P	THE RELUCTANT DRAGON	Ernest H. Shepard
Constance Hiser		NO BEAN SPROUTS, PLEASE!	Carolyn Ewing
Eric A. Kimmel		CHARLIE DRIVES THE STAGE	Glen Rounds
Eric A. Kimmel		HERSHEL AND THE HANUKKAH GOBLINS	Trina Schart Hyman
Steven Kroll		BIG JEREMY	Donald Carrick
Steven Kroll		THE HOKEY-POKEY MAN	Deborah Kogan Ray
Loreen Leedy	P	THE DRAGON HALLOWEEN PARTY	Loreen Leedy
Loreen Leedy		THE POTATO PARTY AND OTHER TROLL TALES	Loreen Leedy
Loreen Leedy		PINGO THE PLAID PANDA	Loreen Leedy
Myra Cohn Livingston		BIRTHDAY POEMS	Margot Tomes
Myra Cohn Livingston, ed.		HALLOWEEN POEMS	Stephen Gammell
Myra Cohn Livingston, ed.		POEMS FOR FATHERS	Robert Casilla
Myra Cohn Livingston		UP IN THE AIR	Leonard Everett Fisher
Ann M. Martin		MA AND PA DRACULA	Dirk Zimmer
Annie Mitra		PENGUIN MOON	Annie Mitra
Liza Ketchum Murrow		FIRE IN THE HEART	
Liza Ketchum Murrow		GOOD-BYE, SAMMY	Gail Owens
Dorothy Hinshaw Patent		HUMPBACK WHALES	photos by Mark J. Ferrari & Deborah A. Glockner-Ferrari
Dorothy Hinshaw Patent		LOOKING AT ANTS	photos
Dorothy Hinshaw Patent		LOOKING AT DOLPHINS AND PORPOISES	photos
Ken Radford		THE CELLAR	
Glen Rounds	R	THE BLIND COLT	Glen Rounds
Glen Rounds	R, P	THE BLIND COLT	Glen Rounds
Glen Rounds		OLD MACDONALD HAD A FARM	Glen Rounds
Marjorie Weinman Sharmat	R, P	WALTER THE WOLF	Kelly Oechsli
Virginia Driving Hawk Sneve, ed.		DANCING TEEPEES: Poems of American Indian Youth	Stephen Gammell
Robert Swindells		A SERPENT'S TOOTH	
Bill Wallace		DANGER IN QUICKSAND SWAMP	
Bill Wallace		SNOT STEW	Lisa McCue
Lisl Weil		LET'S GO TO THE MUSEUM	Lisl Weil
Lisl Weil		THE MAGIC OF MUSIC	Lisl Weil
Elvira Woodruff		AWFULLY SHORT FOR THE FOURTH GRADE	Will Hillenbrand

AUTHOR		TITLE	ILLUSTRATOR
Betty Ren Wright		ROSIE AND THE DANCE OF THE DINOSAURS	
Carol Beach York		ONCE UPON A DARK NOVEMBER	

1990

AUTHOR		TITLE	ILLUSTRATOR
David A. Adler	P	JACKIE ROBINSON: He Was the First	*Robert Casilla*
David A. Adler		A PICTURE BOOK OF BENJAMIN FRANKLIN	*John & Alexandra Wallner*
David A. Adler		A PICTURE BOOK OF THOMAS JEFFERSON	*John & Alexandra Wallner*
David A. Adler		A PICTURE BOOK OF HELEN KELLER	*John & Alexandra Wallner*
David A. Adler	P	A PICTURE BOOK OF MARTIN LUTHER KING, JR.	*Robert Casilla*
David A. Adler	P	A PICTURE BOOK OF ABRAHAM LINCOLN	*John & Alexandra Wallner*
David A. Adler	P	A PICTURE BOOK OF GEORGE WASHINGTON	*John & Alexandra Wallner*
David A. Adler		THOMAS ALVA EDISON: Great Inventor	*Lyle Miller*
Frank Asch	P	BABY IN THE BOX	*Frank Asch*
Mary Jane Auch		KIDNAPPING KEVIN KOWALSKI	
Mary Jane Auch		A SUDDEN CHANGE OF FAMILY	
Lorna Balian		WILBUR'S SPACE MACHINE	*Lorna Balian*
Tom Birdseye		A SONG OF STARS	*Ju-Hong Chen*
Tom Birdseye		TUCKER	
Mimi Brennan		THE GOLDEN EGG: A Comic Adventure	*Mimi Brennan*
Miriam Chaikin		HANUKKAH	*Ellen Weiss*
Marita Conlon-McKenna		UNDER THE HAWTHORN TREE	*Donald Teskey*
Gillian Cross		TWIN AND SUPER-TWIN	*Maureen Bradley*
Ann Curry		THE BOOK OF BRENDAN	
Tomie dePaola	P	FRANCIS: THE POOR MAN OF ASSISI	*Tomie dePaola*
Tomie dePaola		LITTLE GRUNT AND THE BIG EGG: A Prehistoric Fairy Tale	*Tomie dePaola*
Olivier Dunrea	P	MOGWOGS ON THE MARCH!	*Olivier Dunrea*
Leonard Everett Fisher		JASON AND THE GOLDEN FLEECE	*Leonard Everett Fisher*
Leonard Everett Fisher		THE OREGON TRAIL	*photos & illustrations*
Gail Gibbons	P	FARMING	*Gail Gibbons*
Gail Gibbons		HOW A HOUSE IS BUILT	*Gail Gibbons*
Gail Gibbons		WEATHER WORDS AND WHAT THEY MEAN	*Gail Gibbons*
Gail Gibbons	P	VALENTINE'S DAY	*Gail Gibbons*

AUTHOR		TITLE	ILLUSTRATOR
Libby Gleeson		ELEANOR, ELIZABETH	
The Brothers Grimm, retold by Eric A. Kimmel		NANNY GOAT AND THE SEVEN LITTLE KIDS	Janet Stevens
Brett Harvey		MY PRAIRIE CHRISTMAS	Deborah Kogan Ray
Margaret Hodges		THE KITCHEN KNIGHT: A Tale of King Arthur	Trina Schart Hyman
Diane Hoyt-Goldsmith		TOTEM POLE	photos by Lawrence Migdale
Eric A. Kimmel	P	ANANSI AND THE MOSS-COVERED ROCK	Janet Stevens
Eric A. Kimmel		THE CHANUKKAH GUEST	Giora Carmi
Eric A. Kimmel		FOUR DOLLARS AND FIFTY CENTS	Glen Rounds
Steven Kroll		BRANIGAN'S CAT AND THE HALLOWEEN GHOST	Carolyn Ewing
Steven Kroll		IT'S APRIL FOOL'S DAY!	Jeni Bassett
Selma Lagerlöf, retold by Ellin Greene		THE LEGEND OF THE CHRISTMAS ROSE	Charles Mikolaycak
Loreen Leedy		THE DRAGON THANKSGIVING FEAST: Things to Make and Do	Loreen Leedy
Loreen Leedy		THE FURRY NEWS: How to Make A Newspaper	Loreen Leedy
Myra Cohn Livingston, ed.		DOG POEMS	Leslie Morrill
Myra Cohn Livingston, ed.		POEMS FOR GRANDMOTHERS	Patricia Cullen-Clark
Myra Cohn Livingston		MY HEAD IS RED AND OTHER RIDDLE RHYMES	Tere LoPrete
Sandra McCuaig		BLINDFOLD	
Bruce McMillan		ONE SUN: A Book of Terse Verse	photos by Bruce McMillan
Annie Mitra		TUSK! TUSK!	Annie Mitra
Liza Ketchum Murrow		DANCING ON THE TABLE	Ronald Himler
Sally Farrell Odgers		DRUMMOND: The Search for Sarah	Carol Jones
Dorothy Hinshaw Patent		SEALS, SEA LIONS, AND WALRUSES	photos
Dorothy Hinshaw Patent		YELLOWSTONE FIRES: Flames and Rebirth	photos by William Muñoz and others
Deborah Kogan Ray		MY DADDY WAS A SOLDIER: A World War II Story	Deborah Kogan Ray
Glen Rounds		I KNOW AN OLD LADY WHO SWALLOWED A FLY	Glen Rounds
Glen Rounds	P	OLD MACDONALD HAD A FARM	Glen Rounds
Marjorie Weinman Sharmat		I'M SANTA CLAUS AND I'M FAMOUS	Marylin Hafner
Margret Shaw		A WIDER TOMORROW	
Robert Swindells		FOLLOW A SHADOW	
Bill Wallace		THE CHRISTMAS SPURS	
Daisy Wallace, ed.	P	GHOST POEMS	Tomie dePaola
Daisy Wallace, ed.	P	MONSTER POEMS	Kay Chorao
Daisy Wallace, ed.	P	WITCH POEMS	Trina Schart Hyman

AUTHOR		TITLE	ILLUSTRATOR
Lisl Weil		LET'S GO TO THE LIBRARY	Lisl Weil
Edel Wignell		ESCAPE BY DELUGE	
Elizabeth Winthrop	P	BEAR AND MRS. DUCK	Patience Brewster
Elvira Woodruff		THE SUMMER I SHRANK MY GRANDMOTHER	Katherine Coville
Elvira Woodruff		TUBTIME	Suçie Stevenson
Betty Ren Wright		THE GHOST OF ERNIE P.	

1991

AUTHOR		TITLE	ILLUSTRATOR
David A. Adler		CHRISTOPHER COLUMBUS: Great Explorer	Lyle Miller
David A. Adler		A PICTURE BOOK OF CHRISTOPHER COLUMBUS	John & Alexandra Wallner
David A. Adler	P	A PICTURE BOOK OF BENJAMIN FRANKLIN	John & Alexandra Wallner
David A. Adler	P	A PICTURE BOOK OF THOMAS JEFFERSON	John & Alexandra Wallner
David A. Adler		A PICTURE BOOK OF JOHN F. KENNEDY	Robert Casilla
David A. Adler		A PICTURE BOOK OF ELEANOR ROOSEVELT	Robert Casilla
Aesop, adapted by Janet Stevens	P	ANDROCLES AND THE LION	Janet Stevens
Mary Jane Auch		SEVEN LONG YEARS UNTIL COLLEGE	
Zachary Ball	R	BRISTLE FACE	
Betty Bates		HEY THERE, OWLFACE	Leslie Morrill
Tom Birdseye		WAITING FOR BABY	Loreen Leedy
Miriam Chaikin	P	HANUKKAH	Ellen Weiss
Kenn Compton		HAPPY CHRISTMAS TO ALL!	Kenn Compton
Gillian Cross		WOLF	
Russell Freedman		THE WRIGHT BROTHERS: How They Invented the Airplane	photos by Wilbur & Orville Wright
Leonard Everett Fisher		CYCLOPS	Leonard Everett Fisher
Gail Gibbons	P	EASTER	Gail Gibbons
Gail Gibbons		FROM SEED TO PLANT	Gail Gibbons
Gail Gibbons	P	MONARCH BUTTERFLY	Gail Gibbons
Gail Gibbons		WHALES	Gail Gibbons
The Brothers Grimm, retold by Barbara Rogasky	P	THE WATER OF LIFE	Trina Schart Hyman
Constance Hiser		DOG ON THIRD BASE	Carolyn Ewing
Constance Hiser		GHOSTS IN FOURTH GRADE	Cat Bowman Smith
Diane Hoyt-Goldsmith		PUEBLO STORYTELLER	photos by Lawrence Migdale
Trina Schart Hyman	R	HOW SIX FOUND CHRISTMAS	Trina Schart Hyman

AUTHOR		TITLE	ILLUSTRATOR
Eric A. Kimmel		BABA YAGA: A Russian Folktale	Megan Lloyd
Eric A. Kimmel		BEARHEAD: A Russian Folktale	Charles Mikolaycak
Eric A. Kimmel		THE GREATEST OF ALL: A Japanese Folktale	Giora Carmi
Steven Kroll		PRINCESS ABIGAIL AND THE WONDERFUL HAT	Patience Brewster
Steven Kroll		THE SQUIRRELS' THANKSGIVING	Jeni Bassett
Loreen Leedy		THE GREAT TRASH BASH	Loreen Leedy
Loreen Leedy		MESSAGES IN THE MAILBOX: How to Write a Letter	Loreen Leedy
Deborah Lisson		THE DEVIL'S OWN	
Myra Cohn Livingston, ed.		POEMS FOR BROTHERS, POEMS FOR SISTERS	Jean Zallinger
Anita Lobel		THE DWARF GIANT	Anita Lobel
Elizabeth Lutzeier		THE COLDEST WINTER	
Ann M. Martin		ELEVEN KIDS, ONE SUMMER	
Bruce McMillan		PLAY DAY: A Book of Terse Verse	photos by Bruce McMillan
Angela Shelf Medearis		DANCING WITH THE INDIANS	Samuel Byrd
Liza Ketchum Murrow		THE GHOST OF LOST ISLAND	
Dorothy Hinshaw Patent		AFRICAN ELEPHANTS: Giants of the Land	photos by Oria Douglas-Hamilton
Dorothy Hinshaw Patent		WHERE FOOD COMES FROM	photos by William Muñoz
Nina Pellegrini		FAMILIES ARE DIFFERENT	Nina Pellegrini
Polly Robertus		THE DOG WHO HAD KITTENS	Janet Stevens
Barbara Rogasky	P	SMOKE AND ASHES: The Story of the Holocaust	photos
Glen Rounds		COWBOYS	Glen Rounds
Glen Rounds	P	I KNOW AN OLD LADY WHO SWALLOWED A FLY	Glen Rounds
Glen Rounds	R	WASHDAY ON NOAH'S ARK	Glen Rounds
Glen Rounds	R, P	WASHDAY ON NOAH'S ARK	Glen Rounds
Marjorie Weinman Sharmat		I'M THE BEST!	Will Hillenbrand
Patti Sherlock		FOUR OF A KIND	
Virginia Driving Hawk Sneve, ed.	P	DANCING TEEPEES: Poems of American Indian Youth	Stephen Gammell
John Warren Stewig		STONE SOUP	Margot Tomes
Bill Wallace		TOTALLY DISGUSTING!	Leslie Morrill
Rosalind C. Wang		THE FOURTH QUESTION: A Chinese Folktale	Ju-Hong Chen
Lisl Weil		WOLFERL: The First Six Years in the Life of Wolfgang Amadeus Mozart	Lisl Weil
Elizabeth Winthrop		BEAR'S CHRISTMAS SURPRISE	Patience Brewster
Elizabeth Winthrop		A VERY NOISY GIRL	Ellen Weiss

AUTHOR		TITLE	ILLUSTRATOR
Elvira Woodruff		BACK IN ACTION	*Will Hillenbrand*
Elvira Woodruff		SHOW-AND-TELL	*Denise Brunkus*
Elvira Woodruff		THE WING SHOP	*Stephen Gammell*
Betty Ren Wright		THE CAT NEXT DOOR	*Gail Owens*
Betty Ren Wright		THE SCARIEST NIGHT	
Andrea Wyman		RED SKY AT MORNING	

1992

AUTHOR		TITLE	ILLUSTRATOR
William Accorsi		FRIENDSHIP'S FIRST THANSKGIVING	*William Accorsi*
William Accorsi		MY NAME IS POCAHONTAS	*William Accorsi*
David A. Adler		BENJAMIN FRANKLIN: Printer, Inventor, Statesman	*Lyle Miller*
David A. Adler	S	UN LIBRO ILUSTRADO SOBRE CRISTÓBAL COLÓN (A PICTURE BOOK OF CHRISTOPHER COLUMBUS)	*John & Alexandra Wallner*
David A. Adler	S, P	UN LIBRO ILUSTRADO SOBRE CRISTÓBAL COLÓN (A picture BOOK OF CHRISTOPHER COLUMBUS)	*John & Alexandra Wallner*
David A. Adler	S	UN LIBRO ILUSTRADO SOBRE MARTIN LUTHER KING, HIJO (A PICTURE BOOK OF MARTIN LUTHER KING, JR.)	*Robert Casilla*
David A. Adler	S, P	UN LIBRO ILUSTRADO SOBRE MARTIN LUTHER KING, HIJO (A PICTURE BOOK OF MARTIN LUTHER KING, JR.)	*Robert Casilla*
David A. Adler	S	UN LIBRO ILUSTRADO SOBRE ABRAHAM LINCOLN (A PICTURE BOOK OF ABRAHAM LINCOLN)	*John & Alexandra Wallner*
David A. Adler	S, P	UN LIBRO ILUSTRADO SOBRE ABRAHAM LINCOLN (A PICTURE BOOK OF ABRAHAM LINCOLN)	*John & Alexandra Wallner*
David A. Adler		A PICTURE BOOK OF SIMÓN BOLÍVAR	*Robert Casilla*
David A. Adler	P	A PICTURE BOOK OF CHRISTOPHER COLUMBUS	*John & Alexandra Wallner*
David A. Adler	P	A PICTURE BOOK OF HELEN KELLER	*John & Alexandra Wallner*
David A. Adler	P	A PICTURE BOOK OF JOHN F. KENNEDY	*Robert Casilla*
David A. Adler		A PICTURE BOOK OF FLORENCE NIGHTINGALE	*John & Alexandra Wallner*
David A. Adler		A PICTURE BOOK OF JESSE OWENS	*Robert Casilla*
David A. Adler		A PICTURE BOOK OF HARRIET TUBMAN	*Samuel Byrd*

AUTHOR		TITLE	ILLUSTRATOR
Mary Jane Auch		THE EASTER EGG FARM	Mary Jane Auch
Mary Jane Auch		OUT OF STEP	
Durga Bernhard		WHAT'S MAGGIE UP TO?	Durga Bernhard
Emery Bernhard		LADYBUG	Durga Bernhard
Joanne Compton		LITTLE RABBIT'S EASTER SURPRISE	Kenn Compton
Marita Conlon-McKenna		WILDFLOWER GIRL	Donald Teskey
Tomie dePaola	P	AN EARLY AMERICAN CHRISTMAS	Tomie dePaola
Tomie dePaola		PATRICK: Patron Saint of Ireland	Tomie dePaola
Eileen Dunlop		FINN'S ISLAND	
Leonard Everett Fisher	P	THESEUS AND THE MINOTAUR	Leonard Everett Fisher
Leonard Everett Fisher		TRACKS ACROSS AMERICA: The Story of the American Railroad 1825–1900	photos & illustrations
Russell Freedman	P	INDIAN CHIEFS	photos & illustrations
Russell Freedman		AN INDIAN WINTER	paintings by Karl Bodmer
Patricia Gauch		UNCLE MAGIC	Deborah Kogan Ray
Gail Gibbons	P	FLYING	Gail Gibbons
Gail Gibbons		SHARKS	Gail Gibbons
Gail Gibbons		STARGAZERS	Gail Gibbons
Gail Gibbons	P	WEATHER WORDS AND WHAT THEY MEAN	Gail Gibbons
The Brothers Grimm, retold by Janet Stevens		THE BREMEN TOWN MUSICIANS	Janet Stevens
The Brothers Grimm, retold by Eric A. Kimmel	P	NANNY GOAT AND THE SEVEN LITTLE KIDS	Janet Stevens
Florence Parry Heide	P	THE SHRINKING OF TREEHORN	Edward Gorey
Constance Hiser		CRITTER SITTERS	Cat Bowman Smith
Constance Hiser		SIXTH-GRADE STAR	
Diane Hoyt-Goldsmith		ARCTIC HUNTER	photos by Lawrence Migdale
Diane Hoyt-Goldsmith		HOANG ANH: A Vietnamese-American Boy	photos by Lawrence Migdale
Eric A. Kimmel		ANANSI GOES FISHING	Janet Stevens
Eric A. Kimmel		BOOTS AND HIS BROTHERS: A Norwegian Tale	Kimberly Bulcken Root
Eric A. Kimmel	P	THE CHANUKKAH GUEST	Giora Carmi
Eric A. Kimmel		THE OLD WOMAN AND HER PIG	Giora Carmi
Eric A. Kimmel		THE SPOTTED PONY: A Collection of Hanukkah Stories	Leonard Everett Fisher
Eric A. Kimmel		THE TALE OF ALADDIN AND THE WONDERFUL LAMP: A Story from the *Arabian Nights*	Ju-Hong Chen
Steven Kroll		THE MAGIC ROCKET	Will Hillenbrand
Loreen Leedy		BLAST OFF TO EARTH!: A Look at Geography	Loreen Leedy

AUTHOR		TITLE	ILLUSTRATOR
Loreen Leedy		THE MONSTER MONEY BOOK	Loreen Leedy
Myra Cohn Livingston, ed.		IF YOU EVER MEET A WHALE	Leonard Everett Fisher
Myra Cohn Livingston		LET FREEDOM RING: A Ballad of Martin Luther King, Jr.	Samuel Byrd
Myra Cohn Livingston		LIGHT & SHADOW	photos by Barbara Rogasky
Elizabeth Lutzeier		THE WALL	
Ann Martin		RACHEL PARKER, KINDERGARTEN SHOW-OFF	Nancy Poydar
Bruce McMillan		BEACH BALL—LEFT, RIGHT	photos by Bruce McMillan
Bruce McMillan	P	ONE SUN: A Book of Terse Verse	photos by Bruce McMillan
Liza Ketchum Murrow		ALLERGIC TO MY FAMILY	
Mary Neville		THE CHRISTMAS TREE RIDE	Megan Lloyd
Dorothy Hinshaw Patent		NUTRITION: What's in the Food We Eat	photos by William Muñoz
Polly M. Robertus	P	THE DOG WHO HAD KITTENS	Janet Stevens
Nancy K. Robinson		THE GHOST OF WHISPERING ROCK	Ellen Eagle
Glen Rounds		THREE LITTLE PIGS AND THE BIG BAD WOLF	Glen Rounds
Marjorie Weinman Sharmat	P	I'M TERRIFIC	Kay Chorao
Patti Sherlock		SOME FINE DOG	
Bill Wallace		THE BIGGEST KLUTZ IN FIFTH GRADE	
Bill Wallace		BUFFALO GAL	
Elvira Woodruff		DEAR NAPOLEON, I KNOW YOU'RE DEAD, BUT . . .	Noah & Jess Woodruff
Elvira Woodruff		THE DISAPPEARING BIKE SHOP	
Caryn Yacowitz		THE JADE STONE: A Chinese Folktale	Ju-Hong Chen

1993

AUTHOR		TITLE	ILLUSTRATOR
William Accorsi		RACHEL CARSON	William Accorsi
David A. Adler		A PICTURE BOOK OF FREDERICK DOUGLASS	Samuel Byrd
David A. Adler		A PICTURE BOOK OF ANNE FRANK	Karen Ritz
David A. Adler	P	A PICTURE BOOK OF JESSE OWENS	Robert Casilla
David A. Adler		A PICTURE BOOK OF ROSA PARKS	Robert Casilla
David A. Adler		A PICTURE BOOK OF SITTING BULL	Samuel Byrd
David A. Adler	P	A PICTURE BOOK OF HARRIET TUBMAN	Samuel Byrd
Mary Jane Auch		BIRD DOGS CAN'T FLY	Mary Jane Auch
Mary Jane Auch		PEEPING BEAUTY	Mary Jane Auch
Durga Bernhard		ALPHABEASTS: A Hide-and-Seek Alphabet Book	Durga Bernhard

AUTHOR		TITLE	ILLUSTRATOR
Emery Bernhard		DRAGONFLY	Durga Bernhard
Emery Bernhard		HOW SNOWSHOE HARE RESCUED THE SUN: A Tale from the Arctic	Durga Bernhard
Emery Bernhard		SPOTTED EAGLE AND BLACK CROW: A Lakota Legend	Durga Bernhard
Tom Birdseye		JUST CALL ME STUPID	
Tom Birdseye		SOAP! SOAP! DON'T FORGET THE SOAP!: An Appalachian Tale	Andrew Glass
Kenn & Joanne Compton		GRANNY GREENTEETH AND THE NOISE IN THE NIGHT	Kenn Compton
Kenn & Joanne Compton		JACK THE GIANT CHASER: An Appalachian Tale	Kenn Compton
Gillian Cross		THE GREAT AMERICAN ELEPHANT CHASE	
Tomie dePaola	S	EL LIBRO DE LAS ARENAS MOVEDIZAS (THE QUICKSAND BOOK)	Tomie dePaola
Tomie dePaola	S, P	EL LIBRO DE LAS ARENAS MOVEDIZAS (THE QUICKSAND BOOK)	Tomie dePaola
Tomie dePaola	S	EL LIBRO DE LAS NUBES (THE CLOUD BOOK)	Tomie dePaola
Tomie dePaola	S, P	EL LIBRO DE LAS NUBES (THE CLOUD BOOK)	Tomie dePaola
Tomie dePaola	S	EL LIBRO DE LAS PALOMITAS DE MAÍZ (THE POPCORN BOOK)	Tomie dePaola
Tomie dePaola	S, P	EL LIBRO DE LAS PALOMITAS DE MAÍZ (THE POPCORN BOOK)	Tomie dePaola
Tomie dePaola	P	LITTLE GRUNT AND THE BIG EGG	Tomie dePaola
Eileen Dunlop		GREEN WILLOW	
Leonard Everett Fisher	P	CYCLOPS	Leonard Everett Fisher
Leonard Everett Fisher		DAVID AND GOLIATH	Leonard Everett Fisher
Leonard Everett Fisher		STARS & STRIPES: Our National Flag	Leonard Everett Fisher
Gail Gibbons		FROGS	Gail Gibbons
Gail Gibbons	P	FROM SEED TO PLANT	Gail Gibbons
Gail Gibbons		THE PLANETS	Gail Gibbons
Gail Gibbons	P	SHARKS	Gail Gibbons
Gail Gibbons		SPIDERS	Gail Gibbons
Gail Gibbons	P	WHALES	Gail Gibbons
Brett Harvey	P	MY PRAIRIE CHRISTMAS	Deborah Kogan Ray
Brett Harvey	P	MY PRAIRIE YEAR	Deborah Kogan Ray
Constance Hiser		THE MISSING DOLL	Marcy Ramsey
Constance Hiser		SCOOP SNOOPS	Cat Bowman Smith
Margaret Hodges		THE HERO OF BREMEN	Charles Mikolaycak
Margaret Hodges	P	THE KITCHEN KNIGHT: A Tale of King Arthur	Trina Schart Hyman

AUTHOR		TITLE	ILLUSTRATOR
Diane Hoyt-Goldsmith		CELEBRATING KWANZAA	photos by Lawrence Migdale
Diane Hoyt-Goldsmith		CHEROKEE SUMMER	photos by Lawrence Migdale
Eric A. Kimmel	P	ANANSI GOES FISHING	Janet Stevens
Eric A. Kimmel		ASHER AND THE CAPMAKERS: A Hanukkah Story	Will Hillenbrand
Eric A. Kimmel	P	BABA YAGA: A Russian Folktale	Megan Lloyd
Eric A. Kimmel	P	FOUR DOLLARS AND FIFTY CENTS	Glen Rounds
Eric A. Kimmel		THE GINGERBREAD MAN	Megan Lloyd
Eric A. Kimmel		THREE SACKS OF TRUTH: A Story from France	Robert Rayevsky
Eric A. Kimmel		THE WITCH'S FACE: A Mexican Tale	Fabricio Vanden Broeck
Steven Kroll		QUEEN OF THE MAY	Patience Brewster
Steven Kroll		WILL YOU BE MY VALENTINE?	Lillian Hoban
Loreen Leedy	P	THE FURRY NEWS: How to Make a Newspaper	Loreen Leedy
Loreen Leedy		POSTCARDS FROM PLUTO: A Tour of the Solar System	Loreen Leedy
Myra Cohn Livingston		ABRAHAM LINCOLN: A Man for All People	Samuel Byrd
Myra Cohn Livingston	P	SPACE SONGS	Leonard Everett Fisher
Ann Martin	P	RACHEL PARKER, KINDERGARTEN SHOW-OFF	Nancy Poydar
Bruce McMillan		MOUSE VIEWS: What the Class Pet Saw	photos by Bruce McMillan
Angela Shelf Medearis	P	DANCING WITH THE INDIANS	Samuel Byrd
Liza Ketchum Murrow		TWELVE DAYS IN AUGUST	
Dorothy Hinshaw Patent		KILLER WHALES	photos by John K.B. Ford
Dorothy Hinshaw Patent		LOOKING AT PENGUINS	photos by Graham Robertson
Glen Rounds	P	COWBOYS	Glen Rounds
Glen Rounds		THREE BILLY GOATS GRUFF	Glen Rounds
Glen Rounds	R	WILD HORSES (originally WILD HORSES OF THE RED DESERT)	Glen Rounds
Virginia Driving Hawk Sneve		THE NAVAJOS (a First Americans book)	Ronald Himler
Virginia Driving Hawk Sneve		THE SIOUX (a First Americans book)	Ronald Himler
Janet Stevens		COYOTE STEALS THE BLANKET: A Ute Tale	Janet Stevens
Bill Wallace		NEVER SAY QUIT	
Elizabeth Winthrop		ASLEEP IN A HEAP	Mary Morgan
Elizabeth Winthrop		THE BATTLE FOR THE CASTLE	
Elvira Woodruff		GHOSTS DON'T GET GOOSEBUMPS	Joel Iskowitz
Elvira Woodruff		THE SECRET FUNERAL OF SLIM JIM THE SNAKE	
Betty Ren Wright		THE GHOST OF POPCORN HILL	Karen Ritz
Betty Ren Wright		THE GHOST WITCH	Ellen Eagle

AUTHOR		TITLE	ILLUSTRATOR

1994

David A. Adler		HILDE AND ELI: Children of the Holocaust	Karen Ritz
David A. Adler	P	A PICTURE BOOK OF ANNE FRANK	Karen Ritz
David A. Adler		A PICTURE BOOK OF ROBERT E. LEE	John & Alexandra Wallner
David A. Adler		A PICTURE BOOK OF JACKIE ROBINSON	Robert Casilla
David A. Adler		A PICTURE BOOK OF SOJOURNER TRUTH	Gershom Griffith
Mary Jane Auch	P	THE EASTER EGG FARM	Mary Jane Auch
Mary Jane Auch		MONSTER BROTHER	Mary Jane Auch
Patricia Baehr		MOUSE IN THE HOUSE	Laura Lydecker
Emery Bernhard		EAGLES: Lions of the Sky	Durga Bernhard
Emery Bernhard		THE GIRL WHO WANTED TO HUNT: A Siberian Tale	Durga Bernhard
Emery Bernhard		REINDEER	Durga Bernhard
Emery Bernhard		THE TREE THAT RAINS: The Flood Myth of the Huichol Indians of Mexico	Durga Bernhard
Tom Birdseye		A REGULAR FLOOD OF MISHAP	Megan Lloyd
Tom Birdseye & Debbie Holsclaw Birdseye		SHE'LL BE COMIN' ROUND THE MOUNTAIN	Andrew Glass
Joanne Compton		ASHPET: An Appalachian Tale	Kenn Compton
Tomie dePaola		CHRISTOPHER: The Holy Giant	Tomie dePaola
Tomie dePaola	P	PATRICK: Patron Saint of Ireland	Tomie dePaola
Eileen Dunlop		FINN'S SEARCH	
Russell Freedman	P	THE WRIGHT BROTHERS: How They Invented the Airplane	photos by Wilbur & Orville Wright
Gail Gibbons		EMERGENCY!	Gail Gibbons
Gail Gibbons	P	FROGS	Gail Gibbons
Gail Gibbons	P	THE PLANETS	Gail Gibbons
Gail Gibbons	P	SPIDERS	Gail Gibbons
Gail Gibbons		ST. PATRICK'S DAY	Gail Gibbons
Gail Gibbons		WOLVES	Gail Gibbons
Ellin Greene		BILLY BEG AND HIS BULL: An Irish Tale	Kimberly Bulcken Root
The Brothers Grimm, adapted by Eric A. Kimmel		IRON JOHN	Trina Schart Hyman
Constance Hiser		NIGHT OF THE WEREPOODLE	Cynthia Fisher
Diane Hoyt-Goldsmith	P	ARCTIC HUNTER	photos by Lawrence Migdale
Diane Hoyt-Goldsmith	P	CELEBRATING KWANZAA	photos by Lawrence Migdale
Diane Hoyt-Goldsmith		THE DAY OF THE DEAD: A Mexican-American Celebration	photos by Lawrence Migdale
Diane Hoyt-Goldsmith	P	PUEBLO STORYTELLER	photos by Lawrence Migdale

AUTHOR		TITLE	ILLUSTRATOR
Diane Hoyt-Goldsmith	P	Totem Pole	photos by Lawrence Migdale
James Weldon Johnson		The Creation	James E. Ransome
Saragail Katzman Benjamin		My Dog Ate It	
Eric A. Kimmel		Anansi and the Talking Melon	Janet Stevens
Eric A. Kimmel		Bernal & Florinda: A Spanish Tale	Robert Rayevsky
Eric A. Kimmel	P	The Gingerbread Man	Megan Lloyd
Eric A. Kimmel	P	Hershel and the Hanukkah Goblins	Trina Schart Hyman
Eric A. Kimmel		I-Know-Not-What, I-Know-Not-Where: A Russian Tale	Robert Sauber
Eric A. Kimmel		One Good Tern Deserves Another	
Eric A. Kimmel		The Three Princes: A Tale from the Middle East	Leonard Everett Fisher
Steven Kroll		Lewis and Clark: Explorers of the American West	Richard Williams
Kirby Larson		Second-Grade Pig Pals	Nancy Poydar
Loreen Leedy		The Edible Pyramid: Good Eating Every Day	Loreen Leedy
Loreen Leedy		Fraction Action	Loreen Leedy
Loreen Leedy	P	Messages in the Mailbox: How to Write a Letter	Loreen Leedy
Myra Cohn Livingston		Keep on Singing: A Ballad of Marian Anderson	Samuel Byrd
Bruce McMillan	P	Mouse Views: What the Class Pet Saw	photos by Bruce McMillan
Angela Shelf Medearis		The Singing Man	Terea Shaffer
Dorothy Hinshaw Patent		Looking at Bears	photos by William Muñoz
Malka Penn		The Miracle of the Potato Latkes: A Hanukkah Story	Giora Carmi
Sara Pennypacker		Dumbstruck	Mary Jane Auch
Howard Pyle		The Swan Maiden	Robert Sauber
Glen Rounds	R	The Cowboy Trade	Glen Rounds
Glen Rounds	R, P	The Cowboy Trade	Glen Rounds
Glen Rounds	R	The Prairie Schooners	Glen Rounds
Glen Rounds	R, P	The Prairie Schooners	Glen Rounds
Glen Rounds	P	Three Billy Goats Gruff	Glen Rounds
Glen Rounds	R	The Treeless Plains	Glen Rounds
Glen Rounds	R, P	The Treeless Plains	Glen Rounds
Michael Scott		Gemini Game	
Michael Scott		October Moon	
Virginia Driving Hawk Sneve		The Nez Perce (a First Americans book)	Ronald Himler

AUTHOR		TITLE	ILLUSTRATOR
Virginia Driving Hawk Sneve		THE SEMINOLES (a First Americans book)	Ronald Himler
Janet Stevens	P	COYOTE STEALS THE BLANKET: A Ute Tale	Janet Stevens
Glennette Tilley Turner		RUNNING FOR OUR LIVES	Samuel Byrd
Bill Wallace		BLACKWATER SWAMP	
Bill Wallace		TRUE FRIENDS	
Alexandra Wallner		BETSY ROSS	Alexandra Wallner
Elizabeth Winthrop		I'M THE BOSS!	Mary Morgan
Courtni C. Wright		JOURNEY TO FREEDOM: A Story of the Underground Railroad	Gershom Griffith
Courtni C. Wright		JUMPING THE BROOM	Gershom Griffith
Andrea Wyman		FAITH, HOPE, AND CHICKEN FEATHERS	

1995

David A. Adler		CALCULATOR RIDDLES	Cynthia Fisher
David A. Adler		CHILD OF THE WARSAW GHETTO	Karen Ritz
David A. Adler	P	A PICTURE BOOK OF FREDERICK DOUGLASS	Samuel Byrd
David A. Adler		A PICTURE BOOK OF PATRICK HENRY	John & Alexandra Wallner
David A. Adler	P	A PICTURE BOOK OF ROSA PARKS	Robert Casilla
David A. Adler		A PICTURE BOOK OF PAUL REVERE	John & Alexandra Wallner
David A. Adler	P	A PICTURE BOOK OF ELEANOR ROOSEVELT	Robert Casilla
Mary Jane Auch		HEN LAKE	Mary Jane Auch
Mary Jane Auch	P	PEEPING BEAUTY	Mary Jane Auch
Gwendolyn Battle-Lavert		OFF TO SCHOOL	Gershom Griffith
Emery Bernhard		SALAMANDERS	Durga Bernhard
Tom Birdseye		TARANTULA SHOES	
Lucy Jane Bledsoe		THE BIG BIKE RACE	Sterling Brown
Kay Chorao		NUMBER ONE NUMBER FUN	Kay Chorao
Joanne Compton		SODY SALLYRATUS	Kenn Compton
Gillian Cross		NEW WORLD	
Tomie dePaola		MARY: The Mother of Jesus	Tomie dePaola
Tomie dePaola	P	CHRISTOPHER: The Holy Giant	Tomie dePaola
Tomie dePaola	P	THE PARABLES OF JESUS	Tomie dePaola
Eileen Dunlop		WEBSTERS' LEAP	
Leonard Everett Fisher		MOSES	Leonard Everett Fisher
Lucy Frank		I AM AN ARTICHOKE	
Russell Freedman	P	AN INDIAN WINTER	paintings by Karl Bodmer
Russell Freedman	P	BUFFALO HUNT	paintings & drawings

AUTHOR		TITLE	ILLUSTRATOR
Gail Gibbons		BICYCLE BOOK	Gail Gibbons
Gail Gibbons	P	EMERGENCY!	Gail Gibbons
Gail Gibbons		SEA TURTLES	Gail Gibbons
Gail Gibbons	P	ST. PATRICK'S DAY	Gail Gibbons
Gail Gibbons		THE REASONS FOR SEASONS	Gail Gibbons
Gail Gibbons	P	WOLVES	Gail Gibbons
The Brothers Grimm, retold by Eric A. Kimmel		THE GOOSE GIRL	Robert Sauber
Brett Harvey	P	CASSIE'S JOURNEY: Going West in the 1860s	Deborah Kogan Ray
Linda Oatman High		HOUND HEAVEN	
Linda Oatman High		MAIZIE	
Diane Hoyt-Goldsmith		APACHE RODEO	photos by Lawrence Migdale
Diane Hoyt-Goldsmith	P	DAY OF THE DEAD: A Mexican-American Celebration	photos by Lawrence Migdale
Diane Hoyt-Goldsmith		MARDI GRAS: A Cajun Country Celebration	photos by Lawrence Migdale
James Weldon Johnson	P	THE CREATION	James E. Ransome
Eric A. Kimmel	P	ANANSI AND THE TALKING MELON	Janet Stevens
Eric A. Kimmel		THE ADVENTURES OF HERSHEL OF OSTROPOL	Trina Schart Hyman
Eric A. Kimmel	P	THE GREATEST OF ALL: A Japanese Folktale	Giora Carmi
Eric A. Kimmel		RIMONAH OF THE FLASHING SWORD: A North African Tale	Omar Rayyan
Steven Kroll		ELLIS ISLAND: Doorway to Freedom	Karen Ritz
David Lavender		THE SANTA FE TRAIL	photos & illustrations
Loreen Leedy		2 × 2 = BOO!: A Set of Spooky Multiplication Stories	Loreen Leedy
Loreen Leedy		WHO'S WHO IN MY FAMILY?	Loreen Leedy
D. Anne Love		BESS'S LOG CABIN QUILT	Ronald Himler
D. Anne Love		DAKOTA SPRING	Ronald Himler
Joseph Plumb Martin, George F. Scheer, ed.	R	YANKEE DOODLE BOY	Victor Mays
Joseph Plumb Martin, George F. Scheer, ed.	R, P	YANKEE DOODLE BOY	Victor Mays
Angela Shelf Medearis		THE ADVENTURES OF SUGAR AND JUNIOR	Nancy Poydar
Angela Shelf Medearis		POPPA'S NEW PANTS	John Ward
Angela Shelf Medearis	P	THE SINGING MAN	Terea Shaffer
Jo Ann Muchmore		JOHNNY RIDES AGAIN	
Dorothy Hinshaw Patent		EAGLES OF AMERICA	photos by William Muñoz
Malka Penn		THE HANUKKAH GHOSTS	

AUTHOR		TITLE	ILLUSTRATOR
Malka Penn	P	THE MIRACLE OF THE POTATO LATKES: A Hanukkah Story	Giora Carmi
Glen Rounds		SOD HOUSES ON THE GREAT PLAINS	Glen Rounds
Eve Sanders		WHAT'S YOUR NAME?: From Ariel to Zoe	photos by Marilyn Sanders
Virginia Driving Hawk Sneve	R	HIGH ELK'S TREASURE	Oren Lyons
Virginia Driving Hawk Sneve		THE HOPIS (a First Americans book)	Ronald Himler
Virginia Driving Hawk Sneve		THE IROQUOIS (a First Americans book)	Ronald Himler
Virginia Driving Hawk Sneve	P	THE NAVAJOS (a First Americans book)	Ronald Himler
Virginia Driving Hawk Sneve	P	THE SIOUX (a First Americans book)	Ronald Himler
Janet Stevens		FROM PICTURES TO WORDS: A Book About Making a Book	Janet Stevens
Jonathan Swift, retold by Margaret Hodges		GULLIVER IN LILLIPUT	Kimberly Bulcken Root
Alexandra Wallner		BEATRIX POTTER	Alexandra Wallner
Rosalind C. Wang		THE TREASURE CHEST: A Chinese Tale	Will Hillenbrand
Connie Nordhielm Wooldridge		WICKED JACK	Will Hillenbrand
Betty Ren Wright		NOTHING BUT TROUBLE	Jacqueline Rogers
Courtni C. Wright		WAGON TRAIN: A Family Goes West in 1865	Gershom Griffith

1996

AUTHOR		TITLE	ILLUSTRATOR
David A. Adler	P	CALCULATOR RIDDLES	Cynthia Fisher
David A. Adler		FRACTION FUN	Nancy Tobin
David A. Adler		A PICTURE BOOK OF DAVY CROCKETT	John & Alexandra Wallner
David A. Adler		A PICTURE BOOK OF THOMAS ALVA EDISON	John & Alexandra Wallner
David A. Adler	P	A PICTURE BOOK OF SOJOURNER TRUTH	Gershom Griffith
Mary Jane Auch		EGGS MARK THE SPOT	Mary Jane Auch
Mary Jane Auch	P	HEN LAKE	Mary Jane Auch
Debbie Holsclaw Birdseye & Tom Birdseye		WHAT I BELIEVE: Kids Talk About Faith	photos by Robert Crum
Tom Birdseye	P	SOAP! SOAP! DON'T FORGET THE SOAP!	Andrew Glass
Kay Chorao		THE CHRISTMAS STORY	Kay Chorao
Gillian Cross		PICTURES IN THE DARK	
Tomie dePaola	P	THE MIRACLES OF JESUS	Tomie dePaola
Eileen Dunlop		THE GHOST BY THE SEA	
Eileen Dunlop		TALES OF ST. PATRICK	
Leonard Everett Fisher		NIAGARA FALLS: Nature's Wonder	photos & illustrations
Lucy Frank		WILL YOU BE MY BRUSSELS SPROUT?	

AUTHOR		TITLE	ILLUSTRATOR
Russell Freedman		THE LIFE AND DEATH OF CRAZY HORSE	Amos Bad Heart Bull
Suhaib Hamid Ghazi		RAMADAN	Omar Rayyan
Suhaib Hamid Ghazi	P	RAMADAN	Omar Rayyan
Gail Gibbons		CATS	Gail Gibbons
Gail Gibbons		DESERTS	Gail Gibbons
Gail Gibbons		DOGS	Gail Gibbons
Gail Gibbons	P	HOW A HOUSE IS BUILT	Gail Gibbons
Gail Gibbons	P	PREHISTORIC ANIMALS	Gail Gibbons
Gail Gibbons	P	THE REASONS FOR SEASONS	Gail Gibbons
Linda Oatman High		THE SUMMER OF THE GREAT DIVIDE	
Pamela Smith Hill		GHOST HORSES	
Margaret Hodges	P	THE HERO OF BREMEN	Charles Mikolaycak
Ellen Howard		THE LOG CABIN QUILT	Ronald Himler
Diane Hoyt-Goldsmith		CELEBRATING HANUKKAH	photos by Lawrence Migdale
Diane Hoyt-Goldsmith		MIGRANT WORKER: A Boy from the Rio Grande Valley	photos by Lawrence Migdale
Eric A. Kimmel		COUNT SILVERNOSE: A Story from Italy	Omar Rayyan
Eric A. Kimmel	P	IRON JOHN	Trina Schart Hyman
Eric A. Kimmel		THE MAGIC DREIDELS: A Hanukkah Story	Katya Krenina
Eric A. Kimmel	P	THE OLD WOMAN AND HER PIG	Giora Carmi
Eric A. Kimmel		ONE EYE, TWO EYES, THREE EYES: A Hutzul Tale	Dirk Zimmer
Eric A. Kimmel		ONIONS AND GARLIC: An Old Tale	Katya Arnold
Eric A. Kimmel		THE TALE OF ALI BABA AND THE FORTY THIEVES: A Story from the Arabian Nights	Will Hillenbrand
Sheila Solomon Klass		A SHOOTING STAR: A Novel About Annie Oakley	
Steven Kroll	P	LEWIS AND CLARK: Explorers of the American West	Richard Williams
Kirby Larson		CODY AND QUINN, SITTING IN A TREE	Nancy Poydar
David Lavender		SNOWBOUND: The Tragic Story of the Donner Party	photos & illustrations
Loreen Leedy	P	THE EDIBLE PYRAMID: Good Eating Every Day	Loreen Leedy
Loreen Leedy	P	FRACTION ACTION	Loreen Leedy
Loreen Leedy		HOW HUMANS MAKE FRIENDS	Loreen Leedy
Loreen Leedy	P	POSTCARDS FROM PLUTO: A Tour of the Solar System	Loreen Leedy

AUTHOR		TITLE	ILLUSTRATOR
Loreen Leedy	P	2 × 2 = Boo!: A Set of Spooky Multiplication Stories	Loreen Leedy
Myra Cohn Livingston		FESTIVALS	Leonard Everett Fisher
D. Anne Love		MY LONE STAR SUMMER	
Angela Shelf Medearis		HAUNTS: Five Hair-Raising Tales	Trina Schart Hyman
Angela Shelf Medearis		TAILYPO: A Newfangled Tall Tale	Sterling Brown
John Milton, adapted by Margaret Hodges		COMUS	Trina Schart Hyman
Taylor Morrison		ANTONIO'S APPRENTICESHIP: Painting a Fresco in Renaissance Italy	Taylor Morrison
Gareth Owen		ROSIE NO-NAME AND THE FOREST OF FORGETTING	
Dorothy Hinshaw Patent		PRAIRIES	photos by William Muñoz
Barbara Rogasky		THE GOLEM	Trina Schart Hyman
Glen Rounds	R	ONCE WE HAD A HORSE	Glen Rounds
Glen Rounds	R, P	ONCE WE HAD A HORSE	Glen Rounds
Glen Rounds	P	SOD HOUSES ON THE GREAT PLAINS	Glen Rounds
Margaret Shaw-MacKinnon		TIKTALA	László Gál
Virginia Driving Hawk Sneve		THE CHEROKEES (a First Americans book)	Ronald Himler
Virginia Driving Hawk Sneve		THE CHEYENNES (a First Americans book)	Ronald Himler
Janet Stevens		OLD BAG OF BONES: A Coyote Tale	Janet Stevens
Janet Stevens	P	FROM PICTURES TO WORDS: A Book About Making a Book	Janet Stevens
Todd Strasser		HEY DAD, GET A LIFE!	
Michael O. Tunnell & George W. Chilcoat		THE CHILDREN OF TOPAZ: The Story of a Japanese-American Internment Camp Based on a Classroom Diary	photos & illustrations
Alexandra Wallner		AN ALCOTT FAMILY CHRISTMAS	Alexandra Wallner
Alexandra Wallner		THE FIRST AIR VOYAGE IN THE UNITED STATES: The Story of Jean-Pierre Blanchard	Alexandra Wallner
Linda White		TOO MANY PUMPKINS	Megan Lloyd
Elizabeth Winthrop		BEAR AND ROLY POLY	Patience Brewster
Elvira Woodruff	P	THE WING SHOP	Stephen Gammell

1997

David A. Adler		EASY MATH PUZZLES	Cynthia Fisher
David A. Adler	P	FRACTION FUN	Nancy Tobin
David A. Adler		HIDING FROM THE NAZIS	Karen Ritz
David A. Adler		A PICTURE BOOK OF LOUIS BRAILLE	John & Alexandra Wallner

AUTHOR		TITLE	ILLUSTRATOR
David A. Adler	P	A PICTURE BOOK OF JACKIE ROBINSON	Robert Casilla
David A. Adler		A PICTURE BOOK OF THURGOOD MARSHALL	Robert Casilla
David A. Adler	P	A PICTURE BOOK OF FLORENCE NIGHTINGALE	John & Alexandra Wallner
David A. Adler	P	A PICTURE BOOK OF PAUL REVERE	John & Alexandra Wallner
Katya Arnold		DUCK, DUCK, GOOSE?	Katya Arnold
Mary Jane Auch		BANTAM OF THE OPERA	Mary Jane Auch
Mary Jane Auch	P	EGGS MARK THE SPOT	Mary Jane Auch
Teresa Bateman		THE RING OF TRUTH	Omar Rayyan
Marion Dane Bauer		TURTLE DREAMS (a Holiday House Reader)	Diane Dawson Hearn
Debbie Holsclaw Birdseye & Tom Birdseye		UNDER OUR SKIN: Kids Talk About Race	photos by Robert Crum
Tom Birdseye	P	A REGULAR FLOOD OF MISHAP	Megan Lloyd
Stella Blackstone		BABY ROCK, BABY ROLL	Denise & Fernando
Lucy Jane Bledsoe		TRACKS IN THE SNOW	
Marita Conlon-McKenna		FIELDS OF HOME	
Leonard Everett Fisher		THE GODS AND GODDESSES OF ANCIENT EGYPT	Leonard Everett Fisher
Martha Freeman		THE YEAR MY PARENTS RUINED MY LIFE	
Gail Gibbons		GULLS . . . GULLS . . . GULLS . . .	Gail Gibbons
Gail Gibbons	P	DOGS	Gail Gibbons
Gail Gibbons		THE MOON BOOK	Gail Gibbons
Andrew Glass		A RIGHT FINE LIFE: Kit Carson on the Santa Fe Trail	Andrew Glass
Linda Oatman High		A CHRISTMAS STAR	Ronald Himler
Margaret Hodges		THE TRUE TALE OF JOHNNY APPLESEED	Kimberly Bulcken Root
Ellen Howard	P	THE LOG CABIN QUILT	Ronald Himler
Diane Hoyt-Goldsmith		BUFFALO DAYS	photos by Lawrence Migdale
Diane Hoyt-Goldsmith		POTLATCH: A Tsimshian Celebration	photos by Lawrence Migdale
Eric A. Kimmel	P	BEARHEAD	Charles Mikolaycak
Eric A. Kimmel		SIRKO AND THE WOLF: A Ukrainian Tale	Robert Sauber
Eric A. Kimmel	P	THE MAGIC DREIDELS: A Hanukkah Story	Katya Krenina
Eric A. Kimmel		SQUASH IT!	Robert Rayevsky
Sheila Solomon Klass		THE UNCIVIL WAR	
Laurie Lawlor		THE BIGGEST PEST ON EIGHTH AVENUE (a Holiday House Reader)	Cynthia Fisher
Loreen Leedy		MISSION: ADDITION	Loreen Leedy

AUTHOR		TITLE	ILLUSTRATOR
Geraldine McCaughrean		UNICORNS! UNICORNS!	Sophie Windham
Angela Shelf Medearis		RUM-A-TUM-TUM	James E. Ransome
Taylor Morrison		THE NEPTUNE FOUNTAIN: The Apprenticeship of a Renaissance Sculptor	Taylor Morrison
Wendy Orr		PEELING THE ONION	
Nancy Poydar		SNIP, SNIP . . . SNOW!	Nancy Poydar
Glen Rounds	R, P	I KNOW AN OLD LADY WHO SWALLOWED A FLY	Glen Rounds
Virginia Driving Hawk Sneve		THE APACHES (a First Americans book)	Ronald Himler
Jonathan Swift, retold by Margaret Hodges	P	GULLIVER IN LILLIPUT	Kimberly Bulcken Root
Janet Stevens	P	OLD BAG OF BONES: A Coyote Tale	Janet Stevens
Michael O. Tunnell		SCHOOL SPIRITS	
Bill Wallace		ALOHA SUMMER	
Alexandra Wallner		LAURA INGALLS WILDER	Alexandra Wallner
Linda White	P	TOO MANY PUMPKINS	Megan Lloyd
John Winch		THE OLD WOMAN WHO LOVED TO READ	John Winch
Connie Nordhielm Wooldridge	P	WICKED JACK	Will Hillenbrand
Courtni C. Wright	P	JOURNEY TO FREEDOM: A Story of the Underground Railroad	Gershom Griffith

1998

AUTHOR		TITLE	ILLUSTRATOR
David A. Adler		A PICTURE BOOK OF AMELIA EARHART	Jeff Fisher
David A. Adler	P	A PICTURE BOOK OF DAVY CROCKETT	John & Alexandra Wallner
David A. Adler	P	A PICTURE BOOK OF LOUIS BRAILLE	John & Alexandra Wallner
David A. Adler	P	A PICTURE BOOK OF ROBERT E. LEE	John & Alexandra Wallner
David A. Adler		SHAPE UP!: Fun with Triangles and Other Polygons	Nancy Tobin
Mary Jane Auch		I WAS A THIRD GRADE SCIENCE PROJECT	Herm Auch
Bob Barner		WHICH WAY TO THE REVOLUTION?: A Book About Maps	Bob Barner
Teresa Bateman		LEPRECHAUN GOLD	Rosanne Litzinger
Marion Dane Bauer		BEAR'S HICCUPS (a Holiday House Reader)	Diane Dawson Hearn
Marion Dane Bauer		CHRISTMAS IN THE FOREST (a Holiday House Reader)	Diane Dawson Hearn
Karen Magnuson Beil		A CAKE ALL FOR ME!	Paul Meisel
Stella Blackstone		BABY HIGH, BABY LOW	Denise & Fernando
Tony Bradman		A GOODNIGHT KIND OF FEELING	Clive Scruton

AUTHOR		TITLE	ILLUSTRATOR
Kay Chorao		The Cats Kids	Kay Chorao
Judy Cox		Now We Can Have a Wedding!	DyAnne DiSalvo-Ryan
Judy Cox		Third Grade Pet	Cynthia Fisher
Leonard Everett Fisher	P	Monticello	photos & illustrations
Leonard Everett Fisher		To Bigotry No Sanction: The Story of the Oldest Synagogue in America	photos & illustrations
Martha Freeman		The Polyester Grandpa	
Gail Gibbons		The Art Box	Gail Gibbons
Gail Gibbons	P	Cats	Gail Gibbons
Gail Gibbons		Marshes and Swamps	Gail Gibbons
Gail Gibbons	P	The Moon Book	Gail Gibbons
Gail Gibbons		Penguins!	Gail Gibbons
Gail Gibbons	P	Sea Turtles	Gail Gibbons
The Brothers Grimm, retold by Eric A. Kimmel		Seven at One Blow	Megan Lloyd
Michael Harrison		It's My Life	
Esther Hershenhorn		There Goes Lowell's Party!	Jacqueline Rogers
Rebecca Hickox		The Golden Sandal: A Middle Eastern Cinderella Story	Will Hillenbrand
Pamela Smith Hill		A Voice from the Border	
Margaret Hodges		Up the Chimney	Amanda Harvey
Diane Hoyt-Goldsmith		Celebrating Chinese New Year	photos by Lawrence Migdale
Diane Hoyt-Goldsmith	P	Celebrating Hanukkah	photos by Lawrence Migdale
Diane Hoyt-Goldsmith		Lacrosse: The National Game of the Iroquois	photos by Lawrence Migdale
Ryan Ann Hunter		Cross a Bridge	Edward Miller
Ryan Ann Hunter		Into the Sky	Edward Miller
Tony Johnston		The Chizzywink and the Alamagoozlum	Robert Bender
Rukhsana Khan		The Roses in My Carpets	Ronald Himler
David Kherdian		The Golden Bracelet	Nonny Hogrogian
Eric A. Kimmel		Easy Work!: An Old Tale	Andrew Glass
Eric A. Kimmel		Ten Suns: A Chinese Legend	YongSheng Xuan
Eric A. Kimmel	P	The Adventures of Hershel of Ostropol	Trina Schart Hyman
Steven Kroll		The Boston Tea Party	Peter Fiore
David Lavender		Mother Earth, Father Sky: The Pueblo Indians of the American Southwest	photos & illustrations
Laurie Lawlor		The Worst Kid Who Ever Lived on Eighth Avenue (a Holiday House Reader)	Cynthia Fisher

AUTHOR		TITLE	ILLUSTRATOR
Loreen Leedy	P	BLAST OFF TO EARTH!: A Look at Geography	Loreen Leedy
D. Anne Love		THREE AGAINST THE TIDE	
Patricia C. & Fredrick L. McKissack		YOUNG, BLACK, AND DETERMINED: A Biography of Lorraine Hansberry	photos & illustrations
Angela Shelf Medearis		POPPA'S ITCHY CHRISTMAS	John Ward
Christine Morton		PICNIC FARM	Sarah Barringer
Lensey Namioka		THE LAZIEST BOY IN THE WORLD	YongSheng Xuan
Milton J. Nieuwsma, ed.		KINDERLAGER: An Oral History of Young Holocaust Survivors	photos
Nancy Poydar	P	SNIP, SNIP . . . SNOW!	Nancy Poydar
Christina Rossetti		WHAT CAN I GIVE HIM?	Debi Gliori
Robin Spowart		INSIDE, OUTSIDE CHRISTMAS	Robin Spowart
Vladimir Grigorievich Suteev, retold by Katya Arnold		MEOW!	Katya Arnold
Vladimir Grigorievich Suteev, retold by Katya Arnold		THE ADVENTURES OF SNOWWOMAN	Katya Arnold
Alexandra Wallner	P	BEATRIX POTTER	Alexandra Wallner
Alexandra Wallner	P	BETSY ROSS	Alexandra Wallner
Alexandra Wallner		THE FARMER IN THE DELL	Alexandra Wallner
John Winch	P	THE OLD WOMAN WHO LOVED TO READ	John Winch
Elvira Woodruff		CAN YOU GUESS WHERE WE'RE GOING?	Cynthia Fisher
Betty Ren Wright		THE GHOST IN ROOM 11	Jacqueline Rogers

1999

AUTHOR		TITLE	ILLUSTRATOR
David A. Adler	P	A PICTURE BOOK OF AMELIA EARHART	Jeff Fisher
David A. Adler		HOW TALL, HOW SHORT, HOW FARAWAY	Nancy Tobin
David A. Adler		A PICTURE BOOK OF GEORGE WASHINGTON CARVER	Dan Brown
David A. Adler	P	A PICTURE BOOK OF THOMAS ALVA EDISON	John & Alexandra Wallner
David A. Adler	P	A PICTURE BOOK OF THURGOOD MARSHALL	Robert Casilla
Mary Jane Auch		THE NUTQUACKER	Mary Jane Auch
Teresa Bateman	P	LEPRECHAUN GOLD	Rosanne Litzinger
Teresa Bateman	P	THE RING OF TRUTH	Omar Rayyan
Jan Carr		FROZEN NOSES	Dorothy Donohue
Jan Carr		SWINE DIVINE	Robert Bender

AUTHOR		TITLE	ILLUSTRATOR
Alden R. Carter		CRESCENT MOON	
Judy Cox		MEAN, MEAN MAUREEN GREEN	Cynthia Fisher
Gillian Cross		TIGHTROPE	
DyAnne DiSalvo-Ryan		A DOG LIKE JACK	DyAnne DiSalvo-Ryan
Joyce Dunbar		EGGDAY	Jane Cabrera
Richard Ferrie		THE WORLD TURNED UPSIDE DOWN: George Washington and the Battle of Yorktown	photos & illustrations
Leonard Everett Fisher	P	THE GODS AND GODDESSES OF ANCIENT EGYPT	Leonard Everett Fisher
Leonard Everett Fisher		GODS AND GODDESSES OF THE ANCIENT MAYA	Leonard Everett Fisher
Martha Freeman		FOURTH GRADE WEIRDO	
Gail Gibbons		BATS	Gail Gibbons
Gail Gibbons	P	BICYCLE BOOK	Gail Gibbons
Gail Gibbons	P	DESERTS	Gail Gibbons
Gail Gibbons	P	MARSHES AND SWAMPS	Gail Gibbons
Gail Gibbons	P	PENGUINS!	Gail Gibbons
Gail Gibbons		PIGS	Gail Gibbons
Gail Gibbons		THE PUMPKIN BOOK	Gail Gibbons
Gail Gibbons	P	STARGAZERS	Gail Gibbons
Chad Henry		DOGBREATH VICTORIOUS	
Rebecca Hickox	P	THE GOLDEN SANDAL: A Middle Eastern Cinderella Story	Will Hillenbrand
Ziporah Hildebrandt		THIS IS OUR SEDER	Robin Roraback
Margaret Hodges		JOAN OF ARC: The Lily Maid	Robert Rayevsky
Margaret Hodges	P	THE TRUE TALE OF JOHNNY APPLESEED	Kimberly Bulcken Root
Isabelle Holland		PAPERBOY	
Diane Hoyt-Goldsmith	P	CELEBRATING CHINESE NEW YEAR	photos by Lawrence Migdale
Diane Hoyt-Goldsmith		LAS POSADAS: An Hispanic Christmas Celebration	photos by Lawrence Migdale
Patricia Hubbard		TRICK OR TREAT COUNTDOWN	Michael Letzig
Ryan Ann Hunter		DIG A TUNNEL	Edward Miller
Charlotte Jones		YUKON GOLD: The Story of the Klondike Gold Rush	photos & illustrations
Eric A. Kimmel		THE ROOSTER'S ANTLERS: A Story of the Chinese Zodiac	YongSheng Xuan
Eric A. Kimmel		THE BIRDS' GIFT: A Ukrainian Easter Story	Katya Krenina
Katherine Kirkpatrick		REDCOATS AND PETTICOATS	Ronald Himler
Steven Kroll		ROBERT FULTON: From Submarine to Steamboat	Bill Farnsworth

AUTHOR		TITLE	ILLUSTRATOR
Laurie Lawlor		WINDOW ON THE WEST: The Frontier Photography of William Henry Jackson	photos by William Henry Jackson
Loreen Leedy		CELEBRATE THE 50 STATES!	Loreen Leedy
Loreen Leedy	P	MISSION: ADDITION	Loreen Leedy
Loreen Leedy	P	WHO'S WHO IN MY FAMILY?	Loreen Leedy
D. Anne Love		I REMEMBER THE ALAMO	
Sheila MacGill-Callahan		THE LAST SNAKE IN IRELAND: A Story About St. Patrick	Will Hillenbrand
Terri L. Martin		A FAMILY TRAIT	
Jeanne Modesitt		IT'S HANUKKAH!	Robin Spowart
Amy Lowry Poole		HOW THE ROOSTER GOT HIS CROWN	Amy Lowry Poole
Nancy Poydar		FIRST DAY, HOORAY!	Nancy Poydar
Vera Rosenberry		RUN ◆ JUMP ◆ WHIZ ◆ SPLASH	Vera Rosenberry
Eileen Ross		THE HALLOWEEN SHOWDOWN	Lynn Rowe Reed
Glen Rounds		BEAVER	Glen Rounds
Karen Gray Ruelle		THE MONSTER IN HARRY'S BACKYARD (a Holiday House Reader)	Karen Gray Ruelle
Karen Gray Ruelle		THE THANKSGIVING BEAST FEAST (a Holiday House Reader)	Karen Gray Ruelle
Brenda Seabrooke		THE VAMPIRE IN MY BATHTUB	
Carol Sonenklar		MY OWN WORST ENEMY	
Judith St. George		IN THE LINE OF FIRE: Presidents' Lives at Stake	photos & illustrations
Jennifer J. Stewart		IF THAT BREATHES FIRE, WE'RE TOAST!	
John Warren Stewig		KING MIDAS	Omar Rayyan
Linda Leopold Strauss		A FAIRY CALLED HILARY	Sue Truesdell
Ruth Freeman Swain		BEDTIME!	Cat Bowman Smith
Laura Torres		NOVEMBER EVER AFTER	
John Updike	R	A CHILD'S CALENDAR	Trina Schart Hyman
Martha Weston		CATS ARE LIKE THAT (a Holiday House Reader)	Martha Weston

2000 (SPRING LIST)

AUTHOR	TITLE	ILLUSTRATOR
David A. Adler	A PICTURE BOOK OF SACAGAWEA	Dan Brown
Mary Amato	THE WORD EATER	
Bob Barner	FISH WISH	Bob Barner
Gwendolyn Battle-Lavert	THE MUSIC IN DERRICK'S HEART	Colin Bootman
Jane Cabrera	OVER IN THE MEADOW	Jane Cabrera
Kathy Caple	THE FRIENDSHIP TREE (a Holiday House Reader)	Kathy Caple
Russell Freedman & Barbara Elleman	HOLIDAY HOUSE: THE FIRST SIXTY-FIVE YEARS	illustrations

AUTHOR		TITLE	ILLUSTRATOR
Martha Freeman		THE TROUBLE WITH CATS	Cat Bowman Smith
Gail Gibbons	P	THE ART BOX	Gail Gibbons
Gail Gibbons	P	PIGS	Gail Gibbons
Gail Gibbons		RABBITS, RABBITS & MORE RABBITS!	Gail Gibbons
Michael Harrison		FACING THE DARK	
Sharon Heisel		PRECIOUS GOLD, PRECIOUS JADE	
Diane Hoyt-Goldsmith		CELEBRATING PASSOVER	photos by Lawrence Migdale
Ryan Ann Hunter		TAKE OFF!	Edward Miller
Paul Brett Johnson		BEARHIDE AND CROW	Paul Brett Johnson
Eric A. Kimmel		GRIZZ!	Andrew Glass
Eric A. Kimmel		MONTEZUMA AND THE FALL OF THE AZTECS	Daniel San Souci
Eric A. Kimmel	P	THE THREE PRINCES: A Tale from the Middle East	Leonard Everett Fisher
Eric A. Kimmel		THE TWO MOUNTAINS: An Aztec Legend	Leonard Everett Fisher
Steven Kroll	P	THE BOSTON TEA PARTY	Peter Fiore
Steven Kroll		WILLIAM PENN: Founder of Pennsylvania	Ronald Himler
Tom Lalicki		SPELLBINDER: The Life of Harry Houdini	photos & illustrations
Peter Ledwon & Marilyn Mets		MIDNIGHT MATH: Twelve Terrific Math Games	Peter Ledwon & Marilyn Mets
Loreen Leedy	P	THE MONSTER MONEY BOOK	Loreen Leedy
Ellen Levine		DARKNESS OVER DENMARK: The Danish Resistance and the Rescue of the Jews	photos
D. Anne Love		A YEAR WITHOUT RAIN	
Sheila MacGill-Callahan	P	THE LAST SNAKE IN IRELAND: A Story About St. Patrick	Will Hillenbrand
Walter Dean Myers		THE BLUES OF FLATS BROWN	Nina Laden
Susan Goldman Rubin		FIREFLIES IN THE DARK: The Story of Freidl Dicker-Brandeis and the Children of Terezin	pictures by Freidl Dicker-Brandeis and the children of Terezin & photos
Virginia Frances Schwartz		SEND ONE ANGEL DOWN	
John B. Severance		SKYSCRAPERS: How America Grew Up	photos & illustrations
Vladimir Grigorievich Suteev, retold by Katya Arnold		ME TOO!	Katya Arnold
John Wallace		TINY RABBIT GOES TO A BIRTHDAY PARTY	John Wallace
Martha Weston		SPACE GUYS (a Holiday House Reader)	Martha Weston

BIBLIOGRAPHY
1935-1985 · Russell Freedman

BOOKS, MAGAZINES, NEWSPAPERS

Bader, Barbara. *American Picturebooks from Noah's Ark to the Beast Within.* New York: Macmillan, 1976.

"Book Ban Tears Town Apart." *Publishers Weekly,* September 18, 1954.

"Children Want Realism in Books." *Publishers Weekly,* October 29, 1949.

Editorial, *Newsday,* September 15, 1954.

Eichenberg, Fritz. "Bell, Book, and Candle," 1984 May Hill Arbuthnot Lecture. *Top of the News,* Spring, 1984.

Frank, Jerome P. "Deluxe Dickens." *Publishers Weekly,* July 22, 1983.

Fuller, Muriel. *Lady Editor: Careers for Women in Publishing.* New York: Dutton, 1941.

Fuller, Muriel. "Vernon Ives of Holiday House." *Publishers Weekly,* April 26, 1947.

Gentry, Helen. "Fine Books for Children, Too." *The Horn Book,* July 1935.

Hodges, Betty. "Artist Glen Rounds Has Largely Lived the Lives of His Fictional Characters." *Durham Morning Herald,* April 8, 1984.

"Holiday House Marks Its 25th Anniversary." *Publishers Weekly,* July 4, 1960.

"Holiday House: Stocking Books." *Publishers Weekly,* October 26, 1935.

Ives, Vernon. "Children's Books and the War." *Publishers Weekly,* October 23, 1943.

Ives, Vernon. "The New Look in Children's Books." *Library Journal,* December 15, 1947.

Ives, Vernon. "Teen Age: 15 to 50." *Publishers Weekly,* April 26, 1947.

"N.Y. Textbook Commission Refuses to Ban 'Russia.' " *Publishers Weekly*,
    April 23, 1955.
"Production Portraits: Helen Gentry of Holiday House, New York City,"
    Bookbinding and Book Production, November 1938.

NEWSLETTERS AND CATALOGS

Holiday House News, May 1942; April 1957; March 1958; February 1959;
    and March 1960.
Ives, Vernon. "Our 25th Anniversary." Published in the *Holiday House
    1960–1961* catalog.
Junior Literary Guild catalogs: autobiographical pieces by Jane and Paul
    Annixter, Pauline Arnold and Percival White, Zachary Ball, Betty Bates,
    Irma Simonton Black, Gladys Conklin, Tomie dePaola, Irmengarde
    Eberle, Margaret Embry, Leonard Everett Fisher, Helen Griffiths, Quail
    Hawkins, Florence Parry Heide, Marilyn Hirsh, Jim Kjelgaard, Steven
    Kroll, Julian May, Lois Baker Muehl, Glen Rounds, Marjorie Weinman
    Sharmat, Anico Surany, Vivian L. Thompson, Elizabeth Winthrop, and
    Betty Ren Wright.

UNPUBLISHED SOURCES

Briggs, Walter. "Holiday House: Fine Books for Children." Seminar paper,
    Yale College, April 1980.
Letters, memoirs, speeches: Zachary Ball, John Briggs, Gladys Conklin,
    Margery Cuyler, Helen Gentry, Vernon Ives, Edna Kjelgaard, Jim Kjel-
    gaard, Ed Lindemann, Glen Rounds, William R. Scott, and C. F. Shep-
    herd, Jr.
Interviews: Betty Bates, John Briggs, Kate Briggs, Margery Cuyler, Tomie
    dePaola, Fritz Eichenberg, Leonard Everett Fisher, Helen Gentry, Gail
    Gibbons, Dagmar Greve, Florence Parry Heide, Marilyn Hirsh, Trina
    Schart Hyman, Helen Ives, Vernon Ives, Marjorie Jones, Steven Kroll,
    Ed Lindemann, Charles Mikolaycak, Dorothy Hinshaw Patent, David
    Rogers, Glen Rounds, Marjorie Weinman Sharmat, Robert Spencer,
    Rose Vallario, and Barbara Walsh.

BIBLIOGRAPHY
1985–2000 · Barbara Elleman

Freedman, Russell. *Holiday House: The First Fifty Years*. New York: Holiday House, 1985.

Marantz, Ken A. and Sylvia S. Marantz. *Creating Picturebooks: Interviews with Editors, Art Directors, Reviewers, Booksellers, Professors, Librarians and Showcasers*. Jefferson, NC: McFarland, 1997.

Silvey, Anita. *Children's Books and Their Creators*. Boston: Houghton Mifflin, 1995.

Interviews were conducted with David A. Adler, Mary Jane Auch, Tom Birdseye, John Briggs, Kate Briggs, Mary Cash, Kay Chorao, Claire Counihan, Margery Cuyler, Tomie dePaola, Leonard Everett Fisher, Russell Freedman, Diane Foote, Gail Gibbons, Regina Griffin, Diane Hoyt-Goldsmith, Will Hillenbrand, Ronald Himler, Trina Schart Hyman, Eric A. Kimmel, Steven Kroll, Loreen Leedy, James E. Ransome, Janet Stevens, John Warren Stewig, Michael O. Tunnell, Bill Wallace, Barbara Walsh, Virginia Weinstein, Elizabeth Winthrop, and Betty Ren Wright.

INDEX

Page numbers in **_bold italics_** refer to illustrations